Shakespeare Rediscovered

by

Clara Longworth de Chambrun

About the Author

Clara Longworth de Chambrun is the wife of the Count de Chambrun, one of the outstanding officers of the French army during the World War, a regular army man, now retired with the rank of General, and a direct descendant of Lafayette. She is a member of the prominent Longworth family of Cincinnati, Ohio, the sister-in-law of Alice Roosevelt Longworth, and her international marriage in 1901 caused considerable comment. Her interest in Shakespeare dates from early childhood and she is today one of the world's leading authorities on the subject. The Countess de Chambrun is the holder of a doctor's degree from the Sorbonne. Her most recent book is her volume of memoirs, *Shadows Like Myself*.

BOOKS BY CLARA LONGWORTH DE CHAMBRUN

IN ENGLISH

Shakespeare Rediscovered

Shadows Like Myself

Shakespeare, Actor-Poet

Shakespeare's Sonnets:
 New Light and Old Evidence

Playing with Souls

His Wife's Romance

Breaking the King Row

The Making of Nicholas Longworth

Hamlet

IN FRENCH

Giovanni Florio: un apôtre de la Renaissance
 à l'époque de Shakespeare

Shakespeare, acteur-poète

Hamlet de Shakespeare

Le roman d'un homme d'affaires

La nouvelle Desdémone

Deux bagues au doigt

Antoine et Cléopâtre

L'Échiquier

SHAKESPEARE REDISCOVERED

By *means of* Public Records, Secret Reports
& Private Correspondence Newly
Set Forth *as* Evidence on
His Life & Work

❧ ❧

By CLARA LONGWORTH *comtesse* De CHAMBRUN

Doctor of the University of Paris

WITH A PREFACE BY
G. B. HARRISON

CHARLES SCRIBNER'S SONS · NEW YORK
CHARLES SCRIBNER'S SONS · LTD · LONDON
1938

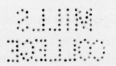

PREFACE

BY G. B. HARRISON

SOME MONTHS ago a party of Notable Persons from Oxford was visiting a University in the United States of America. One of the Distinguished Visitors—an Eminent Elizabethan Scholar—was asked by a Professor of English in that University what he thought of the work of a certain Ignoto.

"Ignoto? I have never heard of Ignoto," replied the Eminent Elizabethan Scholar, who thereupon addressed his companion: "Have you ever heard of Ignoto?"

"No," said his companion, "not I."

So the Eminent Elizabethan Scholar, turning back to the Professor of English, observed coldly:

"We have never heard of the work of this Ignoto. It cannot be of any value."

This conversation (vouched to me for true by the Professor himself) illustrates an attitude common amongst professional scholars; for scholarship is as much a profession as medicine or the law. Scholars have their own qualifications, code and technique. They are taught to deal with facts in certain ways and to step warily from footnote to footnote. Like the Scribes of old, they demand authority for every statement. The method has its advantages. It may not always stimulate the imagination of the reader, but at least he can form his own judgments; and, so long as the scholar is not an interested party, he will probably present

v

his case with a balance and sanity lacking in brighter writing.

Unfortunately, no one is entirely disinterested either in Shakespeare or religion; and even the most austere and self-respecting scholars will distort the evidence to suit their own theories and prejudices. It is therefore more necessary that new notions about Shakespeare, especially when unfamiliar and perhaps disturbing, should be received with an open mind, and that books whose authors are not professional academic persons should have as unprejudiced a hearing as is humanly possible.

Those who know Madame de Chambrun's Sorbonne thesis *Giovanni Florio, an Apostle of the Italian Renaissance in England,* or have read her *Shakespeare, Actor-Poet,* and more recently *My Shakespeare, Rise!* are familiar with some of the theories set forth in this book. The most important chapters, to my mind, are the earlier, in which she sets out much evidence for supposing that John Shakespeare of Stratford-upon-Avon was a zealous Catholic, and that William Shakespeare was brought up in the Old Faith, which he never wholly deserted, and that the course of his life was much affected by his religion. Until recent years religious partisanship has been so strong in England that it has hardly been possible for such a question to be examined without heat, but the belief that Shakespeare's family were Catholic is nowadays generally gaining ground. The evidence which Madame de Chambrun now brings together will, I think, convince any impartial reader, if not of the whole claim, at least that the story of religious persecution during Shakespeare's lifetime needs to be rewritten in the fullest possible detail. If Madame de Chambrun's thesis is accepted many exciting possibilities follow. The old traditions of the deer-stealing, the trouble with Sir Thomas Lucy, the flight from Stratford, the origin of Justice Shallow, take on a new meaning; and the search for the facts of Shakespeare's early life must start again in new places.

The most interesting of the less important suggestions made by Madame de Chambrun is that Shakespeare's own copy of Holinshed's *Chronicles* still exists. If so, it is a rare personal relic of the greatest sentimental and literary value. So far as such matters can be finally proved I believe that the book has as much right to be accepted as Shakespeare's as the famous three pages in the manuscript of *Sir Thomas More*. The palæographical evidence that a prescription for the sore legs of a horse is in Shakespeare's writing is neither stronger nor weaker than the evidence for other specimens of his writing, since the only indisputable examples are six signatures and the words "by me," all written late in life. Palæographical evidence based on such slight foundations must be taken with faith, for hand-writing experts disagree more than most.

The literary evidence is far more convincing, and here I had the advantage, through Madame de Chambrun's kindness, of examining the book for myself before she began to prepare her case. The pages describing the reigns which Shakespeare dramatized have obviously been turned over again and again. The bottom corners are so worn that one can see even from the edges of the closed volume where the book was most used. The original reader, it may be noted, turned pages by using a licked finger at the bottom of the outer margin and pushing the page up. In these parts of the volume many of the most striking passages which Shakespeare himself used are underlined and noted, and the pages are often spotted and stained with ink (or beer). On the other hand, the reigns which Shakespeare did not dramatize are notably clean and seldom marked. There are so many passages noted that one is forced to the conclusion either that some contemporary laboriously collated Holinshed's *Chronicles* with Shakespeare's plays or that some one had identical interests and was attracted by the same phrases or, which is the simplest explanation, that Shakespeare himself once owned this book. The chances are not utterly remote. Of the thousand or so copies (at the most) of the 1587 edition he must have used one. The detailed argument the reader will find for himself in Madame de Chambrun's chapter.

The value, then, of her book is that it brings together a number of new and exciting ideas which are well worth examining. Not all of them will be accepted, or are necessarily right; but there is enough here to set research workers busy for the next twenty years in new directions. If some of her book at first sight appears "wondrous strange" to the student he should follow Hamlet's advice "and therefore as a stranger give it welcome."

G. B. Harrison.

London,
October, 1937

viii

CONTENTS

CONTENTS

ILLUSTRATIONS

ILLUSTRATIONS

PLATE V

COLOPHON OF HOLINSHED'S CHRONICLES

PLATE VI

EXTRACTS FROM THE MUNICIPAL ACCOUNTS OF ABERDEEN SHOWING LAW-RENCE FLETCHER'S NAME AS COMEDIAN SERVITOR TO HIS MAJESTY AND PAYMENT TO THE ENGLISH PLAYERS

PLATE VII

LETTER OF WILLIAM HARVEY TO SIR ROBERT CECIL

PLATE VIII

COVERING PAGE OF THE NORTHUMBERLAND MS.

PLATE IX

FIRST PAGE OF THE NORTHUMBERLAND MS.

PLATE X

SHAKESPEARE'S SIGNATURES

PLATE XI

SHAKESPEARE'S HAND IN THE PLAY OF SIR THOMAS MORE

PLATE XII

Top: CONCLUDING LINES OF SHAKESPEARE'S WILL
Bottom: LEASE MADE OUT AND SIGNED BY FRANCIS COLLINS

PART 1

❧

WARWICKSHIRE

INTRODUCTORY

ANY ONE who puts forth a book about Shakespeare nowadays is expected to begin with an apology. This subject is so outworn and overwritten, it is said, that the works of the great dramatist which are the wise man's delight have too often been made the fool's playground. I think, myself, that nobody has a right to invade it unless there is something completely new to say based on firm historic grounds. The importance of certain personal discoveries which excited small attention until adopted by higher authority must be my most valid reason for this book. Another excuse is that just as there was no malice aforethought in my first offence my later ones come from long-established habit.

I began to love Shakespeare at the age of six, and have continued with unabated enthusiasm until over sixty, but no idea of wielding a pen myself interfered with the pure joy I always experienced in reading the poet's lyric or dramatic production. Even after a rather conscientious study of his principal commentators, I refrained from pushing into the literary arena. Shakespeare came to me as an inherited love, not as a property to be exploited.

Kindly fortune bestowed a grandfather upon me who held the pleasant theory that nothing in Art or Literature is too good for a child, and in undertaking my education he gave me freely of the best.

Joseph Longworth's tales from Shakespeare delivered orally made me despise those of Charles and Mary Lamb, and held me spell-bound by the lyric appeal which his fine voice and

3

diction gave to certain immortal passages supposedly beyond the grasp of the very little girl I was at the opening of the 'eighties. In place of the "Absey Book" we had Knight's Illustrated Edition of the *Plays and Poems of Shakespeare*. I knew all about the Hunting of the Cotswolds, and the troubles of poor Wat, without bothering over the snares of Dame Venus, and could find any play or poem from the Illustrations without recourse to index or number. Soon, through his methods, I was able to read before knowing the name of each letter. It was easy to pick out such lines as "O Romeo, Romeo, wherefore art thou Romeo?" and recognise that name ever after. "To be or not to be" proved a Rosetta stone in deciphering other hieroglyphics and soon with his voice echoing in my memory I could call back the "wingèd words," reading without alphabet as the gipsy musician plays his Liszt concerto with no other musical score than the tune and rhythm. Books were not needed when my grandfather was beside me. He could repeat from memory alone whole scenes from the plays he loved most and pages from the Sonnets and Poems, and—better still—satisfactorily answer all questions about them in a way I have not heard since. When the subject was "out of my welkin" he would say, "You can think that over for yourself when you are older," and memory still holds the key to problems discussed years ago and brings it out unexpectedly now and then to the confusion of certain specialists who know their Shakespeare less well than he.

I can still hear my grandfather reciting certain passages from "Romeo and Juliet" and remember interrupting him one day after the scene where Mercutio before his duel with Tybalt employs several technical Italian fencing terms, to inquire how Shakespeare happened to know a foreign language. His answer satisfied me then and it does so still. What more natural than that the dramatist's intimacy with the Earl of South-

4

ampton led him to frequent the company of the young man's resident teacher, Giovanni Florio—an eminent linguist who had been instructor at Oxford and later settled in London, where he eventually published his admirable translation of Montaigne's *Essays?* It was Giovanni Florio who gave Shakespeare the rudiments of French and Italian, just as it was his large library of foreign books which furnished easy access to the Peninsular authors of whom the English poet made use. This explanation came back to me in 1910 when reading Baconian and other arguments against Shakespeare's authorship of the Plays and Poems, and I began to wonder why partisans of the traditional doctrine neglected such an important factor in the poet's culture since there need be no mystery in Shakespeare's knowledge of Italy, with Florio, so to speak, at his elbow.

With naïve enthusiasm I wrote to a noted scholar of that day, asking why he never made use of Florio's writings to explain the facilities which the poet, without leaving England, possessed for learning the small amount of French and Italian necessary to his purpose. Professor Furness replied that he and other American scholars were unable to consult Florio's original and pre-Shakespearean publications. Apart from a set of stock quotations repeated at second-hand from the eighteenth-century critics, Hunter and Malone, and often incorrectly quoted at that, the works of Florio—with the exception of his celebrated English version of Montaigne's *Essays*—were buried in oblivion.

This started me on the war-path. I resolved to obtain Florio's books for my personal instruction. I had the good fortune to find several of his original works in the Congressional Library and succeeded later in acquiring the extremely rare *First Fruits,* of which, at that time, only a mutilated copy was possessed by the British Museum. I soon found that Florio's conversation manuals contained as much and even more than Shakespeare required and that the list of the grammarian's books shows the original sources of his Italian plots: "In Venice we say on the Rialto, just as Londoners employ the term on the Exchange," quoth Florio, and printed it too in his *World of Words*.

As I proceeded in the study of his *Second Fruits* I gained enlightening glimpses of my pet subject, and observed thirty proverbs which Shakespeare borrowed and a quantity of allusions and parallels throughout the whole dramatic production, which attest the strength and durability of this Italian influence. Of course the passage from Montaigne which Shakespeare borrowed in "The Tempest" was recognised long ago by an early commentator, but I discovered scores of new ones and felt certain that I had enough to prove that the old tradition which says that the pedant Holofernes in "Love's Labour's Lost" was an intentional caricature of Giovanni Florio, was correct.

However, I recognised my limitations: no scholar, but an amateur in possession of a discovery which I was natural critic enough to recognise as a big one. It was pleasant to think how rival editors would clamour to bring out evidence so solidly established! No one clamoured among the publishers of Boston, Philadelphia and New York, where I was met with the same question: In what university had I made my studies?

At last the vice-president of a celebrated Anglo-American house took pity at the spectacle of so much useless energy in a lost cause and explained that unless such a discovery as mine was exploited by a well-known critic or distinguished professor, no scholarly publishing house of any repute would think of accepting it. When I objected with some feeling, that many absurdities about Baconian and other authorships for Shakespeare got into print, he replied with "sweet reasonableness" that what was sensational could always be exploited, but that

6

had nothing to do with erudition. Thus I found myself in the same predicament as the man described by Robert Louis Stevenson in whose possession was a stolen diamond so large that it could not be disposed of. What I had to say about the sources of Shakespeare's Italian culture had not been "regularly and legitimately" acquired and therefore could not be passed on to a "regular and legitimate" publishing house.

Though I found a more open market for such wares in France, where the intrinsic value of an idea seems to be more important than the person who develops it, my defeat rankled and I was eventually led to become a professor myself by following the regular routine of entry and matriculation at the Sorbonne, obtaining the degree of M.A. in 1919. This permitted the preparation, printing and ultimate defence of a thesis which, when accepted, entitled me to rank as a Doctor of the University of Paris.

Meanwhile, for a period of several years, I had been in correspondence with Sir Sidney Lee—who enjoyed at that time the same almost unquestioned authority on Shakespeare that now belongs to Sir E. K. Chambers—and it was an unexpected satisfaction to receive from him on the 12th of June, 1921, the following lines:

"I delight in your development of points already familiar to me in outline, depending for their adequate estimation on the thought, method and erudition which you apply. You have admirably filled a gap in our literary history."

I mention this letter as an "unexpected satisfaction" because, in the course of our previous correspondence, Sir Sidney Lee appeared to attach no importance whatever to the communications I had furnished him in outline! But it proved that a degree *is* useful if one's work is to command attention!

During my years of preparation I learned much about modern methods of Shakespearean comment and noticed that the protagonist of a theory is so anxious to prove that the poet agreed with his own particular views that, instead of attempting to adapt preconceived opinions to known facts, he is tempted to twist facts until they suit previously expressed statements.

Before entering the literary arena I swore very solemnly that I would never suppress or distort such evidence as I might come by. When facts and conclusions went against either taste or preconceived ideas, I promised to alter my ideas instead of tampering with facts. This procedure was detrimental to the defense of my thesis, for I started out with the intention of establishing that both Shakespeare and Florio were friendly frequenters of Holborn House, equally encouraged by the third Earl of Southampton, who was the pupil of one and the patron of the other during the years between 1591 and 1599; this would have made my case stronger. But, as I examined what evidence could be culled from the prefaces written by Florio in divers of his volumes, it became plain that these epistles constantly hark back to a jealous spite against a certain playwright, an impertinent Aristophanes who, together with his comedians, would make game of Socrates himself. This and other allusions convinced me that Florio's sentiments toward the poet who quoted the "golden sayings" more than thirty times and once in the original Italian

Venetia, Venetia,
Qui non ti vede non ti pretia

were anything but friendly. Therefore, at the risk of weakening my own argument, I was obliged to maintain that it was with acrimony on Florio's side and a tolerant spirit of mockery on the other, that Southampton's two protégés regarded each other.

Ever since, I have followed the same procedure, but it

so happened that at the period when my jury complimented me on having at last definitely and permanently established the third Earl of Southampton as Shakespeare's lifelong patron, the fair Youth of the *Sonnets* and of the *Lover's Complaint,* this theory had been practically discarded in England. When I approached the Oxford and the Cambridge Press with a view to translating, or rather re-writing, my thesis in English, all idea that the Earl of Southampton's influence had affected Shakespeare's work after 1594 had seemingly been abandoned. This was made so plain and developed with such heat that I was forced to acknowledge that there must be some reason which made the Southampton theory distasteful and that to disconnect the young man from the national poet had become almost an affair of public interest.

The War being over, I was able to pursue my subject with more persistence and adequacy than during the hostilities, when, not being able to leave Paris, I had to depend only upon such documents as I myself possessed or could find in the Institut, the Mazarine Library or the Bibliothèque Nationale. I began working at the British Museum and Public Record Office and soon became aware that, out of the beaten track followed by historians and biographers, there still remained much to learn about Shakespeare.

I wondered why the State Papers spoke so much of a certain Richard Topcliff, of whom up to that time I had never heard, but whose name appears oftener than that of any other member of the Privy Council and is connected with examinations of "Sedicious Seminaries" upon whom such notables as Bacon sat in judgment, and "syfted" at her Majesty's pleasure. Many were the familiar names of the poet's neighbourhood mentioned in this connection—Clopton—Englefield—Somerville—Arden—Throckmorton and a certain Hugh Hall, clerk. It seemed that just as all roads once led to Rome, the politi-

cal preoccupations of the Queen's ministers centred among the
poet's kin in Warwickshire—and in London, remained attached
to the doings of Arundells, Copleys, Gages and Montagues,
that particular world, in short, related to Henry Wriothesley,
Shakespeare's first patron. Gradually—very gradually—it was
borne in upon me that these are precisely the connections which
it had become expedient to disavow. In following the Southampton trail, the "man who loves Elizabeth" may discover
more than he wishes and incidentally find out why honey-
tongued Shakespeare was publicly reproached for refusing to
shed a single poetical tear on the Sovereign's hearse:

> Nor doth the silver-tonguéd Melicert
> Drop from his honied muse one sable teare,
> To Mourn her death who gracéd his desert,
> And to his laies opened her Royal eare.
>
> Shepherd, remember our Elizabeth,
> And sing her rape, done by that Tarquin, Death![1]

To make a long story short, my studies during the last six
years led me into an unsuspected world, until now never
explored for traces of Shakespeare although conscientiously
investigated by Richard Challoner, John Gerard, Alban Butler
and C. A. Newdigate.

A new Record Society, under the auspices of Edwin H. Bur-
ton, D.D.F.P. Hist. S., and Thomas L. Williams, M.A., whose
labours consist in publishing precisely those State papers and
public Archives formerly deemed politically imprudent to
touch, has furnished material that enlightens Shakespeare's life
and works and largely served to build this volume.

I am no iconoclast. If these findings were of a nature to shed
an unfavorable light on the national poet, perhaps I would
have regretfully dropped the subject and kept the information

[1] "England's Mourning Garment," Chettle.

to myself. It is because this new picture displays "the man Shakespeare" in a way which is completely opposed to the perversions of Frank Harris and Oscar Wilde that I venture to present it, bringing forward, at the same time, certain evidence which explains many mysterious points and shows that the poet's life was as full of romance, dramatic action and high endeavour as the most heroic of his works.

It remains for me now to express my gratitude to those whose aid has permitted me to bring so many hitherto unknown documents before the public. Through the intercession of Doctor Cowley, Corpus Christi furnished me as early as 1914 with a photograph of Fulman's manuscript. The Public Record Office kindly communicated facsimiles of Hall's confession, the 1592 Comptrollment Roll and Arden Arraignment. I am beholden to Her Grace the Duchess of Northumberland for permission to examine the manuscripts at Alnwick Castle; to the Most Honourable the Marquess of Salisbury for the photograph of a letter from Sir William Hervey contained among the Hatfield papers; to the Provost of Aberdeen and the Librarian of King's College in the same royal borough, for similar advantages; to Captain William Jaggard, of Stratford-upon-Avon, for the privilege of keeping, for a six months' study, his incomparable volume of Holinshed's *Chronicles;* to Mr. Frederick Wellstood and the Trustees and Guardians of Shakespeare's birthplace for the privilege of publishing a page of the Bellamy Lease with a sample of Francis Collins' writing and signature; to Father Herbert Thurston, S.J., for keeping me informed upon his studies of John Shakespeare's will, and Father C. A. Newdigate, S.J., who has enlightened my ignorance on many points concerning Elizabethan martyrology. The Greenoch Library kindly furnished me with a facsimile of the W. S. signature contained in their Plutarch, which now, for the first time, may be compared to other apocrypha. (*See Plate I, at end of volume.*)

I must also thank the authorities of the British Museum, particularly Mr. Robin Flower and Mr. Idriss Bell, Doctor G. B. Harrison of King's College and Doctor Craster of the Bodleian Library for kindly help and advice, and Miss Nellie O'Farrell of the Public Record Office for her patient collaboration. Nor must I forget what I owe to the Folger Shakespeare Library of Washington, D. C., the Bibliothèque Nationale and the expert testimony of such palæographers as Messrs. L. Rigault, L. François, F. Gébelin, Count Franzoni and Mlle. d'Alverny, for their expert advice on Shakespeare's marginal writing in Holinshed's *Chronicles*.

CHAPTER ONE

SHAKESPEARE AND
THE ELIZABETHAN STATUTES

THE OMISSION of true historical background from modern portraits of Shakespeare and the failure to apply reasoned comparative criticism to the study of his epoch have led to a curious paradox: the ordinary reader is more ignorant concerning the life of the greatest dramatic writer of any age, than he was under the Commonwealth, Queen Anne or the Georges. It is difficult indeed for those who, for upward of five generations, have enjoyed complete liberty of conscience and seen tolerance practised towards all religious confessions, to realise how entirely each subject's life differed in Shakespeare's England from anything which we now conceive. Even a cursory study of the series of edicts, injunctions and proclamations issued by royal authority and enforced during Elizabeth's long reign suffices to show that the poet lived under a political system of fiscal extortion and occasional terror which must be taken into account if we would comprehend a large portion of those writings in which the cry for justice and freedom sounds so often and so loud. It is impossible to understand the conditions of civil life in the midland shires if we forget that two-thirds of the Queen's subjects virtually dwelt outside of the law after the passage, in 1559, of the ACT OF SUPREMACY and its corollary, the ACT OF UNIFORMITY.

The circumstances of Shakespeare's education, marriage, and

flight from Stratford, his rôle in the Irish campaign and Essex conspiracy, must be examined in connection with simultaneous events occurring throughout England, not judged by the standards which today govern Great Britain, France, and the United States.

The Parliament which opened in January, 1559, passed two Acts which completely altered the conditions of civil life. In the first it was declared that any person, after June of the same year, who *"by writing, printing, teaching, preaching, express words, deed or act advisedly, maliciously and directly affirm, maintain or defend the authority, preeminence, power or jurisdiction spiritual or ecclesiastical of any prince, prelate, person, State or potentate whatsoever, heretofore claimed within this realm"* should be subject to the forfeiture of his goods or a year's imprisonment. At a second offence the penalty called *praemunire* or misprision was enforced and, after a third disavowal of spiritual allegiance to the Queen only, the culprit was liable to the full penalties of high treason. A test oath was demanded from each ecclesiastic, temporal judge, "Justiciar" or mayor, and every other person having the Queen's fee or wages. It was later extended to those who took university degrees, members of Parliament, schoolmasters and teachers of children. This oath, generally referred to as the *Supremacy Oath,* stands thus in the Elizabethan prayer-book:

"I, M . . ., do utterly testify and declare in my conscience that the Queen's Highness is the only supreme governor of this realm, and of all other Her Highness' Dominions and Countries, as well in all spiritual or ecclesiastical things or causes, as temporal, and that no foreign prince, person, prelate, state or potentate hath or ought to have, any jurisdiction, power, superiority, pre-eminence, or authority, *ecclesiastical or spiritual,* within this realm, and therefore I do utterly renounce and forsake all foreign jurisdictions, powers, superiorities and authorities, and do promise that from henceforth I shall bear faith and true allegiance to the Queen's Highness, her heirs and lawful successors, and to my power, shall assist and defend all jurisdictions, pre-eminences, privileges and authorities, granted or belonging to the Queen's Highness, her heirs and successors, or united or annexed to the Imperial Crown of this Realm, so help me God, and the contents of this book."[1]

Sir Simonds d'Ewes, the recorder who declares himself impartial, writes thus of the ACT OF SUPREMACY in his *Parliamentary Journal*:

"The passage of the Bill was opposed by the Archbishop of York, Marquess of Winchester, the Earl of Shrewsbury, Viscount Montague, the Bishop of London, the Bishop of Ely, the Bishop of Worcester, the Bishop of Llandaff, the Bishop of Coventry and Lichfield, the Bishop of Exeter, the Bishop of Chester, the Bishop of Carlisle, the Lord Morley, the Lord Stafford, the Lord Dudley, the Lord Horton, the Lord Rich and the Lord North.

"In which may there still be observed the obstinacy and boldness of the Popish bishops who opposed all things that tended but to the least reformation of Idolatry and Superstition or abolishing the usurped authority of the Bishop of Rome. [It seems that the Abbot of Westminster was absent, because his negative voice, which was never wanting, was not here mentioned.] Of the temporal Lords the most settled to Popery seem to have been the Viscount Montague and the Earl of Shrewsbury."

The ACT OF SUPREMACY was obviously directed against those who acknowledged the spiritual authority of the See of Rome, whereas the language in which the ACT OF UNIFORMITY was couched though vague was more insidious, for it implicitly

---

[1]This oath remained in the Statute-Book until 1690, but after 1606 it was practically replaced by the *Oath of Allegiance* enacted after King James's accession.

included Jews, Baptists, Brownists and Barrowists[2]; according to its terms, the same punishment demanded by the ACT OF SUPREMACY was imposed upon those who practised ANY FORM OF WORSHIP NOT IN CONFORMITY WITH THE REVISED PRAYER BOOK. Several times during the reign, this anomaly led to debates in the House over the true interpretation of the original ACT OF UNIFORMITY, but those who read the *Parliamentary Journals* will find these passages where its real signification, together with that of a later bill devising what punishments might be inflicted to keep subjects in due obedience, are clearly defined:

"*Mr. Speaker* explained that other than popish recusants could not be comprised therein for the Bill and the Preamble run only in this manner: Against such as are *enemies opposed to our State and adherents of the Pope.*

"*Mr. Dalton* would have recusants that are Brownists comprised in the Bill as well as Popish recusants and, to that end, would have the Preamble altered . . .

"*Dr. Lewin* made a long speech. His end was only to have the Brownists and Barrowists as well provided against as Papists, but whether in this Bill or in some other, he left to the wisdom of the House.

"*Sir Walter Raleigh* spoke to this effect: In my conceit the Brownists are worthy to be rooted out of the Commonwealth but what danger may grow to ourselves it were fit to be considered . . . That law is hard that taketh life and sendeth into banishment where men's intentions shall be judged by a Jury . . . I am sorry for it, I am afraid there is near twenty thousand of them [Brownists] in England, and when they

---

[2]Brownists were a sect who derived their name from Robert Browne, gentleman, who had been educated at Cambridge. In 1580 he left the Established Church maintaining that her discipline was "too Popish."

Henry Barrow, whose name was given to a more radical sect, died in 1593, in open conflict with the sovereign's pretensions to religious supremacy.

be gone, who shall maintain their wives and children?"[3]

The final upshot of the 1592 debate was: "Touching the explanation of a branch of the STATUTE made in Anno 23 Regin. Eliz. for reducing her loyal subjects to their due obedience *is only for such as are of the Romish religion.*"

Thus the contention frequently made by Shakespearean commentators, that the accusation brought against the poet's father for recusancy might have been as a Puritan rather than a Papist, is entirely baseless.

"I hate policy. I had as lief be a Brownist as a Politician" ... "The fellow is something of a Puritan"—"If I thought that I would beat him like a dog," says Shakespeare, reflecting the sentiments of those who loved to see his England merry according to the ancient fashion.

When the Queen's government began enforcing the new laws after June, 1559, it was hoped that the fourteen remaining Bishops would consent to follow the tide of self-interest and persuade the higher clergy to do likewise. This hope proved elusive. Only the Bishop of Llandaff conformed to the new laws and took the oath; the rest were automatically removed from their Sees together with ten deans, twelve archdeacons, forty-seven prebendaries and fifteen heads of colleges. Out of ten thousand parishes only eighty rectors were found ready to submit themselves to the Statutes of Elizabeth. The recruits who filled their places were often men without either learning or aptitude for the ministry and who merely sought a living; many did not know how to use the new prayer-book any better than their congregations had learned to follow the responses.

In 1571 Mr. Snagg rose in Parliament and complained that

[3]*The Complete Journal of the votes, speeches and debates, both of the House of Lords and House of Commons throughout the whole reign of Queen Elizabeth of glorious memory,* collected by that eminent Member of Parliament Sir Simonds d'Ewes, Bart., p. 517.

the laws were being set at naught, notably: "That service shall not be said or Sacrament ministered in other sort than in the Book of Common Prayer is prescribed." He showed how differently the same was used in many places from the prescribed rule, as where no part of those prayers were observed, "but some such other prayers as the minister shall think good in place thereof. Whereupon have great divisions, discords, and dislikes grown amongst and between great numbers."

The Nonconformist mentality developed rapidly; many desired to pray as the Spirit moved them, not according to any prescribed ritual either Anglican or Romish. But such rural districts as were not invaded by the spread of Puritanism remained attached to former ways and to their old Pastors whom they strove to retain. All awoke slowly to the dangers of the new legislation and went their ways placidly until some political event provoked sudden and drastic action and aroused country folk to the fact that the ancient order had indeed changed.

Things moved slowly however. The Queen, who had begun her reign with a Privy Council equally divided—having retained all her sister's clerical advisers and added Protestants of her own choosing, such as Leicester, Burleigh, Walsingham and Nicholas Bacon—was always ready to temporise except when made to fear for her life.

Her counsellors were astute enough to content themselves with watchful waiting until assured that Parliament (convened in 1558) had a majority solid enough to back their policies.

The régime in its early stages needed money, not blood, to assure prestige, and the exaction of fines from Catholics, rich or poor, was the most practical way of securing it.

Only two witnesses were required to prove that a man or woman had assisted at Mass and the hundred-mark fine went in large proportion to the denouncer, so that cupidity often played a greater part than religious zeal, and personal enmity the greatest of all.

AN ACT FOR THE ASSURANCE OF THE ROYAL POWER OF ALL STATE AND SUBJECT WITHIN HER HIGHNESS'S DOMINIONS reinforced the ACT OF SUPREMACY four years later. After this the Supremacy oath was imposed upon all who drew the Queen's pay and the slightest suspicion cast upon a functionary's loyalty to the Church as by Law established brought about the offender's indictment, a fact which may explain the difficulties of such office-holders as shared the cult practised by John Shakespeare, the poet's father.

The passage of these measures brought three words currently into the language of that time, one of which only is commonly heard in ours. Those who did not regularly attend the Protestant church *as by law established* were RECUSANTS, those who refused to acknowledge the Queen's spiritual authority were termed PAPISTS and the large class of spies and informers recruited by Richard Topcliff, chief of Walsingham's intelligence service, whose henchmen were placed at the disposal of local authorities, were termed PURSUIVANTS.

During the first decade after the ACTS OF SUPREMACY and UNIFORMITY had been passed, arrests were not followed by any capital punishment. In 1561, an old priest, Thomas Woodhouse, was committed to the Fleet prison, and another, Cuthbert Mayne, was indicted at the same time for "having brought into the kingdom a vain and superstitious thing called an *Agnus Dei* blessed by the Bishop of Rome, and having publicly said Mass and administered the Lord's Supper contrary to the Statutes of our Sovereign Lady Elizabeth and against her peace and crown"; but it was only after eleven years in prison, during which time public sentiment was prepared for the new policy, that both men were executed for high treason; and hangings with the accompaniment of dismemberment, "at the Queen's pleasure," became frequent.

York, Winchester, Durham and London saw some of the best minds of England—from Thomas Plumtree and Doctor Storey of Oxford to Edmund Campion and Robert Southwell —suffer, with many humbler folk, the extreme penalty of the law; so that when Elizabeth Tudor handed in her account in 1603, she could point to an impressive list of priests, laymen, and even gentlewomen who had met a felon's or a traitor's death under the Statutes which bear her name.[4]

The apologists of the régime cannot plead that the severe persecution inflicted was justified by the threat of foreign invasion, for the particular cases which can be connected with Shakespeare's life took place between 1580 and 1585—from eight to three years before the Spanish Armada menace.

However, it is not in my province to accuse or excuse Walsingham, Burleigh, Bacon or Leicester, but to show with an impartiality, perhaps easier to attain by a writer who is neither English nor Catholic, how their policies affected the domestic and civil life of so many of the Queen's subjects. Though it be an ungrateful task to recall such dark shadows on the brilliant Elizabethan picture, they were part of the scene in which the poet lived, moved and had his being. Those persons, I repeat, who, in England, France and America enjoy that freedom of conscience under law for which Shakespeare laboured with his pen and Essex with his sword, should weigh

---

[4]Margaret Ward, guilty of the charitable offence of carrying food to an imprisoned priest—for in those days captives who had nothing in their purse were obliged to rely on private charity in order to eat—was hanged at Tyburn. Mrs. Swithin Wells and Mrs. Wiseman died under sentence. Anne Lyne was hanged for harbouring, but Margaret Clitherow, who refused to plead in court, saying that she would never make twelve jurymen party to her death, was subjected to the *Peine forte et dure*—placed under a sharp stone and under immense weights until, after fifteen minutes, she succumbed.

the acts of Henry VIII's two daughters with the same measures; by declaring Mary *bad* and Elizabeth *good* we imply that the poet who constantly lifted up his voice against the tyrannies of the latter reign did not know his own time.

In harping on the victims of Mary's bigotry, Ridley, Cranmer and Latimer, those who claim to like "fair play" might remember Lacy, Campion and Southwell, and recall that under her Protestant successor more than 2000 English subjects were forced into exile, deprived of all means of support or left to die in Newgate, the Marshalsea prison or Wisbeach Castle. Meanwhile 200,000 pounds had been extorted in fines from recusants remaining in the realm, and civilians of all classes, from dukes and gentlemen to tailors, weavers, joiners, printers, yeomen, boatmen, farm-labourers and stable-lads perished on gibbet or block, not to mention the Queen of a sister kingdom, under the SUPREMACY ACT. But the class that suffered proportionately the most was naturally the "clerics" and the school-teachers formerly recruited from the minor religious orders.

One of the first country vicars to be removed was Sir Roger Dyos of Stratford-on-Avon, who had been placed by Queen Mary as incumbent of the Parish Church in 1553 and had baptised "Jone Shakxpere," the first child of John Shakespeare and Mary Arden, on September 15, 1558. Queen Elizabeth appointed John Beetchgirdle in 1560 and local authority decreed that the old incumbent's wages should be "stayed." Dyos' suit for recovery, backed by Sir Edward Greville and Sir Robert Throckmorton, lasted many years, but on the Chamberlain's accounts the quittance of Sir Roger Dyos' debt may be found: thirteen pounds seventeen shillings and ninepence, with cost of "wax to seal it and a box to bear the same."

Meantime a scholastic appointment was made in Stratford which was to prove singularly important for the educational facilities of the greatest British poet. The Bishop's Registry at Worcester shows the nomination of Simon Hunt, who had taken his Bachelor's degree at Oxford, to teach at the Stratford Grammar School.

"xxix die ejusddem mensis, anno predicto emanavit licencia Simoni Hunt in artibus bacch docendi litteras instruendi pueros in Schola grammaticali in Villa de Stratford super Avon."

When Simon Hunt in 1577 was forced to take refuge on the Continent, his life work, all unknown to himself, was already accomplished. He had given young Shakespeare the foundation of a learning which was to take him further than the best University course.

Stratford was something of an intellectual center. A local Mæcenas, Sir Hugh Clopton, who instituted a purse both for Oxford and Cambridge, had endowed the school so handsomely that the master received a salary which was double that of Eton. This ensured good teaching; the school was open free to all sons of respectable burghers and the funds for its upkeep were in John Shakespeare's hands. The elements of education acquired by the grammar-school boys were by no means negligible. The text-books in use give a key to the students' culture: Lilly's *Sententiae Pueriles* and *Latin Grammar* formed the basis for classical education and furnished considerable knowledge of Seneca, Terence, Cicero, Plautus, Ovid and Horace from all of whom were copious extracts.

" 'Tis a phrase of Horace but I learned it in my Latin grammar."

exclaims one of Shakespeare's characters on reading a classical couplet, and his first biographer astutely observes that "this was probably the author's case." A letter written by an eleven-year-old comrade asking his father to bring some books back from London to his little brother, who became Shakespeare's son-in-law, would do honour to an older boy nowadays. On leaving school Richard Field, the tanner's son, was able to enter the printing house of Thomas Vautrollier who had the monopoly of the publication of educational works and French translations.

Thomas Quinney is found, by Mr. Fripp, quoting from Melin de Saint-Gelais, and like indications that the grammar-school boys were by no means without general culture are numerous. The old method of writing "fair" or in gothic characters was taught throughout Shakespeare's time, a mode which was looked upon as vulgar by Londoners, where the poet's calligraphy marked him as a rustic among university graduates.

Golding's rhymed translation of *Ovid* obviously helped him read the Latin text and the original version used as a school-boy remains at the Bodleian with the attestation dated 1602 that it belonged to him. "This little book of *Ovid* was given to me by W. Hall who says it was once Will Shakespeare's."

Plutarch's *Lives of Noble Graecians and Romans,* and Holinshed's *Chronicles* were authorities in Stratford, the more so that old Raphael Holinshed dwelt in the neighboring hamlet of Packwood. Thomas Wilson's *Arte of Rhetorike for the use of all such as are studious of Eloquence* was freely employed if we are to judge from the deep traces to be found in Shakespeare's plays and poems.

Even if Shakespeare was forced to abandon school at fifteen, the knowledge then acquired was equivalent to good University preparation, for the graduate at sixteen with an M.A. degree was by no means rare at Oxford and Cambridge. The testimony of one of his earliest biographers, John Aubrey, learned from Christopher Beeston, a lifelong associate in London, declares that Shakespeare was by no means weak in the Latin tongue but taught it in the country, would seem to indicate that he had acted as "monitor" and helped Simon Hunt to teach the younger boys.

With the departure of the Magister of the old school, a new régime began at Stratford under a puritan teacher, Thomas Jenkins. He is supposed to have been pictured with his Welsh accent as Sir Hugh Evans in *The Merry Wives;* this does not give a very high idea of the "progress" in learning which the flight of the old Catholic schoolmasters, throughout England, brought about.

Fortunately the revolution was counteracted by the efforts of one man, for in 1568 a champion had arisen who undertook to maintain the Catholic Faith and save his country's learning by the same occasion. This was William Allen.[5] His name until the nineteenth century was such anathema on his native soil that it was not until 1823 that an English editor dared even include it among those that represent the "mettle of her pasture."

Up to that time Burleigh and Walsingham's chief opponent is simply left out of the Elizabethan picture and the poet's

[5]*Portraits of Illustrious Personages of Great Britain,* Edmund Lodge, London, 1823.

Like those of Campion and Southwell, William Allen's parents were gentlefolk of the intellectual type: John Allen of Brockhouse and Janet Lister of Westby. Their son, born at Rossel in Yorkshire, showed exceptional talent early. After three years at Oriel College, Oxford, his studies were of such phenomenal character that he was unanimously elected Fellow of the House, University Proctor, and Principal of St. Mary's Hall before he was twenty-five.

Longing for England brought him back from exile to Oxfordshire and Lancashire where he disseminated many of his books—*Certain Brief Reasons—In Defense of the lawful authority of the Priesthood,* etc.

Protected for a time by the still powerful Duke of Norfolk he was eventually forced to leave the country permanently and, in 1587, was created Archbishop of Mechlin; but, a year later, he retired to Rome, according to the historian Camden "quite worn out with the heats and dissensions of the English fugitives, both scholars and gentlemen," and died when scarcely over sixty "of a broken heart."

Anthony Wood, after repeating in the *Athenæ Oxonienses* some of the invectives thundered against Cardinal Allen, added: "Let writers say what they please, certain it is that he was an active man, and of great parts and high prudence; that he was religious and zealous in his profession, restless until he had performed what he had undertaken; that he was very affable, genteel and winning, and that his person was handsome and proper, which with an innate gravity commanded respect from all that came near him."

24

life-stage is set by his biographers without any reference to a writer whose work anticipated the gradual progress of a century in English prose, and who introduced good taste into a controversial discussion at a time when the Puritan pen and pulpit relied solely on vituperation.

After a short career, the death of Queen Mary put a sudden end to Allen's hope of church preferment just when the archbishopric of York was about to be bestowed upon him. But his vocation was scholastic. First at Louvain, then at Mechlin he taught the refugees from England who could no longer be admitted to Cambridge and Oxford. His scheme for a new national education germinated and took shape and, with dogged determination, he overcame all obstacles and built up a university for his banished fellow-countrymen with a seminary for priests annexed thereto.

Through many vicissitudes this English college subsisted at Douai until the French Revolution. But, during certain years when the political agitations in the Netherlands threatened the safety of the institution, the personnel was divided between Rome and Reims. Subsequently a branch was opened at Valladolid. At the period when the principal house was established at Reims—1578-1594—the organization reached its height of excellence. The English New Testament, printed in 1582, was so superior in scholarship to the Puritan or Bishop's version that when the King James translation gave a standard Bible to England, the Oxford theologians fell back constantly on the Reims translation, completed in 1609. The alumni of Reims were men of the highest literary quality.

When Shakespeare designates a pair of young students as possessing, to a remarkable degree, knowledge of the Greek and Latin classics, he causes them to be introduced as graduates of Reims: "I freely give unto you this young scholar that

25

hath been long studying at Reims; as cunning in Greek and Latin and other tongues as his comrade in music and mathematics . . ." "The Taming of the Shrew."

In the same play, the dramatist outlines an ideal program for his young scholar and it is easy to see, by the declared intentions of Lucentio, and by his servant's counsels of moderation, what the college course comprehended at Reims if not at Padua!

> Here let us breathe and haply institute
> A course of learning and ingenious study.
> Virtue, and that part of philosophy
> Will I apply, that treats of happiness
> By virtue specially to be achiev'd.

Tranio at once responds by suggesting that while sucking the sweets of philosophy and admiring the moral discipline which virtue counsels, time should be left for the arts; might not the student arrange, while studying Aristotle, to cast a glance at Ovid now and then, and cultivate logic and rhetoric in conversation without a text-book as guide? He further observes that poetry and music quicken the intellect as much as mathematics and metaphysics.

In short, the idea suggested is just that laid down by Jesuit schools on the continent, where a full humanistic education was given to worldlings, while to those who might be going forth to martyrdom, rigid training, self-discipline, fastings and mortifications, served to prepare the devotee for the thorny path he was to tread.

The success of the English college was a severe blow to the Queen's Council which, by excluding papists from the home universities, expected that learning would die out among the younger generations of Catholics; so, when it became evident that instead of this, 120 students were graduating yearly from the university and that the seminary ordained an average of from fifty to sixty priests, the contest between two great personalities began: William Allen represented by his school, *versus* Walsingham's Information Service equipped with men and money to combat a force which was purely intellectual.

What a conflict it was! In recounting the principal moves on the great chess-board and showing each attack and counter-attack, I shall make no attempt to establish which side was right or most right, but merely try to show that history cannot be understood if half the documents which went into its making are left out of modern study.

In order to know what sort of existence was led by Shakespeare's family, their neighbours in the shire and friends in London, we must examine into the rigour with which each new Edict, Proclamation or Injunction given by her Majesty affected the rural districts and the printing world: when read by their light many of the troubles into which Mary Arden's son was plunged, from deer-stealing episode to marriage problem, are clarified, and Shakespeare's connection with the Essex conspiracy whose leaders held King James's pledge, in case of success, to accord religious freedom to both Catholic and Puritan, is explained.

The laws as they already stood in 1570 sufficed for the putting down of the Northern Rising and the execution of the protesting Duke of Norfolk, together with that secular priest who had acted as chaplain to the insurgents.

The natural retaliation of the See of Rome was to issue a Bull of Excommunication against the Queen, February 25, 1570, and the duel continued.

Elizabeth parried this blow by more radical legislation, declaring that henceforth the word *heretic* as applied to the sovereign or the introduction of any document from the See of Rome constituted High Treason.

Under the new acts John Felton, gentleman, and John Storey, Doctor of Laws and president of Broadgate Hall, Oxford, were condemned. John Nelson, a Jesuit, newly arrived from the Seminary, was brought to the scaffold, and Thomas Sherwood, a young layman, apprehended on his way there, met the same fate.

The next step came in 1581, with the passage of an ACT TO KEEP HER HIGHNESS' SUBJECTS IN THEIR DUE OBEDIENCE, more commonly known as the ACT OF PERSUASIONS; thenceforth, it became high treason to "reconcile or be reconciled to the Romish religion" (23 Eliz. C.1.) and it was under this Act, as we shall see, that Burleigh and Walsingham prosecuted as traitors or felons many Englishmen who prided themselves on being free-born and whose idea of patriotism as well as religion, led them to risk existence in the attempt to keep the Faith of Thomas à Becket alive in Britain.

It may be noted, by the way, that Elizabeth's parliament declared Becket "a rebellious priest and traitor to his king."

When Walsingham awoke to the fact that the insufficiently educated clergy of the new school were no match for the graduates of the overseas college, he had recourse to another policy. It was declared that too much schooling is dangerous to the State and the "Cardinal's men" by belonging to the Church of Rome, were, *de facto,* guilty of high treason.

He was astute enough to apply this idea in the beginning to the graduates of the overseas seminary and did not extend it to the parish priest at home until the time was ripe and the way prepared to expound the same theory in England. Though the faith daily became more difficult to practise it was hard to credit that the saying of Mass—declared, in the Protestant Prayer-book, founded on "foolish fables" and "dangerous deceits"—was treasonable, and to shelter a priest a hanging matter.

Walsingham's efforts were intelligently bent on persuading

British subjects that plots to murder the Queen were being hatched in the school at Reims. It is never very difficult to make Englishmen believe that there is something radically wrong with the man who lives abroad even when his exile has been enforced. That his old country parson has suddenly become untrue to his cloth takes a little longer.

The Queen's ministers correctly judged that there would be time to deal effectively with the Marian priest when example had been made of a few Jesuits and the working of this far-sighted policy proved that Walsingham and Burleigh had little to learn from Machiavelli.

The spies sent into the Low Countries and on to Rome understood what news they were expected to give, and hastened to broadcast it by the methods then in vogue: the free and general distribution of tracts concerning the turpitude of the seminaries. The "English Romayne Life" is a typical example of this widespread literature. More mystery was made of what was preparing at Reims. It was hinted that a whole army of priests bringing vengeance, death and destruction to the sea-walled garden England would soon be landing on her shores.

This government propaganda was so effective that even Catholics at home shivered at what might be the outcome. That these missionaries of 1580 had undertaken their perilous adventure, not to kill, but to die if need were, seemed unbelievable until it was proved.

A few seminary priests had already filtered into England one by one and were engaged in charitable work in the prisons when the larger mission headed by John Parsons and Edmund Campion arrived. Had the latter come as sole chief of the peaceful army the results might have been less tragic.

For Campion was the man of the hour with a soul unspotted from the world, crystal clear mind, a tongue of flame and a heart big and tender enough to embrace all his fellow-countrymen. "If I, who have run thousands of miles to do you good, shall be rewarded with rigor, I have no more to say but to recommend your case and mine to Almighty God . . . to the end that we may at last be friends in heaven when all injuries shall be forgotten." This was the spirit in which he set forth in a small boat from St. Omer and landed at Dover before dawn on the 25th of June, whereas Parsons dealt more freely, in speech at least, with fire and brimstone.

The master-stroke, made by Campion upon arrival, is worthy of remembrance. His English soul rebelled at the idea of sneaking by stealth into his native country on an errand which had been so widely bruited as treasonable and murderous, and the action he took was so far from being "jesuitical" according to the current meaning of the term, that it forced admiration from his foes by its courage, made his friends rejoice, and brought to his enterprise the sympathy of thousands who admire what might be called a good "sporting spirit."

In an open letter addressed to the Queen and her Privy Council, Campion published his exact intentions upon coming to England, in the form of a public confession, and proved at the same time the weakness of Burleigh's spy system, when opposed to one man of his mettle. Though there were no radios in those days, CAMPION'S BRAG, as it was called, was carried from mouth to mouth with extraordinary celerity throughout the length and breadth of England.

He began by offering to save the Government trouble and expense, by freely confessing the exact intention of himself and his English missionaries: thus Walsingham might have gratis all the information which he was paying an army of spies to ferret out. In the first of the nine points in which Campion "truly and resolutely opens his full purpose" he explains that he has joined the Society of Jesus after eight years' study, abandoned all interest or possibility of wealth, honor, pleasure or worldly felicity, and sworn to do the work assigned to him by his superiors. In the third article he declares: "My charge is of free cost to preach the gospel, minister the Sacraments, instruct the simple, reform sinners, confute errors. I never had mind and am strictly forbidden to deal in any respect with matters of State or policy." He then offers to plead the cause of the Church before the Privy Council, the Doctors and Masters chosen from both Universities, "that a fair light and plain dealing may be cast upon these controversies." Lastly, he appeals to the Sovereign herself, "because it hath pleased God to enrich the Queen my Sovereign Lady with notable gifts of nature, learning, and princely education; that her zeal for truth and love of her people shall incline her Noble Grace to disfavour some proceedings hurtful to the realm and procure towards us oppressed more equity. Many innocent hands are lifted up to heaven for you daily by those English students which beyond the seas are gathering virtues sufficient either to win you to heaven or to die upon your pikes. For be it known to you that we have made a league cheerfully to carry the cross you shall lay upon us and never to despair of your recovery while we have a man left to enjoy your Tyburn or be racked by your torments or consumed in your prisons. The expense is reckoned, the enterprise is begun, it is of God, it cannot be withstood. So the Faith was planted, so it must be restored."

Campion's fame, obscured by long absence, had been great in the Universities and at Court among scholars and men of fashion, but until then it had never reached the market towns and remote manor-houses where his BRAG now penetrated.

It was a psychological moment in British history. The Queen was wavering and hesitated to subscribe to Walsingham's Church policy. Her personal taste was strongly opposed to the

31

puritanical elements which were rapidly becoming preponderant in Anglican affairs. She liked to have candles and a cross on her private altar. She could not abide the idea of a married Bishop and was opposed to preachers who refused to wear a cassock; above all, she deplored the decadence of learning in the Established Church and in the Universities.[6] Her admiration for good scholarship was unfeigned and on a long-ago visit to Oxford she had heard Edmund Campion, then the pride of the University, as public orator. The Queen recognised in him just the sort of scholar who might build up the Established Church in the form she approved and which was later called "high." At this period Elizabeth was seriously contemplating her French marriage scheme which could not be carried out without Mass at its solemnisation. This idea, for her at least, contained no novelty. She had been crowned with Catholic ceremonial by the Archbishop of Carlisle, and solemnly sworn to protect her Catholic clergy. She was therefore ready to discuss terms with Edmund Campion, if he could be brought to terms.

How Campion fulfilled his mission need not be repeated here. From the time that he lodged in Chancery Lane and preached quite openly in a hall hired for the purpose by Lord Paget, he was scarcely disquieted, which proved that there was certain connivance found at Court, perhaps the Queen did not despair of winning him over to her side by her offer of a bishopric in the Established Church. During a six months' tour in the shires he was the guest of William Catesby, Lord Vaux of Harrowden, Sir Thomas Tresham, and scores

[6]Richard Southam, who was vicar of Charlecote in Shakespeare's time, answered the Bishop's interrogations as to his competence on September 9, 1585:

"I have taken no degree of schoole neyther in Oxforde nor Cambridge. I have no lyscence to preach," adding that none could challenge the right of "my good patron and master Sir Thomas Lucy Knighte" to bestow the cure and vicarage upon whom he wished. (Page 265, J. W. Gray, *Shakespeare's Marriage and Departure from Stratford*. Chapman & Hall.)

of others,[7] and was able to inform his superiors: "The exceeding reverence all Catholics do unto us is scarcely creditable."

But the price on his head attracted John Eliot who levied a force of sixty men-at-arms. They surrounded Lyford, the house of Mrs. Yate, and arrested Campion at the conclusion of a last sermon: "Jerusalem, Jerusalem, thou that killest the prophets!" Transported to London with a paper crown on his hat with the inscription: CAMPION THE SEDITIOUS JESUIT, and thrown into a dungeon where, for the period of four days, he could neither stand nor lie down, he was conveyed to Leicester House and invited to fulfil his former boast and debate upon religious matters before the Queen sitting in state among her Privy Councillors, with Leicester and Bedford beside the throne.

They questioned him on his purpose in coming to England: he replied that his object was the salvation of souls.

Elizabeth broke in with the enquiry: "Did he acknowledge her as Queen?" To this he responded that he did indeed recognise her as his lawful Queen and governess whom he was bound to obey in all temporal matters.

After a short debate, the chief spokesman acknowledged that they were satisfied that he had no treasonable design and found no fault in him but that of being a papist.

Campion replied: "Which is my greatest glory."

Then the offer was made that if he would wipe out the last ten years, abjure the Pope and re-enter the Anglican Church which he had left as a deacon, there should be no bounds to possible preferment—not even Canterbury. On his refusal, Campion was taken back to the Tower, and, five days

[7]According to Burleigh's list the chief supporters and entertainers of Campion were Pierrepoints, Sacheveralls, Langfords, Foljambes, Powdrells, Ayers, Tempests, Rookbys, Vavasours, Bulmers, Babthorpes, Grimstones, Hawkeworths, Harringtons, Worthingtons, Talbots, Heskeths, Houghtons, Westbys and Ringmaidens.

Campion's recent biographer, Mr. Evelyn Waugh, computes that more than twice this number remained undetected.

later, warrant was signed by Leicester and Burleigh to put him to the torture.

Further disputations were staged at the Tower where the best intellectual lights of the universities came to argue. The priest only spoke after having been racked to the fainting-point, and even in those days this was not considered quite fair play; but many attended those jousts until, alarmed at the number of converts made, among them Philip Howard, Earl of Arundel, the disputations were suddenly suspended and false news was freely dispersed to discredit the Jesuit's sincerity. It was announced that Campion had committed suicide; then that he had accepted the Queen's offer of an Anglican bishopric; then that he had confessed to far-reaching Catholic plots against the State and denounced those who had given him shelter on his journeys to and from London.

After a last torture, Lord Hunsdon reported that "they might sooner pluck this man's heart out of his bosom, than rack one word out of his mouth that it was against his conscience to utter," and the Council suddenly realised that there was no possible fighting against such a spirit; to extinguish it was the only remedy. He was brought to trial on Tuesday, November 14, with seven fellow missionaries, Sherwin, Kirby, Bosgrave, Cottam, Johnson, Orton, and Rishton, arraigned at the bar of Westminster Hall and charged with High Treason and plots to murder the Queen. Called upon to take his "Bible Oath," Campion, whose arms had been completely paralysed by the late torture he had undergone, could not lift his hand; Sherwin kissed it reverently and raised it for him, while his leader exclaimed: "I protest before God and His holy angels, before Heaven and Earth, before the world and this bar where I stand, which is but a small resemblance of the terrible judgment of the next Life, that I am not guilty of any part of the treason contained in the indictment, or of any other treason whatever." "The plain reason of our standing here is religion and not treason" said Sherwin, and Sir Christopher Wray, Chief Justice of the King's Bench, ordered him to "spare speech."

Campion was hanged at Tyburn on December 1, together with Ralph Sherwin, fellow of Exeter College, and Alexander Bryant, a graduate of Harte's Hall, Oxford.

The Council, having proved the mettle of these men, decided on more stringent methods through which the old Faith which had begun to appear so strong should be "utterly eradicated and stamped out," and it is notable that the first civilians to receive capital condemnation after the ACT OF PERSUASIONS had been passed, were closely akin to Shakespeare's mother, Mary Arden of Wilmcote.

The tragic story of her cousins Edward Arden of Park Hall, on the border of Worcestershire, his wife Mary and their son-in-law, John Somerville of Edreston, four miles from Stratford, must needs be recalled; it furnishes material enough to clarify the so-called mysteries of William's youth and explains why local tradition which is so persistent and consistent concerning certain episodes between 1580 and 1585 is, at the same time, reticent about circumstantial details of an enmity which existed between the Bailiff of Stratford and the local Justice of the Peace who brought "criminals" to trial.

During two generations at least, these details, well known to Stratford and the adjacent counties, were spoken of with extreme caution. Country folk think it "unchancy" to mention those under religious or political ban. Besides, High Treason charges, leading to execution, brand the victim's immediate family with the unsavoury epithet "corrupt in blood"—they are talked of with bated breath or, better, seldom referred to. However superior the social sphere of Park Hall Ardens may have been to that of the Ardens of Wilmcote, the humbler

35

branch was not eager to claim "kin with their betters" when trouble came to them, and the taint of treason was only wiped out under King James who restored Sir William Somerville, Shakespeare's friend, to the estates forfeited under Elizabeth by his brother John.

CHAPTER TWO

THE CASE OF SOMERVILLE AND ARDEN

No BLOT defaced the Arden scutcheon when, in the reign of "Lord Philip and Mary," John Shakespeare, who wrote himself a yeoman and possessed the broad acres of Snitterfield farm and bushes, married Mary, daughter of Robert Arden, Esq., of Wilmcote. The domain of Asbies came to the couple, sowed and tilled as it lay, with a fine house and farm buildings upon it and that symbol of rural superiority, a dove-cot.

After their marriage at Aston-Cantlow, the parish church of his Snitterfield farm, John Shakespeare and Mary his wife moved to Stratford and acquired the house of rough-cast and brick whose dark oaken beams and pointed gable-ends recall the picturesque dwellings of old Normandy. Set in orchards with a large garden at the back, it stood between the forge worked by Richard Horneby, the blacksmith, and the tailor's shop of William Wedgewood. An early childhood impression is recorded by their son in "King John" where the nocturnal arrival of a royal messenger is pictured:

> I saw a smith stand with his hammer thus
> The whilst his iron did on the anvil cool,
> With open mouth swallowing a tailor's news;
> Who, with his shears and measure in his hand,
> Standing on slippers,—which his nimble haste
> Had falsely thrust upon contrary feet,—
> Told of many thousand warlike French . . .

The functions of John Shakespeare can be traced in the archives during ten years honorable service to his borough, ale-taster to the county—an important function in a rural population which exercised rigid control of the purity of their universal beverage—then "Chamberlayne" or treasurer of the town council, then High Bailiff, and finally chief Alderman, his name after 1567 is prefixed with a "Mr." He was active when the plague raged, contributed to the relief of the poor when times were hard, and was chosen, as a just man, to arbitrate local disputes and appraise his neighbors' goods. John was the first bailiff who authorised troupes of players to give their show at the Guild Hall before the Council and, afterwards, if found seemly, licensed them to perform and charge the customary admission at the Swan, Bear or Crown Taverns. On four several occasions the Queen's players, those of Leicester, Nottingham and Worcester, wearing on their sleeves the badge of each particular patron, marched up Bridge Street, a led mule bearing the gear and properties. The Bailiff who received them was privileged to attend the revels at Kenilworth officially.

Rosy, "merry-cheeked" and garrulous, old John appeared to the poet Mennis when he entered the glove shop and was told that son Will had always been a good honest fellow but some folk durst not crack a jest with him.

This picture is given us by the archdeacon of Rochester, Thomas Plume (*circa* 1657).

Had rubicund John, after the losing battle fought with life and poverty, fallen into excess to which his taste-in-ale predisposed him? Had he speculated in grain, as Sir Sidney Lee supposes, or adopted looser ways of life that he dared no longer jest with the family breadwinner?

Prosperity reigned at least during the first decade after John Shakespeare's marriage; he sold the Snitterfield and Wilmcote timber to the corporation, and monthly, when Guild chapel bell rang for council at nine in the forenoon, donned his gown and hastened to join his comrades at the Hall or, in plague time (which came all too often), met them outside in orchard or garden.

Every man practised a trade or industry in the little "corporate state" which was the direct outgrowth of the religious guilds, and looked on sloth as a major vice.

There were weekly markets at the High Cross which stood at the North End of Bridge Street, a stone structure covered by a small-tiled shed. Around this, when a proclamation was read or a sermon preached, rough wooden benches were placed to accommodate listeners. The stocks, pillory and whipping post were set so near that the ears of those undergoing punishment might also be edified. Salted meats and raw hides were sold in Rother Market, together with butter, cheese, poultry, fruit and yarn. Country butchers might take a stand on High Street on fair days, held thrice yearly. There was a local association for making soap and tallow. Among the tailors, weavers, skinners, collar and shoemakers, bakers, pewterers, brewers, grocers, mercers, carpenters and painters, no trade mark stood more in honor than the dividers for stretching gloves which Master Chamberlayne Shakespeare drew very delicately after his name when signing the municipal accounts. But all corporate activity enjoyed such credit that even local magnates like Sir Thomas Lucy and Sir Hugh Clopton before him were inscribed among the Woolmen. A stained-glass window bearing the arms of this honourable corporation decorated the shop front where John sat among his hides and fleeces and sold the gloves of his own fabrication. The use of glass marked another point of superiority over the townsfolk for many neighbours were content to stretch parchment on their window-frames.

The Shakespeares had already christened and lost two daughters when their son William was born to them and carried on April 26, 1563, to be baptised at the old collegiate church of the Holy Trinity. Five other children followed, Gilbert, Johanna, Richard, Anne (who died in 1571) and finally Edmund who remained hardly more than a baby at the time of his elder brother's departure, and eventually joined him as a comedian in London.

Stratford was countrified enough for her children to live very close to nature; the beautiful forest in which it is set held few secrets for young Will. Reminiscences of sports and pastimes abound throughout his entire work: games of marbles, play with tops and tenpins, Morris-dancing, Hoodman blind, and hide-and-seek, swimming bouts in the pools of Avon, and winter slides on the frozen ponds, birds'-nesting in the tree-tops, and reveries under melancholy boughs. Will counted the hours by the shepherd's clock of dandelion, followed the lark in her flight to heaven's gate or listened in hushed silence to the nightingale. Perhaps old Adam's faithful service and the wisdom of Corin, whose simplicity and good sense he so cleverly opposed to the worldly sophistication of Touchstone, was drawn from Thomas Whittington, the Wilmcote shepherd who confided his savings to the hands of "Master Shakespeare's wife."

Stratford was reputed as a great sporting center, nobles, gentry, and farmers flocked from fifty miles round to the yearly games on the Cotswold heights, where leaping, boxing and wrestling contests were well rewarded, handling of lance and quarter staff was practised together with hare coursing, horsemanship and falconry, and any youth fortunate enough to possess a greyhound entered him, like Slender, in the Cotswold races.

The technical language of the huntsman in the "Taming of the Shrew," whose prologue is presented outside Wilmcote Inn, and, later, at an adjacent manor house, shows the writer's knowledge of and passion for sylvan sports. The mixed feelings of a healthy boy, who at the same time possessed keen sensitiveness and aptitude for compassion, are constantly shown in the poet's work; but the blame given by Jaques to the usurping tyrant man who persecutes the rightful owners of the forest did not prevent Shakespeare from killing venison at Fulbrook or hunting the poor hare at Cotswold. His sympathetic comprehension of animals is that of the tender-hearted country boy:

> . . . poor Wat, far off upon a hill,
> Stands on his hinder legs with listening ear,
> To hearken if his foes pursue him still;
> Anon their loud alarums he doth hear.
> And now his grief may be compared well
> To one sore sick that hears the passing bell.
>
> Then shalt thou see the dew-bedabbled wretch
> Turn and return, indenting with the way;
> Each envious briar his weary legs doth scratch,
> Each shadow makes him stop, each murmur stay . . .

Art and letters flourished also in the region. Good libraries and Renaissance refinements were to be found in the homes of Trussels, Conways, Grants, Throckmortons, Cloptons and Somervilles. An inventory of the Arden house at Wilmcote shows it to have been decorated with twelve fine paintings and Shakespeare's description of a manor in this locality proves that the collector with his portfolio of engravings was not unknown.

> Dost thou love pictures? we will fetch thee straight
> Adonis, painted by a running brook,
> And Cytherea all in sedges hid
> Which seem to move and wanton with her breath,

Even as the waving sedges play with wind.
—Or Daphne roaming through a thorny wood,
Scratching her legs that one should swear she bleeds
And at that sight shall sad Apollo weep,
So workmanly the tears and blood are drawn.

Among the handsome manor houses which dot the immediate vicinity of Stratford was that of Edreston or Edston.

Its owner, young John Somerville, after graduating at Harte's Hall, Oxford, married Margaret Arden, granddaughter of Sir John Throckmorton and daughter to Edward Arden, Esquire, of Park Hall.

These Park Hall Ardens conformed to the Statutes to the extent of sending their servants to public church, but privately, like most of their neighbours, they remained Catholics and even maintained their chaplain Hugh Hall, of Idlicote, to say private Mass from time to time.

For this privilege Edward Arden doubtless paid the usual fine fixed at a sum between thirty and forty pounds yearly. Official eyes were accustomed to wink upon such profitable irregularities until some unforeseen event or some new and rigorous legislation obliged eyes and ears to open and suddenly brought down the sword of Damocles.

John Somerville's convictions were more absolute than those of his father-in-law. Old-fashioned, easy-going folk could hardly believe that the law really meant what it said, and the cleft between the two generations was soon to open wide.

Enforced idleness is never good for a vigorous young man with small outlet for his energies and the taint of hereditary insanity. Like others of his faith Somerville was forbidden to absent himself except in a radius of a few miles. Civil rights, public service and even foreign travel were denied him for, if any Catholic suspect once left the kingdom, he could not hope to return. Official surveillance was exercised over visits among neighbours. Exile had thinned the ranks of the local clergy. The passage of the ACT OF PERSUASIONS drove Father Hall into hiding or rather caused him to adopt a better formula than a permanent place of concealment; this was to keep constantly on the move among his former parishioners' houses.

The sacraments which Somerville daily demanded were ever more difficult to obtain, and he began raving rebelliously against the Queen. His terrified wife sent for Sir John Conway, a Catholic neighbor, to watch by her husband's bedside and preach calm and reason, but Somerville, with the shrewdness of insanity, feigned sleep one night. The watch was relaxed and before dawn he tiptoed out of the house, roughly roused the stable-boy, ordered two horses saddled, and bade him come along. He was hardly decently dressed and totally without funds, so that he could not have had any well thought-out plan of action. Moreover, the charges had been drawn from the pistols taken from his bedside and, except for a small dagger, he was unarmed. He selected devious and little trodden ways, but stated to the boy his intention of riding to London, frightening him so much by wild gestures and threatening words that, abandoning his master, the lad galloped home.

Somerville reached a small village called Aynhoe-on-the-Hill on the Warwickshire border, and asked at the Inn for lodging and "horse-meat." The advent of this singular rider, who muttered to himself, aroused the inn-servants' curiosity. When Somerville retired, there was soon a small gathering about his door. In his sleep he called the Queen "viper" and "serpent." The gathering became large and the eavesdroppers began to doubt whether it was lawful to listen to such accusations and leave authority uninformed. When Somerville exclaimed loudly: "Her head should be set upon a pole!" a justice of the peace hastily called in, wakened the sleeper and questioned him as to the meaning of the phrase. Somerville spoke

43

earnestly, explained his intention to remonstrate with the Queen, complained of the wrongs inflicted on her good Catholic subjects, and the extortionate fines levied by Leicester. Should she refuse to listen, he stated his intention of "piercing her wicked heart." The listeners declared the unknown traveller a traitor and handled him accordingly. Bruised, battered, and under heavy guard, he was sent to Oxford, then after five days, almost without sleep or food, on to London, escorted by John d'Oily Esquire, acting upon the orders of Sir Thomas Lucy, Justice of the Peace at Stratford-on-Avon, whose report, together with a bill of thirteen pounds, seven shillings, is to be found at the Public Record Office in the Secret Pouch consecrated to the Arden-Somerville affair.

This Thomas Lucy appears again and again as evil genius to William Shakespeare's whole connection. Early biographers agree that Lucy's enmity towards young Will obliged him, by numerous vexations, to flee the country, and, all unknowingly, enabled the poet to make good in the London world of letters, a fact which was recognised by the first authority who consigned the incident to paper and observed the dramatist's revenge in caricaturing his old enemy as "Justice Shallow" in two of his comedies.

In the Arden affair, Sir Thomas acted with fuller powers than rural justiceship would have conferred, having just been appointed on a Commission of forty-four, twelve of whom were Anglican ecclesiastics, to "Put Down Abuses in Religion" and keep a wary eye upon recusant doings.[1]

An order was despatched at once into Warwickshire by Her Majesty's Privy Council, to arrest all those connected with the accused traitors and search the houses of Catholic suspects for evidence of a far-reaching plot.

Thomas Wilkes' report, of which I modernise the spelling

[1] This innovation was declared unconstitutional by Sir Edward Coke.

and abridge, is to be found in full among the *Domestic State Papers,* Elizabeth Vol. 163, No. 55. It is addressed to the "Lord Treasurer and Secretary," from Charlecote, on November 7, 1583:

"May it please your Honour. Your letter of the second of this present I received at Park Hall, the house of Edward Arden the fourth of the name. Even upon my sending away of Arden to your Honour, according to your former directions, and determined how to proceed to the accomplishing of your Honourable directions therein contained, Sir Thomas Lucy, Mr. Griffin, the preacher, and myself took our voyage towards the house of Edward Grant of Northbrokes and Mr. Elgianby accompanied with Mr. Burgwin towards Hall's house we found nothing but one book called 'The Censure,' in his bedchamber over the tester of his bed, which, as it seemed had lain there long before; in a trunk of Elizabeth Somerville, left by her in the house, we found a book entitled 'Hore beate Mariae.' We examined Grant upon his oath (which at first he was unwilling to take) concerning the book which Somerville confesseth he received from him by Elizabeth Somerville.

"It is confessed by Joyce Hill (a servant) that Elizabeth Somerville brought the book to her brother, who, after the reading thereof, was much perplexed in mind, and that the book was conveyed away again by her. I perceive that there will be alleged in his excuse to save him from the danger of the law, that he hath been sithence midsummer affected with a frantic humour, grown, it is said, of jealousy conceived of his wife. True it is that three or four days before he departed from his house, his mind was greatly troubled in so much that he could not sleep . . . His wife had knowledge of his traitorous purpose. As soon as she understood he was gone towards London, she rideth after him in all haste to stay him, and finding him not to have taken the highway towards Lon-

45

don, she, travelling as far as Ilesbury, returned home again.

"Somerville's determination to be confessed by Hall the priest and to receive the Sacrament hath been and is an ordinary thing before attempting treasons, as we find by the history of King John poisoned by a monk and of late by the report published in print where the Spaniard was confessed by a friar and received the Sacrament before he attempted to murder the Prince of Orange.

"The *Agnus Dei* found upon him was given him—it may be supposed—to defend him from the danger which might ensue had he attempted his wicked enterprise, for that I know to be a superstition, opinion and ceremony among the Papists.

"His acquaintance and society with Hall the priest, being noted as he is for a most dangerous practiser a conveyor of intelligence to all the Capital Papists in these parts, as resorted unto them under the cloak of a gardener he converteth reconcileth confesseth saith Mass etc., and is the most likely to have persuaded this wretched traitor to attempt her Majesty's destruction.

"In the search of Hall's house at Idlicote there was nothing found by book, paper or otherwise, that might render him suspected. He himself is at London, lodging at the Bell Carter Lane. So he could not be examined. Howbeit, all other diligence was used to find his books, but nothing could be discovered through those of his house where there lodgeth the mother of Somerville a creature almost past sense and memory in respect of sickness."

This is the only evidence brought forward against Edward Arden and Hugh Hall who were condemned solely on this report. Mary Arden was sentenced to be burned, Francis Arden of Pedmore, Edward's brother, together with Somerville's wife and sister Elizabeth, were committed to prison as

46

accessories of treason.[2] The examination of Hugh Hall taken by
Thomas Wilkes and Thomas Morton, on the last day of
December, 1583, may be found entire among the Domestic
State Papers of Elizabeth 164, 177. The gist is given below:

". . . For reconciling says that he has no authority so to do,
for he thinks that it requires episcopal sanction . . . hath only
heard confessions but of such who were in the Catholic Church
already . . . He hath had no familiarity with Francis Throckmorton these seven or eight years and doth not remember to
have seen him these four or five years. With Mr. John Talbot,
Sir John Throckmorton, Lord Windesor, Mr. Sheldon he hath
most commonly conversed and sometimes said Mass, but held
no conference of state these thirteen years past, only of religion;
with Sir Thomas Cornwallis and Sir Thomas Kidson he held
no conference but of orchards and gardens.

"In Warwickshire he hath not conversed with other than
Edward Arden but denies that he was present at any marriage
with a Mass . . . All this he sayeth to be true, with refusal
of her Majesty's mercy if [what] he says [be] not true. . . ."

The arraignment and doom of the accused are recorded in
the December sessions (*see Plate II, at end of volume*):

"John Somervyle, Edward Arden, Mary Arden and Hugh
Hall being brought to the bar by the lieutenant of the Tower
are severally arraigned. John Somervyle pleads guilty, Edward
Arden, Mary Arden and Hugh Hall plead not guilty *venire*
from the county of Warwick awarded instanter. Verdict GUILTY.
Judgment against the male prisoner and the female prisoner
as is usual in cases of high treason. Execution on the twentieth."

The government desired to find proof of a far-reaching plot
behind this act of individual madness and Walsingham sent
strict injunctions to Stratford that more victims must be found

[2]Comptrolment Roll 219 m. 54 Hilary 26 Eliz.

and further evidence discovered.[3] Thomas Wilkes responded by a secret letter addressed personally to Walsingham. Mrs. Stopes who published the following passage acknowledges that it is a "euphemistic invitation to make the prisoners speak through torture."

"Unless you can make Somerville, Arden, Hall the priest, and Somerville's wife and sister speak about those things which you desire to be discovered it will not be possible for us here to find out more than is already found out." He goes on to explain how the Warwickshire recusants sustain each other and clear their houses of suspicion on the first alarm of search and adds: "Unless you can charge them with matter from the mouths of your prisoners, look not to wring anything from them *here*."

Walsingham, thus thrown upon his own resources, dealt with the case in a different manner. Young Somerville instead

[3]On November 5 a Commission of Oyer and Terminer took in hand "Mrs. Somervylle, Arden, Hawle, and Elizabeth Somervylle"; the latter was asked whether she had seen her father Edward Arden or received any message from him since the apprehension of her husband. Arden was asked whether the priest Hall had married Elizabeth to Somerville at a mass and what Hall had said against Leicester.

Arden was lodged in the Tower on Nov. 7th, according to the warden's accounts. The bills for the journeys to and fro remain as a proof of the busy doings in the shire.

"To William Man, servaunte to Sir Thomas Lucie, viiith November 1583 for charges of himself and two others with four horses in bringing a prisoner from Park Hall twentie miles beyond Warwicke to the Courte of St. James and for returning backe againe xiii li vi s vii d"

"To Thomas Paynter, servaunte to Sir Thomas Lucie, knight, by like warrant dated at St James xviiith November 1583, as well as for chardges and paines in bringing letters in poste for her Majestie's affairs from Colsell, in the countie of Warwick, from his said Mr, to the Lords of the Counsell, being at ye chardge of two horses for himself and a guide, and also attending at the Courte for answers and returning back again iiii li x s."

"To Henry Rogers gent upon like warrant dated at St James xx mo November 1583 being lately imployed in the countie of Warwick for her Majestie's service in searching sondrie houses and places for bookes and writings dangerous to her Majestie and the state . . ." The Chamberlain's accounts at Stratford Upon Avon record: "Paid for Mr Rogers at the Beare for dinner and supper and fyer when he went to Sir John Hawbalke, knight, 2 shillings. More for his horsemeat 2 s 6d."

"To Sir John Browne upon like warrant, dated at St James xixth November for

of being led out to execution where the appearance of a raving
madman would have caused scandal and defeated the political
purpose of the execution was strangled in prison and the government declared that this horrid crime had been perpetrated
by his fellow-plotters lest he might betray the names of all
those who were engaged with him to kill the Queen. Edward
Arden went forth to his death alone, which he met at Smithfield with courage and spirit, protesting his innocence of
anything save being a Catholic. Edward Rishton lays the
"shameful practices about the making away of the worshipful, valiant and innocent gentleman Mr. Arden" to Burleigh's
and Walsingham's policy, while though Dugdale seems to
accuse Hall the priest of having denounced him, the papers in
the trial tend to show the exact contrary. Sir William Dugdale
speaks thus of the Arden affair:

". . . Edward though a gentleman not inferior to the rest

the chardges and paines of himself and guide and two horses for ridinge in poste from
the courte at St James' with letters for Mr Wilkes, one of the clerkes of her Majestie's
Privy Counsell at Cherlcot in the countie of Warwicke, and for attendance there for
two dayes and then returning iiii li."

"To Thomas Wilkes Esquier, clerk to her Majesties Privy Counsell upon the Counsell's warrant . . . who hath bene by her Majestie's speciall commandment imploied
xv whole daies for her Majestie's service in the countie of Warwicke with three
servaunts attending upon him and two persons from London to the saied countie and
also backe againe xxx li."

Finally we read:

"To Edwarde Wingate, clerk of the Cheque of her Majesties guards and Henrie
Lanham, one of the yeomen of her Majesties chamber, upon a warrante signed by Mr
Vice Chamberlain dated at St James, xxviiith November, 1583, for the chardges of
themselves, their two men and horses being sent by order of her Majesties Privy Counsell from the Courte at St James into Northamptonshire for the apprehension and
bringing upp of one Hugh Hall and his man from thence to be examined at the
Courte concerninge her Majesties affairs, and for the chardges of the said Hall, his
man and their horses, in their coming up, vi li, x s, iii d."

Servants were then called upon to testify: they were Humphrey Morris, Richard
Sheldon, Francis Emmes, William Thacker, Hugh Wright, servant to Sir John Conway.

Thacker's evidence was negative: he had "worn Ardens cloth" for six years, and
served Somerville for three; he knew no priest but Hall, had never heard of masses
or conspiracies and like the other servants went himself to service in the public church
"as it is now used,"

49

of his Ancestors in those virtues wherewith they were adorned, had the hard hap to come to an untimely death in 27 Eliz. the charge layd against him being no less than high Treason against the Queen as privie to some foul intentions that Master Somerville his son-in-law (a Roman Catholik) had towards her person: For which he was prosecuted with so great rigour and violence by the earl of Leicester's means, whom he had irritated in some particulars (as I have credibly heard) partly in disdaining to wear his Livery which many of this county of his rank thought in those days no small honour to them, but chiefly for galling him by certain harsh expressions touching his private accesses to the Countess of Essex before she was his wife; that through the testimony of one Hall, a priest, he was found guilty of the fact and lost his life in Smithfield.

"Tristis hic exitus nobilis viri (saith Master Campden) qui sacerdotis in sides illectus & ejusdem testimonia perclusus lecestrii invidiae vulgo vertebatur certum enim est illum lecestrii invidiam nec imerito incurisse qui in omnibus quibus poterat se temere objesserat quasi adultero obtrec tarerat & ut homine novo dextraxerat." (Dugdale, p. 681.)

Having failed in divulging the details of the non-existent conspiracy, Burleigh set about preparing a pamphlet calculated to inflame public opinion against the Warwickshire plotters. His tract: THE EXECUTION OF JUSTICE IN ENGLAND FOR THE MAINTENANCE OF PUBLIC AND CHRISTIAN PEACE may still be read together with a retort published by Cardinal Allen, THE TRUE SINCERE AND MODEST DEFENCE OF ENGLISH CATHOLICS.

It is only fair to say in Father Hall's defence that there is no trace of his having turned state's evidence. Mrs. Stopes supposes that he died under question as, after his last examination all trace of him is lost. His "fewel and candle" appear on the tower accounts for some months after his condemnation but this was a common practice which allowed the jailer to pocket the money which the crown continued paying for the upkeep of state prisoners, who in many cases are known to have been already dead.

CHAPTER THREE

THE MYSTERY OF SHAKESPEARE'S MARRIAGE

IN SPITE OF the severe repression exercised after Campion's death, there remained, in Warwickshire, a sufficient number of priests to practise their vocation with the connivance of their old parishioners. Sir Thomas Lucy himself, as chief of the Commission to put down abuses in religion, gives a picture of what was constantly happening when he complains that eleven priests "lurking" in the shire were celebrating marriages and baptising children. Listed for indictment over his signature is "One Hales, a very old Massing priest who marryed John Wyse, Gentleman, to his last wife, and marryed Thomas Higginson of Burkswell to his wife now living (it is vehemently to be supposed with Masses) and is commonly resorted to at Mrs. Brookesby's in Tamworth and many other places in the county of Warwick. This Hales hath christened divers children in the Popish order."

It seems essential to remember that it was in the Autumn of 1582 when the hue and cry after more victims was hottest and some months before the arrest of the Ardens and Hugh Hall that the Shakespeare-Hathaway marriage took place. It figures on the Bishop's register at Worcester "Nov. 27th, 1582," when his now vanished licence confirmed the legality of this union.

A backward glance at the atmosphere prevailing in those regions is advisable before examining certain documents in the case which still exist. Warwickshire was an old Catholic stronghold, where the majority set aside the new prayer-book and continued doggedly much as before. Many who did not adhere to the ancient faith had little or no sympathy for the newly established Church of England. Old men shook their heads, deeming it was unlawful for a woman to be a "spiritual governor."

Already in 1579, Bishop Whitgift apologised to Burleigh for his inability to maintain strong discipline in the diocese, saying: "Two kinds of men delight to molest and trouble; the contentious Protestant and the obstinate Papist," which shows that even a bishop could not always prevent country-folk from obeying their old pastors. Bullingham, Whitgift's predecessor in the diocese and Archbishop Grindal too, had often given examples of laxity and winked at abuses, notably at the time when Francis Throckmorton of Coughton Court took to wife Anne Sutton and obtained episcopal licence to have the ceremony performed in any church, chapel or oratory of the diocese and by any fit priest. At this time (1571) it was Hugh Hall who was chaplain to Sir John Throckmorton. The episcopal consent is recorded on Bishop Bullingham's register, No. XXXII, Folio 3B. There is little doubt that Hall was the celebrant and there are many reasons to suppose that it was he who officiated at Shakespeare's nuptials.

Joseph William Gray, alone among commentators, has given the question of Shakespeare's marriage full and conscientious study, but his book, *Shakespeare's Marriage and Departure from Stratford,* has long been out of print, and his dictum in reference to the Throckmorton ceremony is often passed over. "I have not succeeded," he writes, "in finding a record of this marriage, which may have been first solemnized according to the rites of the old faith." Mrs. Carmichael Stopes is more categorical in her assertion that *all* entries, where neither church nor celebrant is specifically mentioned, indicate that the Catholic ritual was employed. She makes no doubt that the sole mystery of Shakespeare's marriage was that a priest officiated. I fully concur in her opinion, but I think that stronger reasons for this belief can be produced.

The Roman rite was commonly practised until 1582 by those who could afford to pay fines. Indeed, certain families "compounded" with the authorities for a lump sum per annum—usually forty pounds—and no questions asked. Sir Thomas Gerard, for instance, had been twice in the Tower when he was summoned by the Master of the Rolls to "compound for his recusancy" with a free offer of a sum to be paid yearly to the Queen.[1]

The fact that such baptisms and marriages as Sir Thomas Lucy complained of figured on the diocesan registers at Worcester, although there was no record of them in the local anglican parish, indicates that there was frequent collusion between the bishop's officers and the "massing" priests still active in the shire, and that, upon payment of a small fee, over and above the charge for a regular licence with banns (from four to six shillings at most), the bishop's sanction might be obtained.

The price demanded of William Shakespeare, however, was by no means small. This should be taken into account in any fair examination of the problem, where, when and by whom his union with Anne Hathaway was celebrated.[2] The normal pro-

[1]This offer, signed by his own hand, is now in the Public Record Office. In it "he most humbly submitteth himself to Her Majesty's pleasure but is not able to offer any great sums offering his person to serve Her Highness in any place in the world. And if he shall not be admitted thereto, then he offereth with very good will thirty pounds a year which is a fourth part of the small portion remaining now left to maintain himself and his poor children." Evidently the amount was not sufficient, for the name of his wife, Dame Elizabeth Gerard, heads the list of thirty-three "recusants some time resident about London and Middlesex but now dispersed into other countries."

[2]When official recognition of his marriage was given at Worcester, a bond of forty pounds "to keep blameless our Father in God, Lord John, Bishop of Worcester or his officers," was exacted from the youthful bridegroom.

cedure of a youth whose parents were old-fashioned Catholics has been shown by Shakespeare himself. This was to crave a blessing on his nuptials from a friendly priest of the neighbourhood. Romeo and Juliet, Orlando and Rosalind, Sebastian and Olivia, Claudio and Hero either publicly or privately were united by a priest. And each clerical portrait is drawn with an astonishingly sympathetic touch.

William was only nineteen. Consequently the then Vicar of the parish of Holy Trinity, Sir William Gilbard *alias* Higgs, must have been obliged to conform to the law and refuse to read the service over a minor. At that time all the priests known to the Shakespeare family were under ban.[3] Such a legal point as this could hardly alarm those who were already outside the parish pale, and it remains to search for the individual most likely to have been selected for this office. Beside the many names obligingly furnished by Sir Thomas Lucy himself, there was one "Massing priest" near Stratford toward whom my attention was called from the fact that shortly after Shakespeare's marriage Sir Thomas Lucy was instrumental in getting him condemned. This was that same Hugh Hall of Idlicote—some four miles from Stratford—a relative of whom

[3]The list of priests denounced and indicted reads:

One William Brookes, a Sedicious Seminarie Prieste, sometime servant to Campion the Jhesuite traitor and in the Tower with him.

One Barnarde Hartelely suspected to be a preeste; wore Lady Giffardes' livery coat, but what hath become of him presenters knowe not.

One Barloe, an olde preeste and great perswader of others to Papistrie.

One Humphrey Hawes, *Alias* Moseley, an obstinate papiste and auld massing preeste and now in Warwick gaol. Mountfort Scott a Jhesuite Seminarye and now hangde as it is thought these two resorted often to places in Warwickshire where they have done great hurt.

One Henry Sydnall a wilful recusant thought to be a preeste he is a vagrant now, and cannot be found.

One Sir Robert Whately an old massing priest but hardly to be found.

One Sir John Appletree a Seminarye priest and fugitive, within three years past at the house of one Thomas Oldnall but where he is they know not.

One George Cocke, alias Cawdrey.

One Palmer, thoughte to have been a preeste from beyond the sea and to have had authority from Rhome or Rheimes to reconcile.

afterwards married Susanna Shakespeare. Hugh Hall had resided in the district for upward of thirteen years, and, besides his spiritual calling, was a remarkable hand at orchard-planting and master of the art of designing the formal "knotted garden" in which the poet evidently rejoiced. As resident chaplain in the family of Edward Arden of Park Hall whose daughter Margaret he had married to John Somerville, "Sir Hugh" was the priest most likely to be resorted to by the son of Mary Arden of Wilmcote.[4]

A very old tradition, recorded by Halliwell-Phillipps, affirms that Shakespeare's marriage to Anne Hathaway took place at Luddington, which was the parish both of Temple Grafton and Shottery, Anne's old home. The registers survived until the eighteenth century, when the church was destroyed by fire. But I shall discuss only facts of which documentary evidence still exists: On the 27th day of Novemeber, 1582, through what means we know not, William Shakespeare obtained the paper which was necessary to legalise his marriage with Anne Hathaway. This fact remains established on Bishop Whitgift's register, for the inhabitants of Stratford were under the jurisdiction of the Worcester See: *Item: eodem die similis emanavit licencia inter Wm. Shappere et Annam Whateley de Temple Grafton.*[5] The very next day another and more peculiar paper was endorsed at Worcester, where the young bridegroom had been summoned to give a bond for forty pounds guaranteed by Yeomen Sandals and Richardson, dwellers on the Hathaway

---

[4]See: C. C. Stopes's *Genealogical Study of the Parkhall Ardens in relation to the Ardens of Wilmcote,* "Shakespeare's Family." London, Elliot Stock.

[5]J. W. Gray and Mrs. Stopes have so convincingly developed the natural theory of the clerk's error in writing Whateley for Hathaway that I shall not deal with it further. The identity of Anne Hathaway as the woman married by William Shakespeare is sufficiently established by the Shephard's reference to her in his Will and by the Will of her granddaughter who left numerous legacies to her Hathaway cousins; it might also be pointed out that it is self-evident that the name, as registered in the bond which was worth forty pounds in good English money, has a far greater chance of being properly transcribed than a memorandum which had, at the time, no particular im-

estate. It should be noted that three weeks later such a bond was raised from forty to one hundred pounds.

After enumerating in Latin the usual "letts and hindrances" to a marriage without the requisite reading of banns, the document specifies in plain English that:

"Said William do upon his own proper cost and expense, defend and save harmless the right reverend Father in God Lord John, Bishop of Worcester, and his officers for licensing them, the said Anne and William, to be married together."

No attempt to furnish any historical reason for the peculiar drafting of this bond has ever been advanced. Biographers and commentators have contented themselves with the suggestion that as the marriage licence issued by the Bishop Whitgift was dated less than seven months before the birth of Susanna Shakespeare, the bond was drawn up to protect the diocesan authority from possible reprisals from the family either of William or his bride. This explanation is exceedingly shallow; even were it admissible that the marriage had been hastily contrived to safeguard Anne's reputation, that would not explain why this bond was drawn up "to defend and save the Bishop harmless" in the matter. The size of the sum indicates that the guarantee was taken, not against the possible dissatisfaction of a yeoman's family, but as a material safeguard. It is an indication that something had occurred to frighten Lord John, Bishop of Worcester, who had given an official sanction to yet another ceremony not in accordance with the Elizabethan statutes.

portance to any one, and may be cumbered with a quantity of mistakes of a similar sort.

The recording clerk was certainly a careless scribe. Mr. Gray points out many other discrepancies between the register and the bonds. "Hiccox" is given for "Hitchcocke," "John Baker" is licenced to marry "Joan Baker" instead of "Joan Barbar," the name of "Bradeley," on the bond register, becomes "Darby." "Elcock" is set down as "Edgock," and Mr. Gray points out that the name "Whately" was immediately under the eye of the scribe on a previous entry, when he sat down to consign the names of Shakespeare and his bride to paper.

It remains to seek in the state archives for the trace of some event which might cause Biship Whitgift anxiety and bring him into reproach. Up to that time such laxity as his was common enough in Warwickshire. Had anything happened specially to excite the Queen's Government in 1582? Out of the nineteen executions which the application of the new Act had brought about—ten at Tyburn and nine in the shires, may not just cause for the Bishop's action be found in the hanging at York of Father James Thomson? A contemporary account of this event is given in the Douay dossier published by Bishop Challoner in 1742.[6] The priest had been marched through York early in November, loaded with double chains. He was sentenced on the 25th and execution set for the 27th, the very day when the bond was exacted from Shakespeare. Thus the Bishop of Worcester just had time to learn of a priest's condemnation when his Episcopal licence for the Shakespeare-Hathaway marriage, celebrated by a priest, was imprudently issued. Bishop Whitgift saw himself implicated in a high treason charge and naturally enough did what he could to make the bridegroom's family financially responsible!

If this hypothesis be accepted, it would render superfluous any other explanation of the mystery which surrounds Shakespeare's marriage by showing the true cause of Sir Thomas

[6]It concludes with the words: "Mr. James Thomson was born and brought up in Yorkshire, from thence he went over to the College lately translated from Doway to Rheims where he was made priest and sent back to England in 1581. He was apprehended in the city of York in the house of Mr. Brenton then prisoner for his conscience in the Kidecote. . . . Being examined by the council they asked him whether the cause of his returning to England was not to reconcile the Queen's subjects to the Church of Rome, he answered 'I will tell you ingenuously that I returned in order to do some service to my country.' They asked how many and what persons he had reconciled. He desired to be excused from answering a question by which he might bring others into danger. Then they asked whether he acknowledged the Queen's Majesty for the supreme head of the Church. He answered that he did not acknowledge her for such. 'Very well,' said they, 'you need say no more, you have said enough.' He answered 'Blessed be God.'"

Lucy's severity. When the culprit was brought before the local authorities accused of poaching, the official interrogatory must have immediately divulged his connection with the Ardens and their Chaplain Hugh Hall. This was enough to change an accusation of "deer-stealing" into one of "felony" or "high treason," so that Justice Shallow's threat "I will make a Star-Chamber matter of it," which sounds monstrously exaggerated in the "Merry Wives of Windsor," would in reality have been a natural consequence of the evidence he had heard.

But the few facts that I can bring forward on the poaching story are so important that they will require a special chapter, and meanwhile, not having been prodigal of theories which I cannot substantiate, during my efforts these last twenty years to shed new light on certain aspects of the "Shakespeare problem," I may perhaps be pardoned in this instance for venturing a personal opinion on Shakespeare's wife of whom we would fain know so much and actually know so little that is positive.

If Anne Hathaway had been shrewish, as many nineteenth-century commentators affirm upon no evidence whatever, and the poet had been unwillingly forced into marrying her, I doubt whether after his phenomenal career, he would have returned to the bride of his youth and produced his latest plays which breathe the serenity of calm after tempest.

Certainly if the proverb "a good woman and a happy people should have no history" be true, Shakespeare's wife was a pattern to her sex.

A few scanty records indicate money difficulties during her husband's own hard times and show that when prosperity came, she shared in it at Stratford. The epitaph placed on her tomb has nothing of the heartless formality usual to such compositions. It is written in Latin by Shakespeare's daughter.

Though the prosody is not without fault, it is probable that the learned Doctor Hall aided his wife in this classic effort. It may be Englished thus:

> "Thou who to me the sap of life didst give,
>   Mother, must I requite thee with a stone?
> Good angel, roll it back that she may live
>   Betimes among the stars, beside Christ's throne."[7]

There is here a fleeting reminiscence of her father's idea in "Hamlet" of the angel's flight heavenward, and also of Juliet's suggestion that her belovéd be placed like a constellation in the firmament. The epitaph certainly indicates that Anne was appreciated and loved by her first-born child Susanna—and even by her son-in-law—an excellent tribute! She had undoubtedly gained the confidence of old Thomas Whittington, long employed as a shepherd by her father, for his savings were placed in her hands for safe keeping with the express desire that "Master Shakespeare's wife should distribute them among the poor in Stratford."

Tradition, which tells so little of Anne Shakespeare's life, recalls one sentiment expressed on her deathbed: The earnest desire to be laid as near to her illustrious husband as his own prescription (the poet's grave is dug 15 feet below the chancel) and the rules of the burying-place permitted.

Though we cannot tell why she was chosen, we can deduce that mercenary ambition was a stranger to the young poet's choice. The amount of her dower on marriage was six pounds, thirteen shillings and eightpence, bequeathed by her father, and if we examine the three principal reasons which Shakespeare himself cites as impedimenta which are apt to come between lovers and their vows, it is easy to eliminate the principal ones: class inequality and the interference of the

[7]The Latin text will be found in Chapter V.

respective families of bride and groom. The Hathaways, like the Shakespeares, were of good county stock and rejoiced in a genteel blazon a *hunting horn argent, garnished with tassels.* The rose-embowered charm of their dwelling, with its pastoral surroundings, perfect setting for a youthful idyll, Time himself has respected. In the period of his prosperity, John Shakespeare twice went on Hathaway's bond, and the relations existing later between the families show no trace of the bitterness characteristic of people who have been unwillingly brought together. Pleasant relations continued for two generations, for the poet's grand-daughter left substantial bequests to her "good and affectionate Hathaway cousins."

As to Anne's motives in accepting a share of young William's destiny, they are evident. The earliest descriptions show Shakespeare as "a handsome, well-shaped man with great sweetness in his manners." Even the bearish Jonson testified "he was indeed honest and of a noble and free nature, had an excellent fantasy, brave motions and gentle expression," and the editor Chettle, who had participated in Greene's jealous attack on the young poet, after he became acquainted with the object of his spleen, said: "I am as sorry as if the original fault had been my fault, because myself have seen his demeanour no less civil than he is excellent in the quality he professes. Besides divers of worship have reported his uprightness of dealing which argues his honesty, and his facetious grace in writing that approves his art." The poet was twenty-eight when this was written, but there is no reason to suppose that the personal charm and magnetic attraction which connected his name with the epithets "gentle," "sweet," "honey-tongued," and "well-beloved" had not begun to show when, hardly twenty, he courted Anne.

Much nonsense has been talked about the interlined bequest of Shakespeare to his wife, as if the testator's neglect to mention her name in the body of the will were wounding. There was, however, no reason, since this will was administered by a daughter and son-in-law, with whom Anne Shakespeare made her home, to inscribe any other provision than this personal bequest. The widow had her legal third in the income from the general capital of her husband's estate, her share in his theatrical company and literary assets. The gift of one of his carved bedsteads "with its furniture" is an indication that, in taking it out of the general property left to his daughter Susanna and his son-in-law Doctor Hall, Shakespeare recognised it as an heirloom belonging personally to Anne. Then, as now, in country houses, the best bed or "lit de parade" is placed in the guest-chamber. The second-best is that of the master of the house; so that the poet's donation to Anne does not indicate that this was a *poor* gift, but a *personal* one. It was probably their marriage bed and had perhaps formed part of her original dower in Anne's share of her dead father's estate, along with the marriage portion bestowed in cash.[8]

Although we have no means of knowing what opinion Shakespeare held of his wife, and whether or not Anne Hathaway ceased, after their children's birth, to embody a youthful ideal of a rural sweetheart, we can easily tell what he thought of marriage as an institution—for the poet, who does not permit his readers to "pluck out the heart of his mystery" when marital sentiment is involved, reveals, as a psychological necessity, the sufferings caused by an illicit love. The Sonnets to his "dark enchantress" are a sufficient proof that he regarded marriage as indissoluble; in spite of unfaithfulness to his wife,

[8]A curious item in the will of Richard Hathaway may give light on this question, for it indicates that the owner of Hewlands, at Shottery, now commonly known as Anne Hathaway's cottage, attached particular importance to his beds as heirlooms.

"Item: my will is that all seelings in my hallhowse withe towe joyned beddes in my parlor shall contynewe to stande unremoved duringe the widowhode of Jone my wyffe and the natural lief of Bartholomewe my sonne and john my sonne and the longest lyver of theme."

she remained throughout the being to whom he was linked on earth by their children and beyond the grave by a mystic sacramental tie.

The priest's definition is repeated by Shakespeare in many different forms but is always essentially the same:

> "A contract or eternal bond of love,
> Confirmed by mutual joinder of your hands,
> Attested by the holy close of lips,
> Strengthened by interchangement of your rings,
> And all the ceremony of this compact,
> Sealed in my function by my testimony."

A tradition so persistent that it is still repeated in Stratford tells how a buck to which Sir Thomas Lucy laid claim was borne "cleanly by the Keeper's nose" and served on the John Shakespeares' table at the modest celebration of his son's nuptials.

CHAPTER FOUR

THE SPIRITUAL TESTAMENT
OF JOHN SHAKESPEARE

A STUDY OF THE STATUTES in their application to Warwickshire life is nowhere more illuminating than when we
apply it to the mysterious document generally termed "John
Shakespeare's Will" found under the tiling of the Henley Street
attic. The text was first published and discussed by Edmund
Malone in his edition of Shakespeare's works printed in 1790, at
which time the original was freely exhibited to all who cared
to investigate the writing but which afterwards, for reasons
best known to those responsible for its disappearance, has been
spirited away from public view, leaving in its place two copies
made respectively by Malone and John Jordan, of Stratford.
According to Malone's expert testimony, the writing belonged
to the latter half of the sixteenth century, somewhat resembling the calligraphy of Edward Allen the player, but more
correct and uniform in spelling and punctuation than was
usual at that epoch. It is indeed astonishingly modern in this
respect, a fact which is explained now that we know when,
where and by whom the model of this will was first composed.

Before analysing the text itself, I must recall the circumstances of its discovery in the attic of England's great poet,
more than two hundred and fifty years ago, according to the
first narration of this event.

A workman, named Joseph Moseley, while repairing the roof, found between the rafters and the tiles a small paper booklet, which purports to be the last will and testament of John Shakespeare, ex-bailiff of Stratford and William's father. The five pages of the document were roughly stitched together with pack thread, the outer covering pages were found later. Moseley handed this treasure to one of the Stratford aldermen. It was copied by John Jordan, an enthusiastic but self-educated amateur, who produced an article thereon in the *Gentleman's Magazine.* The booklet was then turned over to Mr. Davenport, the vicar; he, much intrigued, sent it for examination to the best expert of those days, Edmund Malone. In 1790, after long study, the critic (not easily imposed upon, since it was he who denounced the Chatterton and Ireland forgeries) affirmed that it was genuine and his word should have carried enough weight to have justified the preservation of so valuable a find instead of branding it as a forgery and without any possible bearing on the history of the Shakespeare family.

Though termed a will, it is rather a declaration of faith and pious resolution. Evidently the man who signed such a paper was troubled by the fear that pain or torture might wring from human frailty something contrary to his real thought and conscience, or that circumstances might send him to the grave with his account of sins upon his head, like King Hamlet: "unhouselled, unanelled." As a matter of fact, the testament expresses the sentiments that any impartial student might expect to find on John Shakespeare's pen. It reflects the state of mind in which he lived and died, for he was married as a Catholic at the little church of Aston Cantlow, refused to attend Protestant service at Stratford and abandoned public office the day when, in order to retain his alderman's gown, he might have been obliged to take an oath acknowledging the Queen's supremacy in ecclesiastical matters: an oath to which none of his belief could conscientiously subscribe.

I have shown how, in 1592,[1] the name of Master John Shakespeare is found as a favourer of things popish upon the list signed by Sir Thomas Lucy, and sent to the Privy Council by the Warwickshire commission.

Why then should not the will at first glance appear authentic, since it conforms to historical facts and seems in keeping with the ex-bailiff's character? There is nothing astonishing in the idea that such a paper was drawn up in the house at Henley Street, for not only were John Shakespeare and his neighbours living at a time of severe persecution, but they had been terrified by arrests in their very midst.

The difficulty is not with the *spirit* but with the *form* of the document. The style and wording are florid and un-English so much so that the reader is led to exclaim: "How could a Warwickshire yeoman who had never been nearer to the Apennines than London, compose and execute a piece of writing with so strong a flavour of the Italian ecclesiastical renaissance?" It was thus the problem presented itself until recently and I, for one, hesitated to take sides in the discussion.

But today, thanks to the remarkable discoveries of Father Herbert Thurston, S. J., an authority on Elizabethan literature and history, facts and explanation appear together and bring full confirmation of the authenticity of the testament. We must now admit, however, that instead of having been originally composed by John Shakespeare, the signer merely subscribed to a devotional formula, the model of which was current in Warwickshire between 1580 and 1600.

In short, this confession of faith in a dozen paragraphs, each beginning: "I, John Shakespeare," as in most official texts, is a formula distributed to numbers of English Catholics by the

[1]*My Shakespeare Rise*, London, Lippincott, 1936.

members of the English mission of 1580. It was recommended to the faithful by no less an authority than Saint Charles Borromeo, who entertained Father Campion and Father Parsons a fortnight in Milan and gave them counsel and advice before they set forth on the journey to London, which was to prove fatal to sixty English missionaries.

A dangerous paper this, for any man or woman to sign after 1581, when the Act of Persuasions (23 Eliz. CI) made it high treason to "reconcile or be reconciled to the Romish religion," thus placing the Catholic layman in equal jeopardy with the proscribed priest. Woe to the Shakespeares had this document been found! But, whether it was the signer himself who, ultimately, through fear, made away with it, or some other member of the household, it is hard to guess.

The writer (who spells his name "Jhon Shakespear") declares his intention and desire to receive before death the Sacrament of Extreme Unction, affirms his confidence in God's mercy, repudiates any idea of merit on his part and bases his hope of salvation upon the Redeemer's sacrifice. He declares himself ready to endure bodily pains which may be inflicted upon him, proclaims readiness to forgive former injuries, expresses gratitude for past mercies, invokes the intercession of the Blessed Virgin, his guardian angel and patron saint. He exhorts his family and kinsfolk to do good work, pray, and have Masses said for him.

The style is tedious; it contains 2000 words and innumerable repetitions, but the bearing upon the devotional life of English Catholics under Elizabeth's penal code is obvious. It should at least have aroused the curiosity of historians; such casual "scrapping" shows singularly shallow methods of study.

Nineteenth-century biographers treat the testament with "genteel grimness" or brush it away with levity!

"There can be no doubt that the whole of the paper is a

modern fabrication," writes Halliwell-Phillipps in 1865. "Undoubtedly the work of John Jordan, the first Elizabethan forger to achieve notoriety," declares Sir Sidney Lee; and C. R. Haines dismisses it as an "absurd rigmarole obviously intended as a joke on the public, hidden like a dead mouse behind the wainscoting."

Before crying "forgery" it should be remembered that the only real scholar who examined the original text, copied it with his own hand and published it in his edition of Shakespeare's works, was Edmund Malone and he never withdrew his declaration made in 1790 that the five leaves were a genuine sample of late sixteenth-century script! Though perplexed by its tone and florid style, Malone stated that it could not have been invented with a view to literary imposition.

This opinion was sustained some years ago by Father Thurston, who, after sober, scholarly and impartial study, declared in 1911 that the will "could not conceivably have been invented by a Protestant forger," least of all by Jordan, who had shown himself incapable of understanding part of the text or transcribing properly the language in which it is written. He further showed that it was in keeping with the custom of the day for Catholics to subscribe to such formulæ, and quoted the *Exercise of the Christian Life* by Gaspar Loarte, translated into English and published in 1579. But reviewers gave small attention to Father Thurston's argument and the subject was again dropped.[2]

[2]In regard to the forgery theory Father Thurston argues: "When Jordan sent a copy of the document to the *Gentleman's Magazine* in June, 1784, he declared that the original had been given him by Moseley, Moseley being then alive, and professed his readiness to show the original to any one they might send to inspect it. If this was a bluff, it was a very audacious kind of bluff. Halliwell says that the will was Jordan's own composition, but, obviously the wheelwright could not have invented the text of a document which existed in Italian and Spanish two hundred years before his time. On the forgery theory we would have to suppose that he had found an English translation of this distinctively Catholic testament, that he copied it out in archaic writing, inserting in twelve places the name of John Shakespeare, and that

The discovery of the actual model for John Shakespeare's will, found among the records of the British Museum in 1924, caused the question of Jordan's alleged "forgery" to be re-examined. A small paper booklet printed in Mexico City and containing a half-dozen leaves put a new face on the whole matter. It is in Spanish with blanks left for the signer's name. Of the same form, length and substance as the one found two centuries ago in the Henley Street attic, it confirms the authenticity of the Stratford text, and even supplies certain lines or phrases misread by John Jordan. It also has the advantage of showing the title and real purpose of such a will, together with the name of the original author.

The Mexican version begins:

TESTAMENTO O ULTIMA VOLUNTAD DEL ALMA

Hecho en Salud para assegurarse el christiano de las tentaciones del Demonio, en la hora de la muerte; Ordenando por San Carlos Borromeo, Cardenal del Santa Praxedis, y Arcobispo de Milan.

(rude woodcut of the Crucifixion)

Por la Viuda de Bernardo Calderon, en la calle de San Agostino Anno de 1661[3]

The *Cabeza* or preamble declares that the signer, Juan Phelipe Hernandez, whose name is inscribed in extremely

---

he did his work so skilfully that Malone, the prime detector of forgeries, though he had the five little leaves in his hands for months and wrote many times to make inquiries about them at Stratford, was completely imposed upon.—The sobriety and modernity of the spelling augments the improbability that the five leaves sent to Malone were a fabrication. As the Ireland forgeries abundantly show, the tendency of bogus documents is rather to exaggerate the eccentricities of early English orthography. A suppositious spiritual will, forged by Ireland and purporting to be that of William Shakespeare himself, contains this absurd example of exaggerated antique spelling—"O cherishe mee like the sweete chickenne thatte under the coverte offe herre spreadynge wings receyves herre lytelle broode."

[3]"The Testament or last will of the soul Made in health for the Christian to secure himself From the Temptations of the devil at the hour of death Drawn up by Saint Carlo Borromeo Cardinal of St. Praxedis and Archbishop of Milan. Printed with licence at Mexico by the widow of Bernard Calderon, St. Augustine's Street."

faded ink in the blanks left for that purpose, has taken thought while meditating on the uncertain tenure of life, to prepare for death's inevitable hour by declaring to the world his last will:

In the first place, as the foundation of salvation, I, Juan Phelipe Hernandez, declare and confess, in the presence of Almighty God, Father, Son and Holy Ghost, the most Blessed Virgin Mary and court of heaven, that I wish to live and die obedient to the Holy Roman Church. . . .

The twelve items which exist in both Spanish and English versions exhibit a complete parallel.

This discovery led to others. Far from being an absurd rigmarole forged by the Protestant Jordan, the pages bearing John Shakespeare's attestation emanate from an uncontested ecclesiastical source. The original Italian model is printed in the life of Benedetti Sauli, Borromeo's confessor. Another Spanish text, identical with the first, but this time in manuscript form and showing the same blanks in the script for the signer's name, Maria Teresa de Cardenas, was discovered by Father Thurston. Still another printed will, in Swiss dialect, was published at Barraduz, but at a later date, and proves the popularity of Borromeo's pious testament long after the old bailiff's time. I can also cite a seventeenth-century French testament on the same lines.

Among these different versions, the Italian text is of particular interest because it antedates the Stratford copy by several years and shows the numerous mistakes made when the Henley Street document was first deciphered. The three first paragraphs on the covering page were so badly mildewed that the ink was practically faded away and this explains why the transcription was so faulty whereas the rest contains but few mistakes.

Among them, in the fourth paragraph, referring to extreme

unction, John Shakespeare uses a word "gusting" which Malone read as "justing" and Jordan as "feeling."

Speaking of this word, Father Thurston writes: "'To gust' still survives in Scotland; it was of fairly common occurrence in seventeenth-century English. It means to 'taste' or to 'savor' and in the form for anointing of the lips, the priest still prays that the sick person may be forgiven all the offences he has committed by taste and speech (quidquid per gustum et louquellam deliquisti). Neither Malone nor Jordan could have known this and they consequently guessed respectively that the obscure word represented *feeling* or *justing*. There was, as they could see, a tailed letter at the beginning, a tall letter in the middle, and 'ing' at the end."

I might add that the root still remains in common use in "gusto" and also in "disgust," and that Shakespeare himself thrice makes use of the term, "gust" in the same sense used in the Will . . . "sin's extremest gust" (Timon); "when I shall gust it last" (Winter's Tale); "the gust he hath in quarrelling" (Twelfth Night).

The Italian original also shows that Malone had misread two other words in the thirteenth paragraph: instead of "sharp-cutting razor," he deciphered "charge in a censor," an expression quite meaningless in this connection. "Scalpello pungente" explains the obscure significance and restores the proper terms of the English text:

Item: I John Shakespeare doe by this my will and testament bequeth my soul as soon as it shall be delivered and loosened from the prison my body to be entombed in the sweet and amorous coffin of the side of Jesus Christ; and that in this life-giving sepulchre it may rest and live, perpetually enclosed in that eternal habitation of repose there to bless forever and ever that direful iron of the launce which like a *charge in a censor* formes so sweet and pleasant a monument within the sacred breast of my Lord and Saviour.

Paragraph XIII in Italian:

Voglio e lascio che l'anima mia, subito sciolto da questo carcere terreno, sia sepolto nell' amorosa caverna del Costado di Gesu Christo, nella quale vivica sepoltura giaccia e viva perpetuamente confinata in quello requo et riposo, col benedire mille volte quel ferro della lancia che a guisa di *scalpello pungente* fece monumento cosi dolce nell amato petto del mio signore.

The idea of finding a sepulchre in Christ's side is familiar to early Catholic writers while the phrase: "direful iron of the launce" recalls, as Father Thurston points out, the ancient Canticle *Vexilla Regis:*

Quae vulnerata lanceae mucrone diro.

That Malone himself was fully conscious of his unsatisfactory reading, is proved in a letter to Doctor Davenport dated October 21, 1789, where he refers to the difficulties encountered in deciphering the document. "I have been able to make out the whole of the last leaf of this curious paper, in which the ink is very faint, and some of the words almost obliterated, except one line concerning which I have some doubts. The passage is in the 13th Article, and runs thus: 'Here to bless forever and ever the direful iron of the launce which, like a *charge in a censor* forms so sweet and pleasant a monument within the sacred breast of my Lord and Saviour' the words underscored are those I doubt about; are the contents of a censor called anywhere in the sacred writings, its *charge?*"

I am aware that a distinguished authority suggests that the signer of the spiritual confession might conceivably have been the poet's sister, Johanna, afterwards Mrs. Harte, who continued to live in the Henley Street house, the choice of a female saint as patron being the basis for such a hypothesis; for the tenth paragraph of the will presented together with the Span-

ish version shows that the signer had designated Saint Winifred as particular patron.

Two reasons make me take issue with the supporter of the
theory that a girl should have subscribed the document and
written Jhon twelve times in place of her own name. I note
that in William Shakespeare's will he speaks familiarly of
"my sister Jone" or else "my sister Johanna Hart." Would she
not have done the same? And can we suppose that the phrase
"the dirty puddle of my sins" so natural to the functionary
who had followed State orders and destroyed the images of
the Guild Chapel is more applicable to a mere child of eleven
than to a man?

Item: I John Shakespeare do protest that I am willing yea, I do infinitely desire and humbly crave that of this last will and testament
the glorious and ever Virgin Mary, mother of God, refuge and advocate of Sinners (whom I honor especially above all other Saints),
may be the chiefe Executresse, together with these other saints, my
patrons (Saint Winifride) all whome I invoke and beseech to be
present at the hour of my death that she and they may comfort me
with their desired presence, and crave of sweet Jesus that he will receive my soul into peace.

Item: Queiro i dessio summamente y con toda pieted ruego que
de esta mi ultima voluntad, sea Protectora la gloriosa sempre Virgin
Maria y refugio y abogado de los pecadores: a la qual especialmente
demas de los otros santos y santas mis devotos, que son (NN) invoco
y llamo, que se hallen presentes, a la hora de mi muerto, y ruego a
suo Unigenito Hijo, que riciva mi espiritu en Paz.

On the other hand, many men are known to have chosen
Saint Winifrida instead of a male patron among the saints.
Her well was in great repute among the rural population of
the midland shires, and divers miraculous cures there are
recorded.

Bishop Challoner, in his memoirs of missionary priests, notes a case in point, how the Venerable Edward Oldcorne who, for seventeen years exercised his vocation in the country adjacent to Stratford, and was finally executed at Worcester, April 7, 1605, "resolved on a pilgrimage to St. Winifrida's Well to obtain of God the recovery of his health and strength by the intercession of that virgin martyr; when behold! On his way thither, lodging in a Catholic house, he was told by a priest of the family, of a stone which had been taken out of the aforesaid well and kept in that house. Father Oldcorne, after Mass, applied this stone to his mouth, devoutly recommending himself to the prayer of Saint Winifrida, and in half an hour was perfectly cured of his cancer and proceeding on his journey and bathing himself in the well, recovered also his health and strength." These particulars Father John Gerard declared he had both from Father Oldcorne himself and from the priest of the family where he was cured of the cancer.

Considering the local renown of Winifrida, a man like John Shakespeare might readily have selected this early British Martyr as his particular patroness, rather than a male saint.

Another objection as to John Shakespeare's identity with the signer, has been brought forward by Sir E. K. Chambers who imagines that because there is a mention of "parents" in the will, the ex-bailiff of Stratford could not have subscribed the text, as his father and mother had been long dead at the time of Campion's mission. This objection I have already answered in the *Times Literary Supplement* of March 14, 1935, and will repeat here, that, in appealing to his "friends, parents and kinsfolks" John Shakespeare was merely invoking his own contemporaries, *friends, immediate family and kindred,* and employing the formula in general use. It must be remembered that his will was an almost literal translation of a continental text and that in French, Spanish, Italian or Latin the term

74

"parents" has the same signification as "relatives" in English. Its use by John Shakespeare in no way implies that his father and mother were alive when he signed the testament. Even in the Latin of Sallust the word "parens" grew to mean "near relative," an acceptation which was universal when the language became debased. The definition is given thus by the foremost authority on mediæval and renaissance Latin, Du Cange:

"PARENS SANGUINE PROXIMUS, AGNATUS COGNATUS."

As an illustration, the parallel passage of John Shakespeare's will in its French seventeenth-century form which I had the good fortune to discover at the Bibliothèque Nationale, is given:

"Je prie par les entrailles de Jésus Christ *tous mes amis et parens* bien que l'on ne puisse sçavoir quelle sentence je recevrai de craindre que mon âme ne soit envoyée en purgatoire pour longtemps à cause de mes péchés ils veuillent l'aider par œuvres satisfactoires et principalement par le sainct sacrifice de la messe estant le moyen le plus efficace pour délivrer les âmes en peine."

"*Item XII:* I, John Shakespeare do in like manner praye and beseeche all my dear friends, parents and kinsfolks by the bowels of our Saviour Jesus Christ, that, since it is uncertain what lot will befall me, for feere notwithstanding lest by reason of my sins, I be to pass and stay a long while in purgatory, they will vouchsafe to assist and favor me with their holy prayers and satisfactory workes especially with the holy sacrifice of the Mass as being the most effectual meanes to deliver souls from torments and pains."

What a thing it would be for a present-day scholar if he might examine the document discovered in the Shakespeares' attic and compare it with others of the same period, especially with that note found among the chamberlain's accounts of a debt owed to John Shakespeare by the borough, which, according to Mrs. Stopes, bears every indication of having been set down by the creditor himself and remains as the only sample of John Shakespeare's manner of writing. Though as treasurer of the municipality during many years he disbursed the public moneys and paid the teachers at the Grammar school, the accounts themselves were inscribed by the town clerk.

Such a comparison is, alas, forever impossible, for those who branded the will as a Jordan forgery allowed it to perish as such! We only possess as a basis for speculation the two copies made and collated by Jordan and Malone, and the description of its appearance given in a letter of March, 1790, where Malone says:

"The few leaves which were sent to me were very small, tacked together by a thread; the size the eighth part of a sheet and the upper part of the last page but one, almost illegible."

Malone's final verdict was that although the body of the text could not be connected with the writing of any of the poet's family who have left samples—and in this he was surely correct, for the text was manifestly set down by one of the mission priests—he never wavered in his assertion that the document was ancient and certainly not the work of an eighteenth-century forger.

He was sufficiently satisfied of its authenticity to publish the will *in extenso* in his first edition. It was not repeated in his second edition of Shakespeare's works, and this has led modern critics to suppose that Malone himself shared in their doubts. Today all his critical findings are fully substantiated.

It may be safely assumed that the body of the text was written "fair" or "copy-wise" according to the fashion of the times and, as is the case with that of Teresa de Cardenas, with blanks left for the signer at the beginning of each item, and also for the name of the patron saint. If drawn up by one of the missionaries who went into Warwickshire—Free-man, Oldcorne, Davis, Mountford Scott or Campion himself, this would explain why Malone found both chirography and spelling in advance of the period, for it is noteworthy that the education given these English priests in the overseas college tended towards uniform roman script and the modernisation of spelling so striking in the testament.

Two questions are of particular interest: at what date was the paper drawn up and when was it consigned to oblivion? The solution of both is comparatively easy.

This form of spiritual testament could not have been cur-rent in Warwickshire before the arrival of Campion and Par-sons in 1580, and any reader of Mr. Waugh's book on the former will understand the reawakening of enthusiasm which was caused by the fiery eloquence of his oratory.

A renewed impulsion was given to religious zeal by the ar-rival of Robert Southwell four years later.

It is therefore natural to suppose that the use of the spiritual testament by John Shakespeare was the direct result of Cam-pion's or of Southwell's mission. Campion's arrival in 1580 gives the earliest possible date for the drawing up of the old alderman's strange document, and it is logical to suppose that the compromising paper was concealed during the reign of terror that followed the Arden affair, the crux of which was reached in 1586. The ex-bailiff presented a habeas corpus in 1587 and must have been molested more than once before that. We have seen how vigorously Sir Thomas Lucy brandished search warrants over all Catholic suspects between 1583 and 1585, and the part he played in the arrest and execution of Mary Shakespeare's kindred. In the fate of Francis Throckmorton and William Parry, he was not less active.

As both local tradition and ancient authorities affirm that Mary Arden's son fled from his native town to escape from the persecutions of Sir Thomas Lucy, it seems probable that the poet's enforced departure coincided with the time that his father was moved by fear of a search to hide the incriminating testament behind a great beam in his attic instead of carrying it on his person to the grave. Specialists who desire a more learned discussion than I can supply of the discrepancies which exist between the first two paragraphs of the continental text and the Stratford version may be referred to the *Dublin Review,* October-December, 1923, and the *Month* 1911. I will content myself with the transcription of the Spanish and English texts side by side, up to the point in the middle of the third paragraph after which the eleven paragraphs of the Borromeo model and John Shakespeare's Will are identical. (See Appendix.)

But, at the risk of repeating myself, I must again declare that the differences between the first three paragraphs as deciphered by Jordan and the Italian or Spanish texts, far from indicating any fraud or forgery on the part of the transcriber show that Jordan was not scholarly enough to refrain from amateurish divination, nor modest enough to omit what he did not clearly comprehend. Aided as we now are by a contemporary text, it is easy to discern his limitations, and see just where he misread the opening sentences of the will and the exact spot, in paragraph III, from which point he began to transcribe without any serious error.

What other tracts or books did the ex-bailiff receive from the missionary priest who came to Stratford?

I believe that he acquired the translation into English before referred to of the New Testament made by Gregory Martin *"to show the corruptions of divers late translations and for clearing the controversies in religion of these days."*

This portion of the Bible was printed at Reims when the poet was in his twentieth year and liberally dispersed through

England by the missionaries; I myself possess one which came from those regions. A small circumstance, but one of singular interest, indicates that when William Shakespeare made use of the parable of the sowers from the Gospel of St. Matthew, he had the Reims translation in mind and not either the so-called "Breeches" or "Bishops'" Bible. Though verbal, the evidence is striking. Down to the present day all Protestant Bibles employ the word *tares* in speaking of the ill weeds sown among the wheat whereas the Catholic texts use *cockle*.

Now, in the whole course of Shakespeare's work the word *tares* is never found, but when he recalls the parable of the sowers the word *cockle* appears in its place as in the Reims translation.

"The kingdom of heaven is resembled to a man who sowed good seede in his field, but when men were asleepe his enemy came and oversowed cockle among the wheate, and went his way. And when the blade was shot up and had brought forth fruits, then appeared also the cockle . . . and the servants of the goodman of the house coming said to him, Sir didst thou not sow good seede in thy field, whence then hath it cockle?"

In "Love's Labour's Lost" we find:

"Sowed *cockle* reaps no corn."

and again in "Coriolanus" the same term appears in similar connection:

"That cockle of Rebellion, Insolence, Sedition,
Which we ourselves have ploughed for, sowed and scattered."

Though generally disinclined to base any theory on a single word, there are so many instances where the internal evidence of Shakespeare's works proves the extensive culture obtained from his family's connection with the Church of Rome that I may be pardoned for calling attention to the above example, and in repeating what he makes Rosalind say in response to Orlando's admiration of a refined manner of speech and accent which he finds inconsistent with the rôle of the simple shepherd-lad which she is playing:

"I have been told so of many, but indeed an old religious uncle of mine taught me how to speak."

In Shakespeare's own case, the religious member of his family was an aunt instead of an uncle, for it may be remembered that John Shakespeare's sister had been a nun at Wroxhall until the forced dissolution of the Convent, after which the inmates were sent back to their families or thrown upon the world, the sole exception being the prioress who was allowed a slender indemnity from the Crown. Domina Shakespeare who died in Stratford when her nephew was fourteen certainly must have influenced his childhood and when we remember that the grammar-school magister, Simon Hunt, who taught the poet many years, finished his days as instructor in the Overseas college, Shakespeare's mastery of his mother-tongue need no longer be a subject for surprise or wonder.

How and why he became a poacher is equally simple when examined in the new light I am about to bring on this much-discussed subject.

CHAPTER FIVE

THE POACHING INCIDENT

There is no better substantiated evidence concerning Shakespeare's life than that which tells how he went poaching with the young bloods of the region, hung an impertinent ballad on Charlecote gate, and got himself chastised by the local Justice. Documents, both written and oral, in unbroken sequence from 1688 to the beginning of the nineteenth century, irrevocably link the poet's name with venison, rabbits and the local Justice of the Peace.

The Falstaff scenes in "Henry IV" and the "Merry Wives" present the caricature of Sir Thomas Lucy, master of Charlecote, and recall an adventure which actually occurred.

Contemporary correspondence shows that the creator of Falstaff was referred to by his friends under that name; Sir Toby Mathew quotes a saying of "that excellent author Sir John Falstaff," and Elizabeth Countess of Southampton, in a letter during the Irish campaign, tells her husband "enough to make him merry" concerning his friend Sir John Falstaff and his mistress, dame Pint-Pot (a clear allusion, by the way, to the affair with Mistress Davenant of Oxford). An effort to moralise and standardise the poet has been made by certain commentators who have tried to eliminate the poaching incident from his life-history, and one zealous Victorian critic effaced from Aubrey's manuscript, at the Bodleian, the passage which tells of his affair with Mistress Davenant. In doing so, they have only succeeded in destroying valuable evidence on a personality which is well worth knowing. Half a century ago, this class of critic was content to "Bowdlerise" the text, but today the author himself is Bowdlerised until any image with a human likeness is swept from the books which are offered to the rising generation.

The most spontaneous and impassioned of writers, whose lively wit and ripened wisdom still warm readers' hearts throughout the world, is transformed into a lifeless stock or, worse, a literary industry run upon Sovietic principles. This, through no fault of his own, nor any negligence on the part of early biographers, but merely in a misguided effort to reconstruct his character on twentieth-century lines, so that he may better conform to the tenets of our age.

"I can't believe that Shakespeare was a poacher."

"It is unthinkable that he was ever apprenticed to a butcher," or "that he could have held horses outside a playhouse," or "married a girl six years older than himself," or "consecrated his life-work to the Earl of Southampton, even if he does say so in two signed prefaces."

So chants the chorus, each voice presenting the poet according to its own scale, until, as I said, concerted effort obliterates all trace of Shakespeare the man, as known to his friends and comrades.

He is left literally "without a leg to stand on." No wonder that the authorship of his works is disputed and tossed about among rival candidates, Veres, Stanleys, Rutlands and Bacons.

Iconoclasts have been so busy proving that it was materially impossible for any poacher to kill a buck on Sir Thomas Lucy's property, because, as they say, "there never was any deer at

Charlecote" that even the truly charming ballad by Alfred
Noyes reflects their point of view:

"Will Shakespeare's out like Robin Hood,
　　With his merry men all in green,
To steal a deer in Charlecote wood,
　　Where never a deer was seen,—

"They have jailed sweet Will for a poacher,
　　But squarely he fronts the Squire,
With, 'When did you hear, in your woods, of a deer,
　　Was it under a fairy briar?'—

"Sir Thomas he raged! Sir Thomas he swore,
　　But all and all in vain,
For there never was deer in his woods before,
　　And there never would be again."[1]

However, the most comical side of the whole matter is that
no ancient evidence which refers to the incident—and there
were many—ever pretended that Shakespeare's poaching affray
took place on the grounds of Charlecote; the scene of the incursion was "a park belonging to Sir Thomas Lucy," and early
writers designate the ruined lodge on Daisy Hill as the lock-
up where the culprit was incarcerated following the adventure.
This lodge was on the domain called "Fulbrook"[2] which lies
exactly between Charlecote House and the Meadow-Farm of
Snitterfield, belonging to Shakespeare's father. Fulbrook was
seized and occupied by Sir Thomas Lucy in 1584, following
the passage of a bill which he himself proposed to the Parlia-

---

[1]*Tales of the Mermaid Tavern,* Blackwood, 1913.

[2]"Fulbrook." In first Mariae, as I elsewhere showed, the Queene passed it unto
Sir Francis Inglefield knight to hold in capita since which it is come to the Lucies of
Charlecote by purchase, the last Sir Thomas having renewed the park and by the ad-
dition of Hampton woods thereto enlarged it much (Dugdale, p. 509.)

ment of that year. This fact was well known of yore; but on my visits to Stratford, where I made strict inquiry into this special point, not a person seemed to remember the sevenfold evidence I am about to quote.

In his *Picturesque views on the upper or Warwickshire Avon*[3] Samuel Ireland wrote, in 1785:

"On a considerable eminence called Castle Hill, formerly stood Fulbroke Castle, said to have been built by John, Duke of Bedford, third son to Henry the Fourth, Regent of France. This castle was taken down in the reign of Henry the Eighth by Sir William Compton, Knt . . . who had then the custody of the park. After it was pulled down the materials were conveyed to Compton Wyniate from which Sir William erected the edifice now standing.

"The adjoining park, which had been antiently in the possession of Sir Francis Englefield, was, in the time of our immortal bard, Shakespeare, in that of the Lucy's, who had been long settled in the neighbouring village of Charlecote. It was in this park that our bard is said to have been, in a youthful frolic, engaged in stealing deer, and thereby to have drawn upon himself a prosecution from the *then* owner, Sir Thomas Lucy.

"Within this park is now standing, on a spot called Daisy Hill, a farm-house which was antiently the Keeper's Lodge. To this lodge it is reported our Shakespeare was conveyed, and there confined at the time of the charge.

"The Lucy family boasts a very antient and noble descent but perhaps have not, by any of their high connections or military achievements, acquired more celebrity than from the reputation of having prosecuted our divine bard for stealing deer out of the park at Fulbrook."

Thirty years later, Sir Walter Scott wrote in his journal,

[3]London, 1795, p. 151 *et seq.*

84

under date of April, 1828, when, with his daughter Anne, he had undertaken a pilgrimage into Warwickshire:

"Learning from Washington Irving's description of Stratford that the Hall of Sir Thomas Lucy, the Justice who rendered Warwickshire too hot for Shakespeare, was still extant, we went in quest of it.

"Charlecote is in high preservation and inhabited by Mr. Lucy descendant of the Worshipful Sir Thomas. The Hall is about three hundred years old.—A brick mansion with a gatehouse in advance. It is surrounded by venerable oaks, realising the imagery which Shakespeare loved to dwell upon. Rich, verdant pastures extend on every side and numerous herds of deer were reposing in the shade. All showed that the Lucy family had retained their 'land and beeves.' While we were surveying the Antler-Hall with its stained glass and family pictures, Mr. Lucy came to welcome us in person.

"He told me the park from which Shakespeare stole the buck was not that which surrounds Charlecote, but belonged to a mansion at some distance where Sir Thomas resided at the time of the trespasses. The tradition went that he hid the buck in a barn, part of which was standing a few years ago.

"This visit gave me great pleasure, it really brought Justice Shallow freshly before my eyes: *the luces which do become an old coat well*[4] were not more plainly portrayed *in his own armorials* in the Hall window, than was his person in my mind's eye."

It is easy to see from Sir Walter's description how thoroughly alive the tradition remained in his day; it is also interesting to trace it backward to its source.

Two of the best informed historians directly in touch with Shakespeare's Warwickshire contemporaries, namely William Fulman who spent the last years of his life near Stratford, and

[4]"King Henry IV," Act 3, Scene 2.

Richard Davies, vicar of Saperton, Gloucestershire, consigned the story to the archives of Corpus Christi College, before 1690.

Shakespeare's name figures three times in one of the twenty-five manuscript volumes, which constitute the life work of the Reverend Wm. Fulman, a man of distinguished intelligence which developed into exceptional learning under the tutelage of the erudite Anglican clergyman, Henry Hammond, who, having been chaplain in the Southampton family, had authority enough to speak of Southampton's special protégé.

Fulman passed more than half a century in the compilation and annotation of rare documents and correspondence and became an impassioned collector; after 1669 he retired to Meysey Hampton and it was there that he began working with his neighbour Davies. There also he died in 1688 with the request that his learned friend would terminate what was unfinished and donate his collections to his beloved Alma Mater, Corpus Christi.

Fulman's first six volumes treat of civil and religious history and monastical records. Eleven contain data concerning Oxford University in general. Theological discussions, biographical notes, verse transcriptions and miscellaneous memoranda fill the other eight volumes which were all methodically "digested," bound up and carried to Oxford by the rector of Saperton whose collaboration, far from detracting from Fulman's testimony, gives it double value.

It is significant that Shakespeare's name is spelled according to accepted official form, and that the details concerning his minor poetry are impeccably correct. Fulman notes the date and place of publication of *The Passionate Pilgrim* and adds that a collection containing 154 sonnets together with "A Lover's Complaint" was issued at London in 1609. (*See Plate III, at end of volume.*) A short biographical notice follows in which three spaces for precise data were left blank with the evi-

dent intention of completing, or having his friend Richard
Davies complete, the text. The space reserved for the titles of
Shakespeare's dramatic works is not filled in—but two other
blanks were completed in the rapid and straggling handwriting
of Richard Davies which is in strong contrast to the exquisite
and meticulous calligraphy of Fulman who writes thus:

"WILLIAM SHAKESPEARE WAS BORN AT STRATFORD UPON AVON IN
WARWICKSHIRE ABOUT 1563-64.

"FROM A WRITER OF PLAYS HE BECAME A COMPOSER.

"HE DIED APRIL 23 1616 ÆT. 53. PROBABLY AT STRATFORD, FOR
THERE HE IS BURIED AND HATH A MONUMENT. SEE DUGDALE page
520."

This reference, when followed up in Dugdale's *Antiquities
of Warwickshire* at the place indicated, leads to three pages of
exact information concerning all the graves of the Shakespeare
family in Stratford Church, together with an engraving of the
monument with transcription of the poet's epitaph as well as
the verses cut on his tombstone.[5]

[5]"In the North wall of the Chancell is this monument fixt.

Indicio Pylium genio Socratum, arte Maronem
Terra tegit, populus maret, olympus habet.

Stay, passenger why goest thou so fast
Read if you can'st whom envious death hath plac't
Within this monument SHAKESPEARE with whome
Quick nature dyed, whose name doth deck the tombe
Far more than cost, sith all that he hath writ
Leaves living art but page to serve his witt.

Objit A. Dni 1616
Aet. 53, die 23 Apri:

Near the wall where this monument is erected
lyeth a plaine free stone, underneath wch his
body is buried, wth this Epitaph:

Good friend for Jesus' sake forbeare
To digg the dust enclosed here
Blest be the man that spares these stones
And curst be he that moves my bones."

All the epitaphs, whether in English or Latin, of his wife, daughter, son-in-law, Doctor John Hall, and grandson, Thomas Nash, are given. This shows that Fulman in quoting Dugdale was fully conversant with the family names and it also serves to date the entry as slightly posterior to the publication of Dugdale's famous work (1654).

In the first of the blanks left by Fulman, his collaborator adds: "MUCH GIVEN TO ALL UNLUCKINESS IN STEALING VENISON AND RABBITS PARTICULARLY FROM SIR LUCY WHO HAD HIM OFT WHIPT AND SOMETIMES IMPRISONED AND AT LAST MADE HIM FLY HIS NATIVE COUNTRY TO HIS GREAT ADVANCEMENT. BUT HIS REVENG WAS SO GREAT THAT HE IS HIS JUSTICE CLOD-PATE AND CALLS HIM A GREAT MAN AND IN ALLUSION TO HIS NAME BORE THREE LOUSES RAMPANT FOR HIS ARMS."

This remark refers not only to the caricature of Sir Thomas Lucy as Justice Shallow in "Henry IV" and the "Merry Wives" where the white luces of the ancient armorial blazon are playfully confounded with the humbler genus louse, but to the

---

Monumental inscription in the Quire

(on a brass plate in great letters)
"Here lyeth the body of Anne, wife of William Shakespeare, who departed this life the 6 day of Aug. 1623, being of the age of 67 years.

> Uhera tu mater, tu lac vitamq; dedisti,
> Vae mihi pro tanto munere Saxa dabo,
> Quam mallam amoveat lapidem bonus Angelus orem
> Exuat ut Christi Corpus imago tua;
> Sed nil vota valent, venias cito Christe refurget
> Clausa jacet tumulo mater, & astra petit."

On another (in great letters):

"Here resteth the body of Thomas Nash, Esquire.
He mar. Elizabeth the daugh. of John Hall gentleman: He dyed Aprill 4. Anno 1647. Aged 53.

> Fata manent omnes, hunc non virtute carentum
> Ut neq; divitiis abstulittatra dies.
> Abstulit, at referet lux ultima, siste viator,
> Si peritura paras, per mala parta peris."

88

ballad attributed to Shakespeare which declares categorically that *though an ass* the Justice "thinks himself great," adding:

> Though luces a dozen he paints in his coat
> His name it shall lowsie for Lucy be wrote.
> And Lucy the Lowsie a libel may call it
> We'll sing Lowsie Lucy whatever befall it.

On the last blank after this entry Davies again intervenes with the words:

"ON WHICH HE LAYS A HEAVY CURSE UPON ANYONE WHO SHALL REMOOVE HIS BONES. HE DYED A PAPIST." (*See Plate III, at end of volume.*)

This last phrase caused Fulman's notes to be consigned to oblivion after the assertion of Davies had been dismissed by Doctor Dyce with the argument that *"it is contradicted by the whole tenour of Shakespeare's writings."*

On another:
"Here lyeth the body of John Hall gent. he marr. Susanna daughter and coheir of William Shakespeare gent. He deceased November 25. Anno 1635. Aged 60 years.

> Hallius his Situs est medica celeberimus arte
> Expectans regni gaudia, leta Die.
> Dignus erat meritis qui Nestora vinceret annis
> In terris omnes, sed rapit aqua dies;
> Ne tumulo, quid desit, adest fidissima conjux
> Et vitae Comitem nunt quoq; mortis habet."

On another:
"Here lyeth the body of Susanna, wife of John Hall gent. the daughter of William Shakespeare gent. She deceased the 2 day of July Anno 1649. Aged. 66.

> Witty above her sexe, but that's not all,
> Wife to salvation was good Mistris Hall,
> Something of Shakespeare was in that, but this
> Wholy of him with whom she's now in blisse,
> Then, Passenger, ha'st ne're a teare
> To weep with her that wept with all?
> That wept, yet set herself to chere
> Them up with comforts cordiall.
>   Her love shall live, her mercy spread
>   When thou hast ne're a tear to shed."

—*Antiquities of Warwickshire,* by Sir William Dugdale, Vol. II, pages 685–688.

The poaching story first went into print when Nicholas Rowe, before publishing his magnificent edition of the poet's work, prefaced it in 1709 with "Some account of the Life of Mr. Wm. Shakespeare." After repeating certain information gathered by the actor Betterton at Stratford, Rowe continues:

"He had, by a Misfortune common to young Fellows, fallen into ill company and amongst them, some, that made frequent practices of deer stealing, engaged him with them, more than once, in robbing a park that belonged to Sir Thomas Lucy of Charlecote, near Stratford. For this he was prosecuted by that Gentleman, as he thought, somewhat too severely and in order to revenge that ill usage he made a ballad upon him, and, though this, probably the first essay of his poetry, be lost, yet it is said to have been so very bitter that it redoubled the Prosecution against him to that degree that he was obliged to leave his businesse and Family in Warwickshire for some time and shelter himself in London. . . ."

Writing in 1743, William Oldys, to whom we are indebted for so many delightful reminiscences, repeated the tale from other sources, adding that it came from the Duke of Buckingham, who got it from Sir Wm. d'Avenant:

"There was a very aged gentleman living in the neighborhood of Stratford where he died fifty years since who had not only heard from several old people in that town of Shakespeare's transgression, but could remember the first stanza of that bitter ballad, which, reciting to one of his acquaintance he preserved it in writing; and here it is neither better nor worse, but faithfully transcribed from the copy his relation very courteously communicated to me:

> A parliamente member, a justice of peace,
> At home a poor scare-crow, at London an asse,
> If lowsie is Lucy, as some volke miscalle it
> Then Lucy is lowsie whatever befall it;

He thinks himself greate,
But an asse in his state,
We allow by his eares but with asses to mate,
If lowsie is Lucy, as some volke miscalle it
Sing Oh Lowsie Lucy whatever befall it.

"Contemptible as this performance must now appear, at the time when it was written it might have sufficient power to irritate a vain, weak, vindictive magistrate; especially as it was affixed to several of his park gates and consequently published among his neighbours.—It may be remarked likewise that the jingle on which it turns, occurs in the first scene of the 'Merry Wives of Windsor.' "

The *Biographica Britannica* published in 1763 an article on Shakespeare supposed to have been written by Bishop Warburton: ". . . This ballad was not the only shaft which he let fly against his persecutor, whose anger drove him to the extreme end of ruin where he was forced to a very low degree of drudgery for support."

Edward Capell, in his Notes to the "Merry Wives"—1780, tells how the first stanza of the lost ballad was put into his hands by the grandson of its preserver.

"Mr. Jones who dwelt in Tarbick (Tardebigge), a village in Worcestershire a few miles from Stratford on Avon, and dyed in the year 1703 aged upwards of ninety, remembered to have heard from several old people of Stratford the story of Shakespeare's robbing Sir Thomas Lucy's park; and their account of it agreed with Mr. Rowe's with this addition; that the ballad written against Sir Thomas by Shakespeare was stuck upon his park gate which exasperated the knight to apply to a lawyer at Warwick to proceed against him: Mr. Jones has put down in writing the first stanza of this ballad which was all he remembered of it, and Mr. Thomas Wilkes (my grandfather, transmitted it to my father by memory)—who also took it in writing and his copy is this. . . ."

Capell then repeats the stanza; except for some trifling variations in the spelling, the verse transcribed is exactly like the form quoted by Oldys. Capell supplements the information by stating that the people of those parts pronounced Lucy like Lowsie.

Two points may be noticed in reading his stanza: first, as I said, it explains *why* Davies remarked that Shakespeare called the Justice a "great man"—second, that those who exclaim against the idea that Shakespeare as a youth could have written such coarse lines, seem to have forgotten the song in the Tempest which, in rhythm and in spirit, closely resembles his early essay.

> The master, the swabber, the boatswaine and I,
>   The gunner and his mate,
> Lov'd Mall, Meg, and Marian and Margery,
>   But none of us car'd for Kate.
>   For she had a tongue with a tang
>   Would cry to a sailor "Go hang!"
> She lov'd not the savour of tar nor of pitch,
>   Yet a tailor might scratch her wher-e'er she did itch:
>   Then to sea, boys, and let her go hang.

Again the tale was set down between 1746 and 1800 by John Jordan, who claimed to have discovered the complete ballad in a chest-of-drawers which had belonged to Miss Dorothy Tylor of Shottery.

Naturally enough, those who discredit the old ballad-tradition declare that the whole set of verses was merely forged by Jordan himself, but this, we must notice, does not account for the first stanza above quoted, which was transcribed long before Jordan's time both by Oldys and Capell. Hence, even should we admit that the concluding verses were added later from oral tradition, it does not invalidate the testimony they bring that Warwickshire folk long remembered the old story and continued to dress it according to their taste, taking pains to show that whereas the dramatist pictures the Justice as a vain fool, the later verses show the Knight as *dangerous, hated by all and feared by many*.

Both comedy and ballad agree however on one point—the Lucy blazon with its white luces just as it is ascribed by Shakespeare to Justice Shallow, who from his very first appearance in "Henry IV" displays the characteristic tastes and tendencies which belonged, in real life, to Sir Thomas Lucy of Charlecote.

In the "Merry Wives," inordinately proud of his coat-of-arms and his claim to ancient lineage, he replies to the ridiculous Welsh parson who comes as a peacemaker:

"Sir Hugh, persuade me not, I will make a Star-Chamber matter of it! If he were fifty Sir John Falstaffs he shall not abuse Robert Shallow esquire."

"In the County of Gloster, Justice of peace and coram . . ." adds his cousin Slender, eager to give the great man his full official title as keeper of the coram rege rolls or Custos rotolorum.

"Ay, Cousin Slender, and custalorum!" cries Shallow, taking the mispronounced Latin out of his relative's mouth.

"Ay, and ratolorum too, and a gentleman born, Master Parson! who writes himself *armigero* in any bill, warrant, quittance or obligation, armigero!"

"Ay, that I do, and have done any time these three hundred years!"

Slender continues:

"All his successors gone before him hath done't and all his

93

ancestors that come after him may . . . Ay! They may, give the dozen white luces in their coat!"

"It is an old coat!" remarks Shallow complacently, and the Welsh parson hastens to chime in with his mood but mistakes the word.

"The dozen white louses do become an old coat well; it agrees well, *passant;* it is a familiar beast to man and signifies Love."

Shallow hastens to correct him, the luce is no louse, but a fresh-water fish. . . .[6]

The caricature, recognised by Shakespeare's contemporaries, remains unmistakable today, for, the further we examine the life and acts of Sir Thomas Lucy, as recorded in the State Archives, the more he shows forth as the original Justice Shallow and as a man who, not only through personal vanity, but also through what he deemed moral and political principle, might have acted a tyrant's part toward young Shakespeare, son of Mary Arden of Wilmcote.

I shall follow the course of Lucy's life from the traces left in public documents.

The task is not hard, for Sir Thomas was not a man of complex character. All records show that he was particularly keen on one thing—his material advancement as an eminent personage in the Shire. He was a sportsman, a time-server and an eager seeker after "graft." He put his Puritan principles in his pocket under Mary and pretended, under Elizabeth, to favour the Church "as by law established." It is exactly thus that Shallow is represented, forgetting himself and swearing "by Jesu," "by the Mass" or "by the Rood," then, repairing the error with a more sober oath—"by yea and nay." Never having been to a university, he retained a rustic manner of speech, detected in an early letter which shows Sir Thomas interceding with Leicester

[6]"Merry Wives of Windsor," Act I, Scene I.

to order the judge to cheat for his special protégé in an archery contest.[7]

It was natural, therefore, that Shakespeare should make Justice Shallow comment movingly on the death of a champion who seldom failed to hit the bull's eye.

"Jesu, Jesu, dead! a drew a good bow; and dead! a shot a fine shoot:—John o' Gaunt loved him well and betted much money on his head. Dead! a would have clapt in the clout at twelve score and carried you a forehand shaft a fourteen and fourteen and-a-half that it would have done a man's heart good to see!"

Shallow gives vent to a pious reflection which recalls that he has been tutored in religion by no less a person than John Foxe the martyrologist—"Death, as the psalmist saith, is certain to all. All shall die—" then hastens to inquire what price a yoke of bullocks and a score of ewes may be supposed to bring at Stamford fair.

Sir Thomas Lucy's pride in his game preserve is illustrated in the "Merry Wives," where Shallow is shown receiving thanks for a gift of venison.

Sir Thomas Lucy was jealous of his grain harvest and Shakespeare exhibits Justice Shallow keeping back the wages of a servant who has lost a sack of flour, and ordering *more red wheat* planted on the upland, and so, throughout, while sum-

---

[7]This letter, found among the Marquess of Bath's papers at Longleat, is reproduced in extenso at p. 27, *Shakespeare's Warwickshire Contemporaries."*

"To the Right Honorable and his singular good Lord my L. Robert Dudleye, Mr. Of the Quenes horse, etc. . . .

"Right Honorable and singular good lorde pleaseth it youar honor to be advertised that according to youar lordships request and my one promise I have sent you my servaunt Burnell whom I fear will not be hable to doo your Lordshipp such sarvice as I could wish nor as his hart woold sarve, for that by occasion of longe sickness his strength is greatly decayed, and thereby his shuting much Hindered. Your Lordshipp must take hede in making off yor matches that Burnell be not overmarked for that at this instante he is hable to shute no farr ground (which if youar lordshipp forsee I do not mistrust but he will be able to shute with the best) . . .

"I commend you unto almightie God who send you long life in the feare off God with increace of honor according to your Lordship's one commandement during life."

marising what is known of the knight's career, we shall find the dramatist checking each incident and underlining each characteristic trait.

Thomas Lucy was born at Charlecote on the twenty-fourth of April, 1532. His father Sir William drew up a handsome settlement when he married the boy of fourteen to Joyce Acton, a girl of twelve in August, 1546. Through his bride, heiress of Sutton Park, Thomas was already lord of a great estate when his father's death, in 1551, left him, at nineteen, master of Charlecote, which he rebuilt in a sumptuous manner in 1558. In the same year he was chosen sheriff of the county.

In 1565 he was knighted—tradition says in his own house— and appointed Justice of the peace, custos rotolorum and Commissioner of Musters. Thus he began early to play the part in which Shakespeare shows Justice Shallow pressing into military service the conscripts of Falstaff's ragged regiment.

"Good morrow, honest gentlemen," says Bardolph, entering with the muster roll. "I beseech you which is Justice Shallow?"

"—I am Robert Shallow, sir, a poor esquire of this county and one of the King's justices-of-the-Peace. What is your good pleasure with me?

"—My captain, sir, commends him to you; my captain, Sir John Falstaff, a tall gentleman by heaven, and a most gallant leader."

Shallow, with pompous politeness, enquires "How doth the Good knight? May I ask how my lady his wife doth? . . . Look here comes Good Sir John. Give me your good hand; give me your Worship's good hand. By my troth, you look well, and bear your years well. Welcome, good Sir John."[8]

He then introduces his cousin Silence, who is sitting on the commission with him, to muster soldiers for the wars and at the end of the scene Falstaff sums up the magistrate's dis-

[8]Henry IV (part 2), Act III, Scene I.

96

position of bragging satisfaction in his "lands and beeves," promising to get some of Justice Shallow's money through adroit flattery as surely as the large Pike makes his meal of *small fresh water fish*.[9]

In 1571, Lucy was elected knight of the Shire and sent down to a parliament which had been convoked to enact anti-catholic legislation. He sat on a committee organised to "combat abuses in religion" and was influential in pushing the *Act to maintain her Majesty's subjects in due Obedience*. He was equally zealous in drawing up a bill against the practice of Priests wearing the badges of certain noblemen, as a safeguard against arrest.

In 1581 he was appointed Commissioner with truly inquisitorial rights to investigate into the doings of his Warwickshire neighbors, watch over the "Queen's peace," and maintain her Majesty's subjects docile under laws which, at each session of parliament, became more dangerous for Shakespeare's kinsfolk.

Mrs. Stopes, who attempted to "white-wash" Sir Thomas when he secured capital punishment for the Arden family and their chaplain, shows, by the very records quoted in *Shakespeare's Warwickshire Contemporaries*, enough to defeat her own contention.

This remark is not made in any spirit of criticism, for, of all modern commentators, Mrs. Stopes has furnished the most important contributions to Shakespearean research during sixty years of unremitting devotion to her subject. From 1913 until her death we were constantly in touch through correspondence and it would be difficult to estimate what scholars owe to her indefatigable study. I had the honour of furnishing her with material concerning Florio for her book on *Henry, Third Earl of Southampton* and when we met at last, we became sincere friends. Nor did I ever visit London without taking tea in her house in Hampstead. To her comments upon the texts she had discovered, she brought a passion inseparable from

9Allusion to the Lucy blazon.

her adoration of Shakespeare. It made her suffer to think that the poet could have possessed any human failings or frailties and almost unconsciously, she tried to eliminate anything which might, in her opinion, redound to his discredit; that he ever was a poacher was more than she could bear! In the same spirit, she considered that all those neighbours who actually enjoyed the privilege of feasting their eyes on this "divinity" partook of a reflected glory. Thus she would not admit that Sir Thomas Lucy ever disliked and persecuted a young man of such distinguished talent, and her study of the Justice of Peace is one of the most curious examples I know, where patient research and scrupulous exposition of facts are accompanied by a commentary which consistently deforms the evidence presented. She writes that:

"There is nothing to show that he [Sir Thomas Lucy] was not upright in action and conscientious in intention while he obeyed the government represented by Leicester. We must allow somewhat for customs and circumstances of the time and for the blinding effect of religious and party passions; nevertheless he seems to have acted harshly towards recusants."[10] She did admit, however, that perhaps his "energy" in hounding Edward Arden to death was enough to embitter Shakespeare's mind.

The Parliament Session, which began on November 23, 1584, and to which Sir Thomas Lucy was again sent as Knight of the Shire, amply proved, before terminating, that Warwickshire neighbours had good cause to hate and fear Thomas Lucy; they did, if we are to believe Shakespeare's ballad:

> "He's a haughty proud insolent knight of the Shire
> T'home nobodye loves, yet there's many him feare,
> If Lucy is lowsie as some volke miscall it
> Sing O! Lowsie Lucy whatever befall it."

[10]He was indeed directly responsible for seven capital condemnations.

A private bill, for the *Assurance of certain lands not yet defined to Sir Thomas Lucy and others* proved how carefully the
land-grabbing scheme was thought out. It passed a few hours
before the law which dispossessed Clopton, Englefield, and
other Catholic landlords then living in exile. This legislation
was called an *Act against Jesuits, Seminary priests and such like
disobedient persons.* Encouraged by this success, Sir Thomas
drafted another bill for the *Better preservation of Grain and
Game* and again the ballad recalls his complaints against the
Fulbrook poachers:

> "To the Sessions he went and did sorely complain
> His parks had been robbed and his deer they were slain.
> This Lucy is Lowsie as some volke miscalle it,
> Sing O! Lowsie Lucy whatever befall it!"

Even if all the verses of the ballad which refer to this episode
were not made by Shakespeare they certainly do bear the im-
press of early local reminiscence and reflect the indignation of
Stratford neighbours at the knight's frequent oppressions and
extortions. This indignation found voice in the lines which
seem to contain a fairly true representation of the poaching incident; for to the eyes of recusant Stratford, it was not the boy
"much given to all unluckiness in stealing venison and rabbits"
who appeared guilty in these escapades; it was the Justice whom
they found at fault.

The legitimate owner was Sir Francis Englefield, who as
a Catholic had been obliged, like the Cloptons, to flee the country after the legislation of 1571. No formal act of transfer had
yet been made after seizure by the Crown, so that it was natural
that during a period of years the Stratford youth "had the run
of it"; for Fulbrook had been "disparked" in Queen Mary's
time and, according to the ancient game laws, *"any animal within its native wildness might be killed and no man had any
property in the same until it was dead."*

But, when Parliament, in 1584, dispossessed Englefield as *recusant and traitor,* Sir Thomas Lucy acquired possession of the coveted acres. Does not possession constitute nine-tenths of the law? To make his occupation effective, he doubtless, as Ireland says, took up his residence at Fulbrook lodge for a certain time and erected palings, but the property was not confirmed to his grandson by right of purchase from the Crown until the reign of King James.

Meanwhile, the more than doubtful tenure of this new preserve may well explain how and why Shakespeare himself, in *King Lear,* excused his former depredations.

"See how yond justice rails against yon simple thief. . . . Change places and handy dandy, which is the Justice and which the thief?"

Englefield was much beloved in the shire, Sir Thomas was not; so the friends of the exiled proprietor "despoiled the spoiler" in a spirit of glee and self-justification.

"Full often struck their doe and bore it cleanly by the keepers' nose," as Shakespeare wrote in "Titus Andronicus," even if they risked getting whipped for it. But to be the enemy of Sir Thomas involved more than a whipping.

A learned Welsh scholar and Doctor of Law, William Parry, member for Queenborough, Kent, denounced the pending legislation with a fiery eloquence which anticipated Hampden. Free speech was not the order of the day and such an intervention in favour of Liberty is thus consigned by Sir Simonds d'Ewes:

"The Bill against Jesuits, seminary priests and such like disobedient subjects having, through the third reading, passed the House was sent up to the Lords. The bill upon the reading passed the house with little or no argument, except it were from one Dr. Parry who, in very violent terms spake directly against the whole bill affirming it to savour of treasons, to be full of blood, danger, despair and terror or dread to the English subjects of this realm, our brethren, uncles and kinsfolks, and also full of confiscations, but unto whom? not, said he, to her Majesty. Where upon Dr. Parry, by order of this house, was appointed to be sequestered into the outer room into the sergeant's custody."

After having been three times sequestered with pressure brought to bear to change his negative vote, it was declared that he had behaved himself "unreverently and disorderly in the house and should be imprisoned and disabled from being a member."

Parliamentary immunity being thus raised, he was impeached by Sir Thomas Lucy, who also petitioned the Queen to bring him to trial on a high-treason charge.

The execution took place on March 4 in the Court-Yard of Westminster Palace, with the victim protesting to the last that his confession of "plotting" had been extorted under torture and summoning the Queen to answer for his blood on the Day of Judgment (Baga de Secretis, Pouch XXVI).

December, 1584, which is the date when Lucy's bill secured Sir Francis Englefield's lands to his own use, may well be that of the famous poaching incursion ascribed to Will Shakespeare and other Stratford lads, who staged a riot in protest against the new proprietor, ripped down the enclosure, broke into the Lodge of Fulbrook, beat the keepers who tried to bar them out—"But did not kiss the keeper's daughter"—a Shakespearean joke whose point is now lost upon us, but which certainly had one at the time! Both the old ballad and Shakespeare's play show that the word "riot" was applied to the affair.

> He said 'twas a riot,
>   his men had been beat,
> His venison killed
>   and clandestinely eat—*etc.*

Here is the scene between the Justice and the accused poacher in "The Merry Wives":

Shallow—"Knight, you have beaten my men, killed my deer and broke open my lodge!"

Falstaff—"But not kissed your keeper's daughter."

Shallow—"Tut, a pin! This shall be answered; the council shall know of this!"

Falstaff—"If 'twere known in council you'll be laughed at!"

Shallow—"The Council shall hear it; it is a riot."

The Act of 1584 set such a premium upon denunciations and was enforced with such rigor that Mendoza the Spanish Ambassador reported that 11,000 British subjects went to prison or into exile after this date. Among all those whose business was to enforce the law none acted with more consistent zeal than Sir Thomas Lucy.

On September 5, 1585, he was officially thanked for his arrest of the Abingdon brothers as recusants at Hucknoll, and sat upon a commission to punish the "tiplers" of Stratford-on-Avon. Though no longer sheriff in his own county, he became that year sheriff of Worcestershire in right of his wife's large holdings there.

In 1588 he again appeared as Commissioner of Musters and in 1590 was made a member of the Council for the marches of Wales, where recusancy continued to lift a rebellious head.

During all this period the family fortunes of the Shakespeares grew ever darker.

In 1586 John Shakespeare's old comrades at the Council Board nominated Richard Court to take his place, alleging that Mr. Shakespeare omitted to present himself when sessions were called and had done so for a long time past. No plausible reason has yet been offered to explain why a man who, during thirteen years' term of office as Chamberlain, Bailiff and Chief Alderman, never failed in his attendance at the Halls, should suddenly cease to appear at any meeting. The cause which underlay this new line of conduct is self-evident. As a functionary, John Shakespeare might at any moment be required to subscribe to the test-oath, or openly refuse it and take the consequences, but as a private citizen he might hope to remain unmolested unless directly denounced.

Notwithstanding his precautions, the ex-bailiff evidently got into trouble the following year (1587) and had to produce a *habeas corpus* to protect himself from molestation.

In 1592 the name of Mr. John Shakespeare appears third among those denounced for recusancy in the parish of Stratford-on-Avon. Mr. Wheeler, who had been his associate in the municipal council, headed the list with his son. George Bardolph and William Fluellen are also mentioned, an interesting attestation that the dramatist selected these names which he has made celebrated, from among his Stratford neighbours. (*See Plate II, at end of volume.*)

The Christopher Shakespeares figure on this document for the Parish of Packwood.

No doubt whatever can subsist that the accusation brought against the ex-bailiff by the Warwickshire commissioners was as a Catholic suspect, although Mr. Fripp made many zealous attempts to prove that he was a Puritan. Sir Thomas Lucy himself was a convinced Puritan whose activities were directed against Catholics only.

Instructions given to examiners explicitly forbade them to "press any man concerning matters of doctrine or conscience." The three points to be insisted upon were allegiance to the Queen, opinions concerning Papal supremacy, and approval of the maintenance of seminary priests. It was not, indeed, until

103

after 1593 that the first Government stand was taken against two Puritans, Collings and Greenwood, who, as "conscientious objectors" denied the Queen's spiritual supremacy. However, as it was drawn up in 1592, the act under which so many suffered was specifically directed against Catholic recusants, it reads:

FOR THE BETTER DISCOVERY OF WICKED AND SEDITIOUS PERSONS CALLING THEMSELVES CATHOLICS BUT BEING REBELLIOUS AND TRAITOROUS SUBJECTS.

Terror reigned in town and countryside. Once more the fanatical zeal of Sir Thomas Lucy's Commission made itself felt among Shakespeare's relatives.

In April, 1593, an official report tells how the pursuivants searched Coughton Court "where Mistress Arden, wife of Arden the traitor, doth dwell at this present, still obstinate in her recusancy, also her servant, John Brown," and the London Council replied:

"It would seem by your letter to Mr. Topcliffe there was resistance offered at such time as you did search the house; and that they of the household did not carry themselves with that dutiful course and obedience they ought, and that divers superstitious things and furniture for Mass were there found. And it was confessed that a Seminary priest was harboured there who was conveyed out of the way and lieth in a secret place.

"We have thought good to require of you to commit to prison the said Mrs. Arden with the rest of her servants to be proceeded with according to the qualities of their offence which we refer to your discretion."

In 1595 the Warwickshire Commission arrested William Freeman and had him hanged at Warwick, July 13, for *priesthood*. In the same year Lady Joyce Lucy died and was buried at Charlecote. Her epitaph, written and signed like an affidavit by Sir Thomas himself, is declared by Mrs. Stopes to have been conceived "as an answer to wide-spread gossip concerning family disunion." This epitaph may be found in Sir William Dugdale's *Antiquities of Warwickshire* (1653):

"Here entombed lieth the Lady Joyce Lucy," etc., etc., "who departed out of this wretched world to her heavenly kingdom in the year of Our Lord 1595, and of her age 65; all the time of her life a true and faithful servant of her good God; never detected of any crime or vice, in religion most sound, in love to her husband most faithful and true; in friendship most constant; to what in trust was committed to her most secret, in wisdom excelling, in governing of her house and bringing up of youth in the fear of God, that did converse with her, most rare and singular. A great maintainer of hospitality; greatly esteemed of her betters; misliked of none unless the envious. When all is spoken that can be said, a woman so furnished and garnished with virtue, as not to be bettered and hardly to be equalled by any. As she lived most virtuously, so she died most godly. Set down by him that best did know what hath been written to be true.   THOMAS LUCY."

Whatever the reasons which moved the husband to execute such an extraordinary piece of literary composition and furnish, at the same time such a self-revealing document, the epitaph remains interesting as a piece of corroborative evidence displaying the personal style so admirably caricatured every time Justice Shallow speaks in "Henry IV" and "The Merry Wives." A few surviving letters confirm and illustrate the resemblance between Shakespeare's caricature and the elder Sir Thomas Lucy.

He died July 7, 1600, but it seems probable that his son, another Sir Thomas, knighted in 1593, practically succeeded after this event, for nothing subsists in public or private records concerning Thomas Lucy the elder, after the hanging of the priest Freeman in 1595, except notice of a sumptuous funeral.

"I think we may believe that he closed an honorable career by a fitting end," says the charitable Mrs. Stopes.

However that may be, no one wrote his epitaph, Shakespeare alone made the old knight immortal, for, in spite of the censor, who, when the quarto was published, eliminated the passage where the Lucy coat-of-arms is trifled with, it reappeared in the Folio and subsequent editions of "The Merry Wives."

Any impartial student, putting together what is already known and examining it in the light of this new evidence, must conclude that the ancient tradition of Shakespeare's grievances against the local Justice set down by his early biographers and recalled by his own pen, should figure, as of old, in any attempt to reconstitute the dramatist's early life or explain what became of him during the so-called "lost years."

To the material difficulties encountered during the long interval between forced departure from Stratford, arrival at the Playhouse, and his introduction to London as a lyric poet who might vie with Sidney and Spenser, perils were added. Sir Thomas Lucy had a long arm and the suspicion which weighed so heavily upon Shakespeare's family could not fail to cast its shadow upon a refugee who was kin to "Arden the traitor," son to John Shakespeare and Mary Arden, and cousin to John Trussel of Billesley, an obstinate recusant who attached his name to the third edition of Robert Southwell's proscribed book, *Triumph over Death*.

In London, as in the Shires, Walsingham's sergeant had become a living fear.

Leslie Hotson's discovery that the enmity of the Warwickshire Justice of the Peace was pursued by his London Colleague, Judge William Gardiner who had married a Lucy heiress and quartered the famous blazon, shows more than the finder himself read into the episode, but it does indicate that the poet was not always content with the rôle of stander-by when acts of injustice were inflicted on his friends and I am inclined to think that the greatest gift offered to the author by his young Patron was the assurance of peace and tranquillity during ten years' intensive literary production.

PART 2

❧

LONDON

CHAPTER SIX

SHAKESPEARE'S LONDON PATRON

NOTHING IS KNOWN about the exact date of Shakespeare's arrival in London; neither can we do more than guess at the trades he practised to keep body and soul together and earn the contemptuous nicknames "Rude Groom," "Shakescene" and "Johannes Factotum" from a jealous rival. That he held horses outside the theatre to earn a few pence on play days is probable. The testimony that he did so comes from his godson William Davenant who stepped into the great dramatist's theatrical shoes and was strong on the early days of the man he strove to imitate. d'Avenant's Ode "On the Remembrance of Master William Shakespeare" prettily recalls the affectionate admiration of an eleven-year-old boy. His intimate association with John Lowine and Joseph Taylor when he took over the surviving remnants of the Blackfriars' troupe placed him in a position to be more thoroughly informed on the actors' world than any man of his time, for even under Cromwellian autocracy, when the theatre was in eclipse Sir William d'Avenant cleverly evaded the laws against playhouses, reconstituted the dispersed company and under colour of an appeal to patriotism, presented what he called oratorios or Opera Stilo Recitativo at the Tennis Court and Lincoln's Inn.[1]

[1]With the Restoration came violent anti-puritan reaction. Charles II made d'Avenant his poet-laureate and confided to him the task of re-establishing the drama. The Drury Lane Company prided itself on possessing the true Shakespearean tradition concerning

Another early testimony affirms that Shakespeare was "forced to a very low form of drudgery." The internal evidence of his work shows that he was familiar as only a technician can be with the art of printing and it is likely that he gained some practical experience at Vautrollier's shop where his co-Stratfordian Richard Field served as apprentice before publishing his fellow-townsman's books as Master of the printing-house. Perhaps young Shakespeare did some legal scrivening, thus earning the term of "noverint" which is cast at the author of "Hamlet." But ere his rapidly developing talent unleashed the hounds of envy upon him, many were the material difficulties encountered by the Warwickshire lad, before finding a safe haven where fame grew and prospered under the patronage of a family equally distinguished for riches and taste.

On the 18th of April, 1593, Shakespeare asked and obtained licence to print a poem "Venus and Adonis." The subject taken from the tenth book of Ovid's *Metamorphoses* was here treated with a freshness of inspiration, a sense of the beauties of nature through which the local colour of the Cotswold region shines on every page and a technical mastery of languages and rhythm which provoked favourable comparison with England's best poets. The success obtained was prodigious and lifted the author above the still discredited status of theatrical writer to the full glory of recognition as a great lyric artist. Indeed, as a masterpiece of life and youth it has perhaps never had its like.

---

the proper interpretation of the principal characters through "old Mr. Taylor" and Mr. Lowine who had been taught their parts by Shakespeare himself and who passed on the torch directly to Betterton. Through him it went to David Garrick who fired the Kembles, Keanes, Booths, Fechters and Salvinis, and so on in pious succession. The history of d'Avenant's Troupe was written day by day from 1662 to 1708 by the manager and archive-keeper, John Downes, who boasts "never having missed a performance or a rehearsal during 45 years." Betterton's great parts were Pericles, Hamlet, Richard III, King Lear, Macbeth, Timon, Henry VIII and Falstaff, and Downes affirms that each rôle seemed to have been made specially to fit his extraordinary talents, while young Mr. Knyaston, "our beautiful leading lady, interpreted Shakespeare's heroines so remarkably that I dare affirm no woman could have shown such tenderness and sensibility."

Francis Meres, professor of rhetoric at Oxford, declared that if Apollo and the Muses used English they would choose the verse of Shakespeare. It is true that the acid-tongued Middleton in a satire curiously entitled "A Mad World, My Masters" attacked the sensuality of the poem and expressed astonishment at finding such reprehensible literature in the hands of women of fashion. But critical attack seldom diminishes the success of a work when its vogue with the public is already assured. On the contrary, hot debate over the poem increased its sale, the theatrical reviews, so dear to the students of Oxford and Cambridge, took up the subject. In "The Pilgrimage to Parnassus," a burlesque character exclaims "Oh, sweet Mr. Shakespeare, I'll have his picture in my study at the Court. Let this duncified world esteem its Spenser and Chaucer, I'll worship sweet Mr. Shakespeare and to honor him I'll have his 'Venus and Adonis' under my pillow."

In the "Return from Parnassus," where the characters take the names of Shakespeare's company in order to discuss his poetry, Kemp, the clown, declares that "university pens" smell too much of that writer Ovid and talk too much of Proserpina and Jupiter: "Here is our fellow Shakespeare who puts them all down, aye, and Ben Jonson too." If success was chiefly due to Shakespeare's own energy and talent, there was another element which is rarely absent in such a case; that of luck. Fortune certainly favoured the actor-author, when she placed in his path, at exactly the time when his help was most needful, the ideal patron dreamed of by every struggling artist. "Venus and Adonis," the poem under discussion between London and Oxford, was offered to the young Earl of Southampton, as the "first fruit of the poet's invention," with the promise that if found worthy, by such a reader, the author would consecrate every idle hour to honour his young patron with a graver labour.

The Right Honourable Henry Wriothesley, third Earl of

Southampton and Baron Tichfield, whom Shakespeare acknowledged as his sole patron, came into the world under the shadow of a prison; the family had been implicated in the Northern rising which caused so much blood to flow. The second Earl, though permitted on parole to be near his wife at the time of their son's birth (October, 1573), was either in the Tower or under close surveillance until his death in 1581, at which time his heir, then eight years of age, passed under the wardship of the Crown. The vigilance of Burleigh could not, however, prevent him from growing up a Catholic like the rest of his family.

Young Southampton's mother, whose signature attests the first payment made at Court to Shakespeare and Burbage for a theatrical performance, was related to the Copleys, Cornwallis and Arundels, all well known as devoted to the old faith. Her father, Anthony Browne, Viscount Montague, was the only great layman in the House of Lords with enough civic courage to denounce the Acts of Supremacy and Uniformity as "unreasonable, unjust and unnecessary," adding that no greater tyranny can be conceived than to compel a man under penalty of death to swear "to that which his conscience believes to be false."

Through sheer force of personality and unquestioned patriotism, this old warrior of the Armada year made his own and his family's independence respected in spite of the Statutes, until his death in 1592. The Queen looked upon him with a grateful veneration which was proof against both open and insidious attacks. His widow, Lady Magdalene, remained a bulwark of Catholicism and retained much influence at Court.[2]

---

[2] When the outbreak of the gunpowder plot again placed all Catholics under suspicion in King James' reign, orders were given that Lady Montague's loyalty should not be called into question and, although the Crown itself could not exempt her house from official search like the others, she was authorised to select her own servants for that purpose!

She gave two-thirds of her income to the payment of fines, regretting only that what was left might not suffice to keep more proscribed priests under the shelter of her livery at Cowdray and Montague House. Well might William Shakespeare when he arrived with his name on the Warwickshire black list have been grateful for the protection of the house of Montague!

At his coming of age in October, 1593—at which date Shakespeare's first poem appears—the third Earl of Southampton had power to assure success in the world of letters and at the playhouse; he was the bright particular star in the sphere of intellectual London. He could spread a mantle of favouring protection over friends and dependents on account of the privileges which great wealth and unquestioned patriotism had brought to his grandfather, thanks also to his friendship with the Earl of Essex, who, at that time, enjoyed a favour almost equal to that formerly known by Leicester.

Indeed it is no exaggeration to reaffirm what the early biographers of Shakespeare were agreed upon, that his path to success in the London world of letters and on the stage was smoothed, if not entirely due, to Wriothesley influence.

It was young Henry's stepfather, Sir Thomas Heneage (who married the dowager Countess of Southampton in May, 1594), that chose the plays which might be presented before Elizabeth and constantly favoured the troupe for which Shakespeare wrote and in which he acted, and I shall show in Chapter VIII, that the third husband of this Court beauty gave like patronage to Shakespeare's lyric poetry.

I need hardly repeat Rowe's oft-quoted statement, made on the authority of Sir William d'Avenant, that young Harry Wriothesley once gave Shakespeare a thousand pounds "for a purchase he had a mind to." But I am inclined to think that his protection went further, for in that same April of 1593 which marked the high tide of persecution in Warwickshire, trouble ceased for the Shakespeares of Stratford with the appearance of "Venus and Adonis." Not only did the poet gradually free his father from debt, he obtained through the favour of Essex and Camden, then at the Heralds' College, the armorial blazon which had been previously refused, and placed John Shakespeare's family in the county—as is quaintly declared by Nicholas Rowe—among "people of good figure and fashion."

Mrs. Stopes quotes a letter showing with what good nature Lord Southampton did what he could to protect his recusant kinsfolk when he still enjoyed the favour of Robert Cecil to whom these lines are addressed:

"My Lord,

"I had much rather do your Lordship service than be so often troublesome unto you as I am, yet must I now of necessity renew an old suit on behalf of my poor aunt Katherine Cornwallis who, by your Lordship's favour hath hitherto lived free from trouble for her recusancy, but is now by malice likely to be indicted if your Lordship interpose not some means to help her . . . My Lord, I can say no more for her than I have already done, she is an old woman and liveth without scandal." (Cecil Papers, CXVIII, 104.)

The situation was different in 1591 when the new legislation asserting that all persons *calling themselves catholics were but rebellious and traitorous subjects,* was enforced. Old Viscount Montague, dying in the country, could no more make his name feared in the Queen's council and his grandson Harry still a minor, under Burleigh's wardship, was powerless to protect the old schoolmaster Swithin Wells, who, accused of recusancy, took shelter in London under the pretext of instructing his lordship in the French and Italian tongues[3] and was hanged at the

---

[3]I have done what I could to trace the career of Swithin Wells, sixth son of Thomas Wells of Brambridge near Winchester, whose daughters joined the Convent of Brigittine Nuns at Rouen, from contemporary documents:—

"Swithin was 'well informed upon all a young gentleman should know'—fully

entrance of Gray's Inn, charged with having permitted Mass to be solemnised under his roof. Three priests and four gentlemen were executed for this offence. Their story has been often told but never with reference to Shakespeare's patron.

By family tradition as well as taste, Henry Wriothesley adored the drama. His grandfather, a "favourite of Apollo," had in his day been star of the students' troupe at the University and this grandson had such a passion for the theatre that he is described in contemporary correspondence as going to plays every day. After graduating with a Master's Degree from Saint John's at Cambridge, he began reading law at Gray's Inn with a view to the future management of his great estate.

During his sojourn, Shakespeare's "Comedy of Errors," adapted from a comedy of Plautus, was performed and caused some scandal, as professional actors had never appeared at the Inns of Court and the overcrowding was such that due precedence could not be observed. But if this occasion was long remembered as "The Night of Errors," at court the play's

educated in the liberal sciences and perfected in the tongues by years of travel on the continent where his religious devotion was stimulated by a pilgrimage to the holy places. On returning home he opened a school for boys at Monckton Farley and employed himself in teaching Belles-Lettres and music, having for his assistant therein Mr. Woodfen, afterwards priest and martyr. Wells was a man of great good nature, charming in conversation and much addicted to rural sports such as riding, hawking and hunting, and his school where a wife of happy endowments presided, was greatly appreciated by the Catholic gentry of the region, until under suspicion of encouraging papistry it was closed by the local authorities.

"Mr. and Mrs. Wells continued for a time to keep open house for such priests as were in the district until Swithin himself having so often served as guide and accompanied certain priests on their charitable missions became a marked man in the shire, was 'closely questioned' on several occasions and was obliged to change his residence."

Under examination he stated that after abandoning school he lived on the benevolence of his friends and on that of his brother Gilbert, carefully omitting—according to the unwritten law among recusants—to name any names. However, on the list of suspected persons, calendered among the State papers, lodging in Southampton House, Father Stanney, Wells' confessor, confirms this report in a memoir published by Challoner: "After having instructed several persons of quality he was selected, on account of his great skill in languages, as resident professor by Henry Third Earl of Southampton, and lived in his house with much commendation for several years."

success was complete and the Queen, Sir Robert Cecil, the Earl of Essex and Lord Southampton were among those who applauded the choice of Sir Thomas Heneage, who, as vice-chamberlain, brought the rollicking comedy officially on the boards.

In the midst of numberless theatrical successes and in less than a year after the publication of "Venus and Adonis" a graver labour entitled "The Rape of Lucrece" was also issued from the press of Richard Field. The dedication inscribed, like the first, to Lord Southampton, expressed a fervent devotion inspired by a year's growth of beneficent friendship which differed much from the usual stilted formality of that period.

In "Lucrece," Shakespeare shows mastery of a more difficult subject than that formerly treated. "Venus" had presented all the arguments which might induce a young man to abjure celibacy. In "Lucrece," he pointed out the devastation wrought by an illicit passion which leads to death and the violent disruption of family ties. It contains the quintessence of drama, as "Venus and Adonis" reaches the height of lyric art.

These two masterpieces, though neglected in our times, as compared with the dramatic works, were recognised in his own as those of genius. Thirteen editions succeeded one another in what, for those days, was a very brief interval, and the lustre reflected on the person to whom they were addressed served to make Southampton as much an object of admiration as the author himself.

> "Thou glorious Laurel of the Muses' hill,
> Whose eye hath crowned our most victorious pen,
> Bright lamp of virtue in whose sacred skill
> Lives all the bliss of ears, enchanting men,
> Vouchsafe to sweet my work with thy sweet tongue"

solicited Gervaise Markham in 1594, and such prayers were echoed by other aspirants for the young Earl's favour, who imitated Shakespeare's dedications and vainly endeavoured to match his verse.

Thomas Nash, in his "Choice of Valentines," seems to recall Shakespeare's success and excuses his own loose conceits not more lascivious, after all, than those of Ovid.

In 1594 Nash dedicated to Southampton his "Jack Wilton, or the Unfortunate Traveller," a type of picaresque romance which enjoyed a measure of popular favour. Among those who sought the young man's patronage may be mentioned Barnaby Barnes, George Peel, George Wither, Gervaise Markham, Richard Barnfield, Samuel Daniel, Mathias Gwynn, Sir John Beaumont, Arthur Price, Francis Peel, William Petty, George Chapman and Giovanni Florio. It is amusing to compare Shakespeare's 1594 dedication with the unblushing plagiarism offered to the same patron by his Italian tutor. Shakespeare said:

"The love I dedicate to your Lordship is without end, whereof this pamphlet without beginning is but a superfluous moiety, the warrant I have of your honourable disposition, not the worth of these untutored lines, makes it assured of acceptance. What I have done is yours, what I have to do is yours, being part of all I have devoted yours. Were my worth greater my duty would show greater; meantime, as it is, it is bound to your lordship, to whom I wish long life still lengthened with all happiness.

Your Lordship's in all duty
William Shakespeare."

If Shakespeare exaggerated his debt to the man "who gave his pen both skill and argument," Florio's assertion is completely absurd. Certainly Southampton could not have been very helpful in compiling the Italian-English Dictionary:

"To the patrons of Virtue and patterns of honour, Roger

Earle of Rutland, Henrie, Earle of Southampton, and Lucie, Countess of Bedford,

"In truth I acknowledge an entire debt, not only of all my best knowledge, but of all, yea of more than I know or can express to your bounteous Lordship, Most noble, most virtuous, and most Honourable Earl of Southampton, in whose pay and patronage I have lived some years and to whom I owe and vow the years that I have to live. But as to me and many more the glorious and gracious sunshine of your honour hath infused light and life so may my lesser borrowed light, after a principal respect to your benign aspect and influence afford some lustre to others.

"Your Honours' most humble and bounden in true service

Iohn Florio"[4]

In 1921 my thesis on Giovanni Florio as apostle of the Renaissance in England first established the intimate connection between this Italian lexicographer, translator and grammarian, and Shakespeare's life and work. Since that time others have learned more than my researches pursued in America and Paris could bring to light. Miss Frances Yates has proved beyond question that Florio during the years that he declared himself in the young earl's "pay and patronage" also drew a stipend from Burleigh's Intelligence service, placed there apparently not only as a teacher of languages but also to report on the recusant activities of Shakespeare's patron, who, through Elizabeth's reign, remained steadfast to his faith. It was not indeed until the Gunpowder Plot was undertaken by his cousin Copley and others who had been associated with him in the Essex affair that Southampton refused to be enrolled again among malcontents. Perhaps he thought that his family had suffered enough already; in any event a contemporary letter describes

[4] *A World of Wordes or most copious and exact Dictionarie in Italian and English,* Collected by Iohn Florio. Printed at London by Arnold Hatfield for Edward Blount, 1598.

how the "sweet reasonableness of King James" led him to accompany that monarch to the services of the Established Church.[5]

It is indeed impossible to exaggerate the importance of Henry Wriothesley's interest in Shakespeare's career. The tastes and special inclinations of the young man have an immediate reflex on the play in hand. When Southampton was dreaming of serving under Essex in France, the scene of the comedies is transported to Navarre or to the Louvre, as in "Love's Labour's Lost" and "All's Well That Ends Well." When engrossed with law books, the poet's verse bristles with judicial terms and legal phraseology; when, with his tutor Florio, Harry revels in the tales of Boccaccio, Cynthio or Della Porto, the dramatist takes his inspiration from these Italian sources, and later, when Southampton's professor undertook the translation of Montaigne's Essays, Shakespeare threw into his work not only more than a score of passages directly borrowed from these pages, but the whole character of his thought in contact with the French philosopher's theories seems to change and deepen.

Not only did Shakespeare owe to his young patron the success which he so fully acknowledged in his dedications and

[5] A report from the Venetian Ambassador in August 1603 quoted by Charlotte Carmichael Stopes in her life of Henry third Earl of Southampton—p. 269—says:

"Queen Anne has become secretly a Catholic though she goes to the hereticall church with her husband. She insists on educating her daughter as a Catholic and the King keeps the Prince from her as much as he can.

"The King has made himself head of the Anglican church and exacts the oath. Old Howard, who has lately been appointed to the Council and Southampton who were both Catholics declare that God has touched their hearts and that the example of the King has greater weight with them than the disputes of theologians."

A letter to the Privy Council in which Sir Maurice Berkeley defends himself on the score of conversing with Lady Southampton shows that she remained loyal to the old faith.

"I do confess that the Countess of Southampton told me that there was a very severe and terrible bill coming from the higher house against catholic recusants; but, that I promised her to speak against it when it came amongst us, or not to speak for it—I utterly deny. It might have proceeded from some humour to make her discover what perplexity she was, being a catholic, or to make her discover as much as she knew of the humour of the catholic party. . . ."

the Sonnets which are their epitome, many difficulties he encountered in the literary world were aggravated by Southampton's influence. The personal opposition of the clan which Essex called the "Pack" made itself felt too. The bugbear of censorship constantly came in the way of Shakespeare's production, whether on the stage or in print. His art, as he himself complained, was made "tongue tied by authority." A manuscript belonging to his company was discovered, a century ago, in the censor's portfolio. It dealt with the forbidden topic, the life and death of a political hero and religious martyr, Sir Thomas More; Edmund Tilney's hand can still be read warning the players to omit the Ill May-Day scene, or present it at their peril. The censor also dealt harshly with Falstaff under the original name which Shakespeare had chosen for him, "Sir John Oldcastle." Oldcastle, in fact, was a great favourite in the contemporary world of Puritans, and the author, who had been obliged to delete the name of his choice, succeeded in making two allusions to this event which got past the censor "quand même"; once, when Prince Hal addresses Jack as "my old lad of the Castle" and again in the epilogue to "Henry IV, Part II":[6] "If you be not too much cloyed with fat meat, our humble author will continue the story with Sir John in it, and make you merry with fair Katherine of France, where for anything I know, Falstaff will die of a sweat, unless already a' be killed with your hard opinions; for Oldcastle died a martyr and this is not the man." How the censor treated Richard II will appear later.

The play of "Sir John Oldcastle," which, on account of the name, is sometimes attributed to Shakespeare, was, in reality, by Drayton and Munday and served as a reply to "Henry IV" (as George Wyndham pointed out long ago).[7] Presented by the

[6]The Folger Library possesses the text of "Henry IV," shortened in such a manner as to make it the "Comedy of Falstaff," for amateur presentation.

[7]An interesting study of the rivalry between the Admiral's and the Chamberlain's company is also to be found in Dr. G. B. Harrison's *Shakespeare at Work*.

rival company as a Protestant retort to Shakespeare's abuse of the Oldcastle name, it profited by the vogue of the more celebrated play. The Prologue sets forth these facts very plainly:

> . . . . It is no pampered glutton we present,
> No aged counsellor to youthful sinne,
> But one whose virtue shone above the rest,
> A valiant martyr and a virtuous Peere,
> In whose true faith and loyalty exprest
> Unto his Sovereign, and his country's weal
> We strove to pay that tribute of our love
> Your favours merit: let fair truth be graced
> Since forged invention former time defaced.

By way of gracing "fair truth," Prince Hal's escapade is transformed into an episode of a similar character where a priest, who is the villain of the play, turns highwayman, robs the King and is finally hanged.

I know that many readers contend that it does not matter whether, in his life and conduct, Lord Southampton was worthy of the poems he inspired. Against this idea, I would like to protest once and for all. If the author was mistaken in his estimate of Southampton's value, the value of the poems *would* be lessened, and we could not have the same respect for the author's intelligence. Shakespeare is admirable, not only for his poetic talent, but for his sane judgment and extraordinary divination of the human heart. If, in the world about him, the "wisdom of Nestor, the art of Virgil and the genius of Socrates" had not taught him how to distinguish between a romantic hero and a degenerate dilettante, then and then only would Shakespeare not have been Shakespeare. The study of Southampton's character is essential to our knowledge of the poet, and it is easy to learn his reputation in the world and in his own family, for the young Earl was a great personage who moved in a large sphere. There are enough records of his public and private life to form a solid basis of knowledge. Henry Wriothesley's large correspondence, political, domestic and colonial, the memoirs and letters of his contemporaries and the State Archives confirm and endorse Shakespeare's opinion. At a time when descriptive anagrams were so much in vogue, the ones which became current to designate Southampton were "Stamp of Honour" and "Honour in Perfection." He was an enlightened patron of Art for Art's sake, but not more ardent in his cult for letters than in his pursuit of high renown, and the presence of the King himself could not prevent the friend of Essex from chastising the man who spoke ill of Robert Devereux living or dead.[8] He was venerated by his household, loved by his friends and adored by wife and children. Besides the praise of many poets and the grateful tribute of the Faculty of St. John's College at Cambridge which he endowed with a princely library, he is shown as a pattern to succeeding ages by one of his lifelong retainers:

> "So, dear Southampton, since deserved praise,
> Came thronging on thee faster than thy days;
> Since thy immortal virtues still were seen
> When thy grave head was gray, to be most green,
> We fools began to hope that thy life state,
> Was not confinéd to our common fate.

[8]"The Lords of Southampton and Grey, the first night the Queen came hither, renewed old quarrels, and fell flatly out in her presence. She was in discourse with my Lord of Southampton touching the Lord of Essex's action, and wondered, as she said, that so many great men did so little for themselves; to which, Lord Southampton answered, that the Queen being made a party against them, they were forced to yield; but if that course had not been taken, there was none of their private enemies, with whom only their quarrel was, that *durst* have opposed themselves. This being overheard by Lord Grey, he would maintain the contrary party durst have done much more than they, upon which he had the lie at him. The Queen bade them remember where they were, and soon after sent them to their lodgings, to which they were committed with guards upon them. The next day they were brought out and heard before the Council, and condemned to the Tower. But soon after the King sent for them, and taking the quarrel upon him, and the wrong and disgrace done to her Majesty, and not exchanged between them, so forgave it to make them friends, which was accordingly effected and they set at liberty."—*Third Earl of Southampton*, p. 267.

But that thou still should'st keep the world's fair stage,
Acting all parts of goodness, that each age
Succeeding ours, might, in thy actions see
What virtues in them dead, do live in thee."

I see with pleasure that the most recent work undertaken by Dover Wilson and Professor A. W. Pollard, in dealing with Shakespeare problems, acknowledges that "those who have insisted upon the immense influence exercised over Shakespeare by his intimacy with Essex and Southampton are certainly right."

Beneath his amiable exterior Southampton's nature was impulsive, intense and even violent. At seventeen he had already escaped from tutelage in a frustrated attempt to join Essex's expedition to France and fight under the banner of Henry of Navarre. In a letter to Essex dated from Dieppe, March 2, 1592, he regrets having no better present to make than the offer of "myself to be disposed of by your commandment of which I shall be exceedingly proud, endeavouring always by the best means to deserve it."

His devotion to friends was such that no danger or trouble seemed too great for him to undertake. He saved the lives of the Danvers brothers in most romantic fashion. They had been implicated in the death of Sir Henry Long, after a family feud conducted much in the Capulet-Montague fashion. Provocation came from Long's side but the murdered man had powerful friends in Wiltshire and soon the hunt was up and hue and cry started after the two assassins.

Southampton sheltered them at Whitely Lodge, one of his many residences; then organised a series of pretended hunting parties which led them ever nearer the coast until the port of Southampton was reached. There the rescuer chartered a ship to waft his friends to France with recommendations to the King.

At Itchin ferry they were almost caught by a sheriff bearing a search-warrant. Southampton's party did not lack daring. "His lordship's barber Humphrey Drewell and his Italian John Florio" held up the official and threatened to drown him if he attempted to interfere with justice as his Lordship understood it.

While serving King Henry the Fourth, Sir Charles and Sir Henry Danvers remained in close correspondence with their preserver (this shows how easily Shakespeare was by way of learning all that he needed for his play "Love's Labour's Lost"). When they were finally pardoned through French intercession, the Danverses accompanied Southampton on his Irish campaign and threw in their lot in the hazardous conspiracy to force the Queen's abdication for which Sir Charles lost his life. In love as in friendship Southampton's career was typically romantic. While still a minor he was betrothed by his guardian, William Cecil Lord Burleigh, to that powerful minister's granddaughter Elizabeth Vere. During a five-year engagement, the young man constantly pleaded "for a respite," but he only escaped from Cecil's powerful clutch upon the payment of five thousand crowns, the earliest case recorded in England of damage exacted for breach of promise.

Shakespeare's poetic solicitations, encouraging his young patron to marry and found a family, are by some considered to prove that the poet took the side of an ambitious mother in pleading the cause she had so much at heart in the early nineties. However this may be, each event of Southampton's life found an immediate and sympathetic echo in Shakespeare's plays or poems. "A Lover's Complaint," which was printed in the same volume with the 154 Sonnets, is but the story of the young man's romantic attachment to the Queen's beautiful maid-of-honour, Elizabeth Vernon, which kept Court gossip on the qui-vive, culminated in a secret marriage and brought about the young couple's imprisonment in the Fleet. Southampton optimistically wrote to Essex that *"as his offence was light her Majesty's resentment should not be heavy,"* but the Queen's anger at such open flouting of her authority was so violent that she ordered him committed to the Tower, as though guilty of a crime against the State, instead of the civil prison. This is indication enough that the marriage was performed by Mr. Wright the Catholic chaplain attached to the Earl's household, for we have Southampton's sworn testimony that he "knew no priest but Mr. Wright."

Her council refused to confirm the high treason charge and the young couple were sent to finish their honeymoon in the civil prison of the Fleet and, on emerging, were never admitted to Court until, after the Queen's death, they became its most brilliant ornament, but meantime, during the dark days which were to follow the Irish fiasco and the collapse of the Drury House Conspiracy, we shall find Shakespeare constantly placing his talents at the service of his patron to show "the whole body of the time its form and pressure."

The cause of Essex and Southampton led the dramatist to jeopardise his own safety and the fortunes of his troupe, but after Southampton's release and his enjoyment of the full favour of King James, his poet shared it.

And just as, in the early days, Shakespeare owed his dramatic plots to his patron's favourite Italian novels, so, at the close, we find him, once more, making use of Southampton's new interests when the Earl turned his zeal and talent toward colonial enterprise. As secretary of the Virginia Company, it was he who received the report of the barque *Sea Venture* wrecked in "the still-vex'd Bermoothes" of which Shakespeare made such poetic use in "The Tempest."

To what extent Southampton influenced his friend in questions of religion is a problem with which I am incompetent to
deal. No one in our modern world (which differs so much from
his) can pluck out the heart of that mystery—like Rosencrantz
and Guildenstern, we are too far away from Hamlet's soul to
mount the heights whence, from life's dissonance, the poet
struck "one clear chord to reach the ears of God." He and
God alone know that secret.

To show how each Victorian commentator makes the poet's
picture after his own image, it may be smilingly recalled that
Doctor Dyce, who brushed aside the Fulman-Davies evidence as
incredible, did so by explaining that "Shakespeare might have
incidentally let fall expressions unfavourable to Puritanism which
were mis-represented as papistical."

Halliwell-Phillipps gives himself and his readers hope that
"Shakespeare's last moments were soothed by a Puritan Pas-
tor" and Sir Sidney Lee plainly asserts: "We may dismiss
as idle gossip the irresponsible report that he died a Papist"
. . . that he was to the last a conforming member of the
Church of England admits of no question."

The Islamic scholar reads into his works admission of God's
Unity and finds the poet in agreement with the Koranic conception of the social system which recognises the necessity of
class (or what Shakespeare himself calls *degree*) without which
"mankind, like ravenous fishes, would feed on one another."

The Jew perceives an active expression of Hebraic sympathy
in his delineation of some very un-Christian Christians; the
militant Free-Thinker points complacently to Laertes's impulsive denunciation of a "churlish priest" who refuses to go farther
than his rule warrants, as showing the author's hostility to
prelates.

The believer in psychic phenomena as demonstrated by a
modern spiritualistic medium calls Hamlet to witness "that

there are more things in Heaven and Earth than are dreamed of" in Horatio's sceptical philosophy.

The only conclusions a modern commentator can form must be drawn, not from the opinion of a fellow-critic, but from a close study of the poet's work and knowledge of his immediate surroundings. Whether or no Shakespeare was in sympathy with the phrases which he puts in the mouth of such characters as the haughty Bishop of Carlisle or the humble Franciscan, friar Laurence, may remain a matter of controversy, but there can be no shadow of doubt that the author was conversant, as only a person who has lived among Roman Catholics can be, with the form and expression of their faith.

His characters speak like the best masters of ecclesiastical style and when we remember that William Allen and Robert Southwell were in close correspondence with the Arundell and Southampton families this is not a matter for astonishment.

It is also certain that Shakespeare did nothing to offend the taste of his Catholic auditors. All the plays which were taken from sources which still exist and with which comparison can be made show one major difference. The poet has suppressed all anti-clerical allusions in following the original model. In the Italian tale of Giulietta, the heroine makes some very disagreeable reflections on the morality of friars in general and the one to whom she has confided herself in particular. Shakespeare's Juliet dismisses any doubt as to the friar's motives with:

"He has still been tried a holy man."

The original "King John," too, was full of "mud-slinging" at monastic life; all this is struck out in Shakespeare's rearrangement, though he probably sacrificed thereby many a comic effect among the "groundlings."

This is negative evidence, but there is much of a positive kind which shows throughout the plays that the author's sym-

pathies remained with the persecuted, not with the persecutors
—and how could it have been otherwise with one of his magnanimity?

> "How many a holy and obsequious tear
> Hath dear religious love stolen from mine eye,
> As interest of the dead . . ."

says Sonnet 31, and if Shakespeare's tragic stage is so full of
blood and thunder as to seem often unreal and exaggerated, was
it not because, so often haunted by spectacles of violence, he
had been moved to shed "the drops that sacred pity had
engendered"?

It is difficult to realise that to an Elizabethan audience, Portia's prayer for clemency as "mightiest in the Mighty" represented a daringly subversive suggestion on the author's part.
In good truth, mercy might have become Elizabeth better than
her crown, but she gave her subjects no opportunity of judging
its effect.

There are, indeed, countless passages in the production of
this epoch which can only be explained by carelessness on the
part of the censor or a certain collusion suggested by a high
Court influence—to which censorship, even in our day, is not
completely indifferent—and, however hard the task might be to
prove by the internal evidence of the plays, that the author was
a member of the Church of Rome, all must admit that his
familiarity with her tenets is manifested on every occasion.

On the other hand, to prove any Puritan sympathies on the
poet's part would be a difficult task.

Shakespeare's picture of the Carters and Vassals loitering at
the church door, and, out of a spirit of wanton destruction,
defacing *the precious image of our dear Redeemer*," his reference to that "Sepulchre in stubborn Jewry, of the World's
Ransom, Blessed Mary's Son," together with the passage which

130

sums up Norfolk's life and death, have a decidedly Roman tinge:

> Many a time hath banished Norfolk fought
> For Jesu Christ, in glorious Christian field,
> Streaming the ensign of the Christian cross
> Against black pagans, Turks and Saracens;
> And toil'd with works of war, retired himself
> To Italy, and there at Venice gave
> His body to that pleasant country's earth,
> And his pure soul unto his captain Christ,
> Under whose colours he had fought so long.
>
> ("Richard II," Act IV, Sc. 1.)

John of Gaunt's tirade, which is quoted as though it ought to represent the speech of a patriot still triumphing in his country's prestige, is in reality a lament on the civil ruin and useless bloodshed occasioned by persecution.

> This England which was wont to conquer others
> Hath made a *shameful conquest of herself.*

These examples are taken from two plays written at the height of Southampton's influence over the poet, but similar instances may be found throughout the whole dramatic work, most of all perhaps in "The Winter's Tale," where confession and repentance are shown as the sinner's only sure path to salvation. The meditations of Leontes, his tribute to the faithful friend who "priest-like had cleansed his bosom," might find their place in any essay on pious devotion, and it cannot be said that Shakespeare put such passages in "The Winter's Tale" as part of a necessary historical background; on the contrary, this typically Christian talk is a gross anachronism in the mouth of a King who awaited the Oracle of Delphi's response to know whether he had indeed been guilty of his Queen's death.

Sir E. K. Chambers finds strong reason in "Timon of

Athens" to conclude that Shakespeare in his latter days was a *convert* to the Roman form of belief. I cannot agree with his theory. If, as Richard Davies claimed, Shakespeare "dyed a Papist," it is more natural to suppose that it was not through conversion but by a gradual reconciliation to the old faith he had seen practised at Stratford by all his kinsfolk, and in London by his beloved Patron,

your luvg assured
freind
H Southampton

CHAPTER SEVEN

THE SONNET SEQUENCE

SHAKESPEARE'S SONNETS NEVER BEFORE IMPRINTED accompanied by a poem entitled "A Lover's Complaint" were published in 1609 by an editor called Thomas Thorpe.

A certain number of these sonnets had already circulated in manuscript among men of letters. They were vaunted by Francis Meres in *Palladis Tamia* (1598) where these lines may be read:

"The sweet, witty soul of Ovid lives in mellifluous and honey-tongued Shakespeare, witness his 'Venus and Adonis,' his 'Lucrece,' his sug'red sonnets among his private friends."

Meres' praise probably incited an editor to procure some of the sonnets to satisfy public curiosity and, in 1599, William Jaggard succeeded in piecing out a small volume entitled *The Passionate Pilgrim* containing two sonnets which figured later in Thorpe's edition under the numbers 138 and 144, together with four rejected stanzas from "Venus and Adonis," two sonnets which appear in "Love's Labour's Lost," one which was not again reproduced,[1] the beautiful "Good Night" verses and "Crabbed Age and Youth." Whether the latter portion of Jaggard's tiny book, *Sonnets on Sundry Notes of Music,* may be attributed in part to Shakespeare's pen, or whether Jaggard even meant to suggest that they were really his, is a question still open to controversy.

[1]"If music and sweet poetry agree . . ."

One thing is certain: Thorpe's volume enriched the world by 200 stanzas which bear William Shakespeare's best lyric stamp, and although Victorian critics freely apply the terms "thief" and "pirate" to both Thorpe and Jaggard, those who today are equally ignorant of the circumstances which brought Shakespeare's text into the printer's hands should rather praise them for the happy initiative which saved these poems for Posterity.

It is the fashion of our day to treat the Sonnets as an impenetrable mystery, a question so complex that we can hardly hope to reach a solution; as to "A Lover's Complaint," critics seldom or never speak of it at all.

These poems, however, are inseparable, since, as we shall see, the Sonnets contain an eloquent plea for the young patron to marry, and indicate that he may choose any one among the lovely maidens who are eagerly waiting, whereas "A Lover's Complaint" is a plea that he should marry *one* particular young woman, Elizabeth Vernon, a suggestion which the Earl of Southampton complied with, in spite of all obstacles, in 1597.

If the Sonnets are grouped by subject, they fall naturally into logical order, and constitute a spiritual and romantic autobiography, as William Wordsworth declared:

> "Scorn not the Sonnet, reader; with this key
> Shakespeare unlocked his heart."

Nicholas Rowe, the earliest and most sympathetic commentator on the poet's life and work, concluded his brief biography with this suggestive statement: "The character of the man is to be found in his writings."

Now the study of a dramatic work alone, picturing as it does the passions and diversities of mankind, is apt to lead into strange paradoxes. What character in the vast repertoire is the poet's mouthpiece? Is Polonius the prototype of a far-seeing parent and wise statesman? Is Falstaff's clever opportunism given as a model? Or Iago's counsels to abjure honour and honesty, in order to get money in purse, the advice of Iago's creator? and yet, under the deceptive words "Shakespeare says" I have heard these passages quoted as moral precepts, and a candidate for the presidency of of the United States once declared that some of poor old Polonius' most striking commonplaces were the wisest words Shakespeare ever penned. There is, however, one guiding thread which may lead through the maze of dramatic passion. When a precept or sentiment, expressed in the play, accords with a similar expression in the Sonnets, the reader may be confident of the author's real meaning.

One hundred and twenty-seven sonnets offer praise, counsel and occasional blame to that friend of beauty, birth, wealth and wit of whom a very distinct picture is given. They also outline a tale of rivalry in love between poet and patron, lament their falling out and celebrate their subsequent reconciliation. Thirty more are addressed to the dark enchantress who, for a brief period, exercised her charms over the fair youth and held the poet in her toils for a longer time.

This monumental work was not written in a day. Internal evidence shows that some twelve years were covered and careful study of the whole clarifies many a problem such as:

Why are there so many repetitions of the same thought? The author himself answers this question:

> "Oh, know, sweet love, I always write of you,
> And you and love are all my argument;
> So all my best is dressing old words new,
> Spending again what is already spent,
> And as the day is ever new and old,
> So is my love still telling what is told." [76]

The date of composition in certain cases is solved with equal ease.

Sonnet Number 104 celebrates a birthday anniversary, not an ordinary one, but a fixed mark in life, a young man's majority. We know that the Earl of Southampton was born October 7, 1573. As the poet declares that he has been offering praise for three years,

> "Three beauteous springs to yellow autumn turned
> In process of the seasons have I seen.
> Three April perfumes in three hot Junes burned,
> Since first I saw you fresh, which yet are green" [104]

we can infer that poet and patron first met in 1590. Two other fixed dates can be established: the liberation of Southampton from the Tower is celebrated in Sonnet 107. Sonnet 125 obviously refers to King James's coronation.

A more vague analogy between certain plays and poems indicates also when the sonnet was conceived: for instance, where the poet calls up the vision of his patron's face,

> ". . . like a jewel hung in ghastly night,
> Makes black night beauteous and her old face new" [27]

was evidently composed when he was writing "Romeo and Juliet."

Well satisfied with the image, Shakespeare turned it once more to account:

> "Thy beauty hangs upon the cheek of night
> Like a rich jewel in an Ethiop's ear."

Number 122 explains why the poet felt authorised to give away his sonnet manuscript and answers the query as to how Thorpe's volume came to be published by Southampton's step-father. As will be shown in Chapter VIII.

We cannot look for either logical or chronological sequence

in Thorpe's volume since many of the poems on reconciliation are placed before those which tell of the friends' quarrel and estrangement, but, as I said, if grouped by subject, these apparently separate poems may be read as a sequent and intensely dramatic whole. To ignore the collection is not only to miss the quintessence of Shakespeare's poetic genius, but to lay aside the master-key to his entire literary production.

When Thorpe's volume is read aright, the hundred and fifty-four sonnets therein will be found to reveal a sentimental monodrama, composed between Shakespeare's thirtieth and forty-third years. It is due to both masculine and feminine inspiration, "two loves of comfort and despair."

The first twenty sonnets, correctly placed at the beginning of Thorpe's volume, give a portrait of the young benefactor whose high position at Court and in the world of letters enables him to play providence to the actor-poet. Handsome, rich and noble, but also fair, kind and true—a rarer combination, the writer esteems that such a man should leave the world richer than when he came into it, through his own posterity. This group is but a plea for the young Lord, sole heir to a great estate and placed, by his father's death, under royal ward, to marry and refound his family. To allow such a heritage to fall into oblivion constitutes a crime against his fellow men, almost an impiety towards God. Twenty times the same thought is expressed in a vivid way so that the reader, by this literary *tour de force,* is led without fatigue to its complete exposition.

"From fairest creatures we desire increase
That thereby beauty's rose might never die," [1]

"Now is the time that face should form another;" [3]

"She [Nature] carved thee for her seal and meant thereby
Thou should'st print more, not let that copy die." [11]

137

"Who lets so fair a house fall to decay,
Which husbandry in honour might uphold
Against the stormy gusts of winter's day
And barren rage of death's eternal cold?
　O, none but unthrifts! Dear my love you know
　You had a father: let your son say so." [13]

"If I could write the beauty of your eyes
And in fresh numbers number all your graces,
The age to come would say, 'This poet lies;
Such heavenly touches ne'er touch'd earthly faces.'
So should my papers, yellow'd with their age,
Be scorned like old men of less truth than tongue,
And your true rights be term'd a poet's rage
And stretchéd metre of an antique song:
　But were some child of yours alive that time,
　You should live twice, in it and in my rhyme." [17]

Such is the *leitmotiv,* and it should be observed that when in "Venus and Adonis" like counsels are given a young man to heed the call of Mother Nature, the self-same arguments and similar language are employed.

"Upon the earth's increase why should'st thou feed,
Unless the earth by thy increase be fed?
By law of nature thou art bound to breed,
That thine may live when thou thyself art dead;
　And so in spite of death thou dost survive
　In that thy likeness still is left alive."

"Beauty within itself should not be wasted:
Fair flowers that are not gathered in their prime
Rot and consume themselves in little time."

"Seeds spring from seeds, and beauty breedeth beauty
Thou wast begot, to get it is thy duty."

138

There is no descriptive detail insisted on by the poet in drawing Adonis that is not applicable to the young patron to whom "Venus and Adonis" and the "Rape of Lucrece" were inscribed. The author of the fifty-third sonnet even acknowledges that his portrait of the Grecian youth is also that of his sonnet hero.

"Describe Adonis, and the counterfeit
Is poorly imitated after you;
On Helen's cheek all art of beauty set,
And you in Grecian tires are painted new:
Speak of the spring and foison of the year;
The one doth shadow of your beauty show,
The other as your bounty doth appear;
And you in every blessed shape we know.
    In all external grace you have some part,
    But you like none, none you, for constant heart." [53]

Paintings, prints and miniatures still show that the type of good looks possessed by Henry Wriothesley conforms to the descriptions of Adonis, hero of "A Lover's Complaint" and him of the Sonnets as well. His delicate complexion was lit up by blue-gray eyes of extraordinary brilliance, twin suns which radiated wit. According to all the poets who sang his praises, his excellent reading and fine voice enhanced the beauty of their lines. He possessed great taste and aptitude for field sports. His smile was amiable and charming.

The astonishing likeness between Lady Southampton and her son, referred to by Shakespeare in the third sonnet, is confirmed by a glance at Harry's portrait which seems to have been literally traced on that of his mother. Both are in the gallery at Welbeck.

"Thou art thy mother's glass, and she in thee
Calls back the lovely April of her prime," [3]

139

One of Southampton's portraits gives enlightenment on a hitherto inexplicable passage in the sonnet book. When Shakespeare declares, for instance, that his poetry has the unique object of extolling *One of one, still such and ever so,* no commentator has explained the obscure meaning except by the too facile claim of a misprint.

> "Let not my love be called idolatry,
> Nor my belovéd as an idol show,
> Since all alike my songs and praises be
> *To one, of one, still such, and ever so.*" [105]

There is no misprint, however; the phrase is simply the literal translation of Southampton's heraldic device and old French motto: *Ung partout tout par ung,* as it appears on a well-known engraving, of the Earl of Oxford and the Earl of Southampton[2] so that the 105th sonnet is merely a theme with variations played upon the Wriothesley blazon.

In contrast to the young hero so copiously endowed with the graces and gifts of fortune, the poet draws an unflattering portrait of himself:

> "With Time's injurious hand crushed and o'er worn;" [63]

The image reflected by his mirror shows a face "beated and chopt with tann'd antiquity" [62]. His mature appearance was accentuated by early baldness, at thirty-three he probably

[2]Wriothesley portraits, Plate XV, Richard Golding, Oxford, 1920.

"One every where the same, and every where *all.*"

Nothing could be less applicable to William Herbert who is identified by some as the fair youth, than any of Shakespeare's descriptions. The future Lord Pembroke was plain and dark. He was not under the tutelage of the Crown for his father was still living when he came to Court so that the epithet "Child of State" could have for him no signification. He had no coterie of adoring poets in 1591, at which date he was a boy of ten!

looked forty. Over-work, anxiety and frequent insomnia had left deep traces:

"That time of year thou mayest in me behold
When yellow leaves, or none, or few, do hang
Upon those boughs which shake against the cold,
Bare ruin'd choirs where late the sweet birds sang." [73]

Distinct as the physical portrait is the impression of the poet's mind and heart that the sonnets give us. They show a person of extreme sensitiveness and high susceptibility, whose moral qualities balance his intelligence. A man to whom meanness and pettiness are only known through what he has experienced on the part of others. His imaginative intuition and ready sympathy dispose him to see the other man's point of view and his generosity inclines him to grasp the justice of another's claim rather than cling to personal interest. The self-portrait shows a person devoted to his profession and "well contented" in general save for those special occasions when he particularly indicates that for some reason he is "out of suits with fortune," then he seems to be subject to the violent attacks of melancholy from which even an optimistic nature is not exempt.

Although adoring his profession, in which like Hamlet he saw the highest possibilities, both moral and artistic, he suffered from the discredit attaching to the stage.

"Thence comes it that my name receives a brand,
And almost thence my nature is subdued
To what it works in, like the dyer's hand." [111]

He deplored that the exigencies of an actor's life often made him false to his best ideals of art:

"Alas, 'tis true I have gone here and there
And made myself a motley to the view,
Gor'd mine own thoughts, sold cheap what is most dear, . . ." [110]

His legal status remained that of a vagabond, denied the
privilege of Christian burial, whose mortal remains might rea-
sonably become the prey of medical student or anatomist.

"The coward conquest of a wretch's knife." [74]

Honourable sepulture is always spoken of in a tone which
would be inexplicable if it were, to the author, a matter of
course. The haunting fear which evidently pursued him through
life, is shown in "Hamlet" and appears on his tombstone.

The distress his equivocal situation caused him was largely
on his friend's account. Southampton was undoubtedly criti-
cised for so much favouring a player. His application for a coat-
of-arms, was not, as Frank Harris declared, "the petty vanity
of a parvenu," but desire for a real advantage which, as the
Twenty-Sixth Sonnet says,

> "Puts apparel on my tattered loving,
> To show me worthy of thy sweet respect,"

Shakespeare frequently speaks of himself as remaining dumb
before rivals, certain poems indicating that he suffered specially
in his early London days from shyness and remained rather a
listener than a partaker in the wit combats and debates presided
over by Southampton in the literary taverns:

> "I think good thoughts whilst others write good words,
> And like unlettered clerk still cry 'Amen'
> To every hymn that able spirit affords
> In polished form of well-refined pen." [85]

or again:

> "O, learn to read what silent love hath writ:
> To hear with eyes belongs to love's fine wit." [23]

Wearied by imputations on his want of classical learning
(for which Ben Jonson reproached him), the poet expresses

142

more impatience with pedantry than with ignorance, and his bitterest words are reserved to denounce fraud, affectation and hypocrisy. To *overpass the modesty of nature* seems to him a crime whether in life or art, his horror freely expressed for false hair at a time when the sovereign's wardrobe boasted sixty blond wigs must have appeared daring as well as comic:

> "Before these bastard signs of fair were born,
> Or durst inhabit on a living brow;
> Before the golden tresses of the dead,
> The right of sepulchres, were shorn away,
> To live a second life on second head;
> Ere beauty's dead fleece made another gay." [68]

If the Sonnet confessions show the author's many qualities of brain and heart, may they not also help spy out his chief defect?

> "All men have faults, and even I in this," [35]

he exclaims with a certain ingenuous simplicity, when pardoning his friend's shortcomings.

Among all the human passions so marvellously described in the plays, there is one which the dramatist seems to understand better than any, and if Alphonse Daudet and Robert Southwell were right in proclaiming that no one can truly describe a sentiment or an emotion which he has not felt, we must believe that the green-eyed monster jealousy caused the poet keen and constant suffering. Its first manifestation in the Sonnets was professional. It is not, however, a base form of selfishness that his complaints embody.

He is wounded when the poets preferred to himself are unworthy of his patron's notice; when he encounters a better spirit he acknowledges superiority and only regrets that his own verse cannot equal that of the master.

Nevertheless he is fully conscious that his own sincerity is more wholesome than the adulation laid on with a trowel by sycophants and flatterers.

> ". . . yet when they have devised
> What strainèd touches rhetoric can lend,
> Thou truly fair wert truly sympathised
> In true plain words by thy true-telling friend;
>   And their gross painting might be better used
>   Where cheeks need blood; in thee it is abused." [82]

> "I never saw that you did painting need,
> And therefore to your fair no painting set;
> I found, or thought I found, you did exceed
> The barren tender of a poet's debt, . . ." [83]

More than sixteen Sonnets deal with the theme of rivalry in art. Several shafts are aimed at a poet who may be identified with George Chapman, translator of the *Iliad* and author of *The Amorous Zodiac,* whose metaphors are exaggerated and whose similes are generally astronomical. Shakespeare is driven to exclaim how different are his own artistic conceptions from the Euphuistic Muse:

> "Making a couplement of proud compare
> With sun and moon, with earth and sea's rich gems,
> With April's first-born flowers, and all things rare
> Which heaven's air in this huge rondure hems." [21]

An obvious example of the lack of sequence in Thorpe's arrangement is contained in the group dealing with the rival poets. Number 80 describes a "better spirit" under the figure of a stately man-of-war on the sea of the patron's favour, while the poet himself is compared to a humble skiff:

> "Your shallowest help will hold me up afloat,
> Whilst he upon your soundless deep doth ride:
> Or, being wrecked, I am a worthless boat,
> He of tall building and of goodly pride." [80]

The succeeding Sonnets treat of quite other matters until in Number 86 we again meet the ship metaphor.

> "Was it the proud full sail of his great verse,
> Bound for the prize of all too precious You?"

There has been much debate over the identification of this "better spirit." Professor Minto thinks that Chapman is meant, others select Jonson, though I do not believe that Ben was yet on the scene; a recent protagonist has done his best to establish Samuel Drayton's claim, but I am inclined to follow the very ancient opinion of Gerald Massey, who pointed out that Marlowe's "Doctor Faustus" was played at a rival theatre and considers that the greater Spirit

> . . . "by spirits taught to write
> Above a mortal pitch, that struck me dead—"

referred to the poet whom popular superstition considered to owe his art to the assistance of a diabolical familiar.

If so, this would fix the date of this group as anterior to 1594.

A long absence from London is marked when Shakespeare, like Montaigne, travelling on horseback, sadly measures the distance of his provincial tour:

> "The beast that bears me, tired with my woe,
> Plods dully on, to bear that weight in me,
> As if by some instinct the wretch did know
> His rider loved not speed, being made from thee." [50]

On returning, his patron received him with coldness and this brings us to a theme, repeated in so many beautiful forms that it is difficult to select how best to show the poet's thought that he would rather disappear than be a burden or shame to his friend:

> "Thou canst not, love, disgrace me half so ill,
> To set a form upon desired change,
> As I'll myself disgrace: knowing thy will,

> I will acquaintance strangle and look strange,
> Be absent from thy walks: and on my tongue
> Thy sweet belovéd name no more shall dwell,
> Lest I, too much profane, should do it wrong,
> And haply of our old acquaintance tell.
>   For thee against myself I'll vow debate,
>   For I must ne'er love him whom thou dost hate." [89]

Ten sonnets embroider on this theme. Those which follow are more bitter and poignant. The noble lord summons his player, but misses the engagement; Shakespeare comments ironically upon the relative value of their leisure.

> "I have no precious time at all to spend,
> Nor services to do, till you require.
> Nor dare I chide the world-without-end hour
> Whilst I, my sovereign, watch the clock for you,
> Nor think the bitterness of absence sour
> When you have bid your servant once adieu:" [57]

And again in Sonnet 58:

> "I am to wait, though waiting so be hell;
> Not blame your pleasure, be it ill or well."

The masterpiece of the whole collection, from the point of view of linguistic art, is the product of this period of abandonment. At each line the knell of expiring friendship is sounded by the resonant consonants which clang like funeral chimes.

> "No longer mourn for me when I am dead.
> Then you shall hear the surly sullen bell
> Give warning to the world that I am fled
> From this vile world, with vilest worms to dwell.
> Nay, if you read this line, remember not
> The hand that writ it; for I love you so
> That I in your sweet thoughts would be forgot
> If thinking on me then should make you woe.

Oh, if, I say, you look upon this verse
When I perhaps compounded am with clay,
Do not so much as my poor name rehearse,
But let your love even with my life decay,
    Lest the wise world should look into your moan
    And mock you with me after I am gone." [71]

The end comes with Sonnet Number 87:

"Farewell! Thou art too dear for my possessing,
And like enough thou knowest thy estimate.
The charter of thy worth gives thee releasing;
My bonds in thee are all determinate. . . ."

With this severance "the dark lady," cause of the friends'
quarrel, appears. A group of six sonnets describes their rivalry
and develops the theme of jealousy in love.

"And when a woman wooes, what woman's son
Will sourly leave her till she have prevailed?" [41]

"That thou hast her, it is not all my grief,
And yet it may be said I loved her dearly;" [42]

Numbers 133, 134, 143 tell the same tale plainly and, as I
have already pointed out, 144, the veritable key to the whole
situation, was printed as number 2 in "The Passionate Pilgrim,"
enough to show that it deserves an early, not an almost final
rank, in Thorpe's volume.

Place it where the reader will, the story it tells is plain
enough! The handsome patron, before deciding to follow his
poet's advice and seek a wife in his own courtly sphere, indulged
in an amorous adventure which not only left an indelible impression of bitterness in Shakespeare's heart but is reflected as
we shall see in the literature of the time.

"Two loves I have of comfort and despair,
Which like two spirits do suggest me still;

The better angel is a man right fair,
The worser spirit a woman coloured ill.
To win me soon to hell, my female evil
Tempteth my better angel from my side,
And would corrupt my saint to be a devil,
Wooing his purity with her foul pride.
And whether that my angel be turned fiend
Suspect I may, yet not directly tell;
But being both from me, both to each friend,
I guess one angel in another's hell:
    Yet this shall I ne'er know, but live in doubt,
    Till my bad angel fire my good one out." [44]

The series addressed to the so-called "Dark Lady" consists of thirty stanzas. It is separated from those in praise of the fair youth by a double-leaded space and begins at the number 127. Half of them consist in amorous trifling and praise of dark beauty, a dozen more are jealous and reproachful.

There is a complete change of tone in the Sonnets addressed to the "woman coloured ill." Whereas all the poems written to his patron are respectful, the fair youth, even when blamed, never being treated as an equal, in addressing this "worser spirit" the author indicates that she belongs to a social world which is not above his own; quite the contrary.

In order to read the "Dark Lady" group in logical sequence we must begin with those which the editor of the 1609 edition placed at the very end of the collection under the numbers 153 and 154.

This was done with the evident intention of concealing, or at least masking, from contemporary readers, the story of the rivalry which had arisen between poet and patron and which, at the time, caused malevolent gossip.

The series begins on a light tone of badinage. In those days it was hardly admissible that beauty could pretend to dwell under any but a fair complexion:

> "In the old age black was not counted fair,
> Or if it were, it bore not beauty's name;" [127]

The troupe was playing at Bath when the author first alludes to the dark Circe, and remarks how idle it seems to seek a cure for pain in medicinal waters. The only remedy for his heartache lies in the deep pools of shadow, the orbs of his dark mistress.

As Shakespeare's troupe was playing at Bath in September, 1592—a payment to Lord Strange's men is then recorded—this may help place an approximate date on Sonnet Number 153, where what the poet says is singularly illuminated if we restore the missing capital B to "bath."

> "But at my mistress' eye Love's brand new-fired,
> The boy for trial needs would touch my breast;
> I, sick withal, the help of Bath desired,
> And thither hied, a sad distemper'd guest,
>   But found no cure, the bath for my help lies
>   Where Cupid got new fire—my mistress' eyes."

And this leads directly to number 132:

> "Thine eyes I love, and they, as pitying me,
> Knowing thy heart torments me with disdain,
> Have put on black and loving mourners be,
> Looking with pretty ruth upon my pain.
> And truly not the morning sun of heaven
> Better becomes the grey cheeks of the east,
> Nor that full star that ushers in the even
> Doth half that glory to the sober west,
> As those two mourning eyes become thy face.
> O! let it then as well beseem thy heart
> To mourn for me, since mourning doth thee grace,

And suit thy pity like in every part.
Then will I swear beauty herself is black,
And all they foul that thy complexion lack."

We gain insight into the lady's reputation for veracity—
evidently not excellent—and the poet's desire to be considered
younger than he looks:

"When my love swears that she is made of truth,
I do believe her, though I know she lies,
That she may think me some untutored youth,
Unlearned in the world's false subtleties.
Thus vainly thinking that she thinks me young,
Although she knows my days are past the best,
Simply I credit her false-speaking tongue:
On both sides thus is simple truth suppressed.
But wherefore says she not she is unjust?
And wherefore say not I that I am old?
O! love's best habit is in seeming trust,
And age in love loves not to have years told.
Therefore I lie with her and she with me,
And in our faults by lies we flatter'd be." [138]

We learn also that her obstinacy is notorious and every combination of word-play is made on her excessive will and the
poet's christian name.

"Whoever hath her wish, thou hast thy 'Will,'
And 'Will' to boot, and 'Will' in overplus;
More than enough am I that vex thee still,
To thy sweet will making addition thus.
Wilt thou, whose will is large and spacious,
Not once vouchsafe to hide my will in thine?
Shall will in others seem right gracious,
And in my will no fair acceptance shine?
The sea, all water, yet receives rain still
And in abundance addeth to his store;

> So thou, being rich in 'Will,' add to thy 'Will'
> One will of mine, to make thy large will more
> Let no unkind, no fair beseechers kill;
> Think all but one, and me in that one Will." [135]

And again, after a dozen more lines of the same sort:

> "Make but my name thy love and love that still,
> And then thou lov'st me, for my name is 'Will.'" [136]

It may seem curious that after this plain statement there are still those who declare that the man who wrote these sonnets was called Francis, Edward or Roger, but such considerations seldom prevent any partisan from clinging to a preconceived idea.

The "Dark Lady" is praised for her musical taste and for her delicate mastery of the virginals, an early form of spinet which developed into the piano of our days.

> "How oft, when thou, my music, music play'st,
> Upon that blessed wood whose motion sounds
> With thy sweet fingers when thou gently sway'st
> The wiry concord that mine ear confounds,
> Do I envy those jacks that nimble leap
> To kiss the tender inward of thy hand,
> Whilst my poor lips, which should that harvest reap,
> At the wood's boldness by thee blushing stand!
>
> To be so tickled, they would change their state
> And situation with those dancing chips,
> O'er whom thy fingers walk with gentle gait,
> Making dead wood more blest than living lips.
>   Since saucy jacks so happy are in this,
>   Give them thy fingers, me thy lips to kiss." [128]

When the poet's eyes are open to her perfidy, he cannot escape from her toils.

> "In faith, I do not love thee with mine eyes,
> For they in thee a thousand errors note;

151

But 'tis my heart that loves what they despise,
Who, in despite of view, is pleased to dote. . . .
But my five wits nor my five senses can
Dissuade one foolish heart from serving thee,
Who leaves unnerved[3] the likeness of a man
Thy proud heart's slave and vassal wretch to be:
  Only my plague thus far I count my gain,
  That she that makes me sin awards me pain." [141]

Never were love's torments chanted upon a more sincere and
tragic note. The poet's views of marriage were not those of our
twentieth century. He fully believed that he was sinning grievously in forgetting the wife of his youth for the sake of a
woman far less good, and perhaps less beautiful than his Anne.
That "she who had made him sin should cause him to suffer
acutely," seemed to him natural and legitimate punishment for
his moral weakness.

"In loving thee thou knowest I am forsworn,
But thou art twice forsworn, to me love swearing;
In act thy bed-vow broke, and new faith torn
In vowing new hate after new love bearing.
But why of two oaths' breach do I accuse thee,
When I break twenty? I am perjured most;
For all my vows are oaths but to misuse thee,
And all my honest faith in thee is lost,
For I have sworn deep oaths, of thy deep kindness,
Oaths of thy love, thy truth, thy constancy,
And, to enlighten thee, gave eyes to blindness,
Or made them swear against the thing they see;
  For I have sworn thee fair; more perjured I,
  To swear against the truth so foul a lie." [152]

[3]"Unnerved" is my own emendation. The word "unswayed," which is in the original text, means immovable and the poet has just explained that he is incapable of resistance, hence: unnerved. This word is used in the same sense in "Hamlet," when
Priam's death is described: "the unnerved father falls."

In a stanza of realistic and brutal frankness he describes the chain of sensual attachment to which imagination can no longer lend the glamour which alone can idealise and enhance human relations.

"The expense of spirit in a waste of shame
Is lust in action; and till action, lust
Is perjur'd, murderous, bloody, full of blame,
Savage, extreme, rude, cruel, not to trust,
Enjoy'd no sooner but despiséd straight,
Past reason hunted, and no sooner had
Past reason hated, as a swallowed bait
On purpose laid to make the taker mad:
Mad in pursuit and in possession so;
Had, having, and in quest to have, extreme;
A bliss in proof, and prov'd, a very woe;
Before, a joy propos'd; behind, a dream.
    All this the world well knows; yet none knows well
    To shun the heaven that leads men to this hell." [129]

This is followed by an apostrophe to his own soul in which the influence of Father Southwell's poetry is visible and where he recognises the grossness of the body as the chief obstacle against the spirit's aspiration towards divine wisdom.

"Poor soul, the centre of my sinful earth,
Pressed by these rebel powers that thee array,
Why dost thou pine within and suffer dearth,
Painting thy outward walls so costly gay?
Why so large cost, having so short a lease,
Dost thou upon thy fading mansion spend?
Shall worms, inheritors of this excess,
Eat up thy charge? Is this thy body's end?
Then, soul, live thou upon thy servant's loss,
And let that pine to aggravate thy store;
Buy terms divine in selling hours of dross;

Within be fed, without be rich no more;
So shalt thou feed on Death, that feeds on men,
And Death once dead, there's no more dying then!" [146]

On this theme of high renunciation, the series addressed to the so-called "Dark Lady" naturally concludes:

In the portrait shown of the author, we perceive no saint, assuredly, but a man of courage and honesty who knows equally well how to laugh and weep and whose heart was in perfect equilibrium with his brain.

And what of the woman?

When Sir Sidney Lee declared that her influence on the poet's life could have been but a passing one, which left no trace upon any of the great dramas, he seems to forget "Antony and Cleopatra." For in Shakespeare's portrait of the Queen of Egypt it is easy to recognise the same wilful beauty—"la belle laide" already made known to his sonnet readers.

Just as Raphael traced his Madonnas after the model of La Fornarina's features, the dramatist recalls his dark mistress in delineating the "Serpent of the Nile." In describing the enslavement of the Roman triumvir, he remembers his own.

For the frantic passion which disrupts empires and homes differs in no essential from the fatal madness which ravaged the poet's heart and transformed him into the "vassal wretch" of a woman who his reason told him was cruel, false and without scruple.

"Whence hast thou this becoming of things ill,
    That in the very refuse of thy deeds
    There is such strength and warrantise of skill
    That, in my mind, thy worst all best exceeds?
    Who taught thee how to make me love thee more,
    The more I hear and see just cause of hate?
    O, though I love what others do abhor,

With others thou shouldst not abhor my state:
If thy unworthiness raised love in me,
More worthy I to be beloved of thee." [150]

Antony apostrophises Cleopatra in the very same harsh
terms, finding again the ruthless insults set down in the sonnets,
insults which the Cleopatras of the world, whether Queens or
commoners, are ready to pardon, because in their thirst for
domination, invincible desire, which is stronger than reason or
moral contempt, is the most intoxicating homage a lover can
offer.

Through the perspective of years the poet was able to judge
his former passion objectively. He was too great an artist not to
realise what his work had gained from this devastating experience.

Contrary to the false aphorism of Heine who declares that a
poet "out of his great sorrows can only make little songs," out
of his past pain Shakespeare built up a great drama of human
philosophy.

To Antony's bitter cry of lamentation:

"Would I had never met her!"

the friendly philosopher replies:

"Oh, sir. You had then left unseen a wonderful piece of work
which not to have been blessed withal would have discredited
all your travel."

But the romance of the Sonnets ends, as it should, on a note
of serenity. With the death of sinful love, friendship blooms
again. Learning how much his patron has suffered by the breach
between them, the poet hastened to salve the wounds of friendship and self-esteem:

"That you were once unkind befriends me now,
And for that sorrow which I then did feel
Needs must I under my transgression bow,

155

Unless my nerves were brass or hammer'd steel.
For if you were by my unkindness shaken
As I by yours, you've passed a hell of time,
And I, a tyrant, have no leisure taken
To weigh how once I suffered in your crime.
O! that our night of woe might have rememb'red
My deepest sense, how hard true sorrow hits.
And soon to you, as you to me, then tend'red
The humble salve which wounded bosoms fits!
But that your trespass now becomes a fee;
Mine ransoms yours, and yours must ransom me." [120]

And this leads to a masterly climax where, in fourteen son-nets, whose majesty and elevation of sentiment have never been equalled, Shakespeare's magic pen shows how it can conquer death and time, and obtain, for his hymn to friendship, what the well-wishing editor Thorpe declared: "THAT ETERNITY PROMISED BY OUR EVER-LIVING POET."

History shows, and I have just recalled, how, after having been drawn into the political turmoil at the end of Elizabeth's reign, the young nobleman, condemned to perpetual imprison-ment, nearly died from the hardships of the Tower, but hope sprang again when the Queen, "that mortal moon" who bore the sobriquet of Cynthia, suffered eclipse and her successor reversed her cruel sentence.

The advent of King James, which had been foreseen by the augurs as necessarily bringing civil war and its horrors to Eng-land, was established in concord, which was to last more than a score of years and on the tenth of April, 1603, in the peace and calm of a general amnesty, the poet celebrated his friend and patron's release from captivity in one of the balmiest seasons England ever knew.

"Not mine own fears, nor the prophetic soul
Of the wide world, dreaming on things to come,

Can yet the lease of my true love control,
Suppos'd as forfeit to a confin'd doom.
The mortal moon hath her eclipse endur'd,
And the sad augurs mock their own presage;
Incertainties now crown themselves assur'd,
And peace proclaims olives of endless age.
Now with the drops of this most balmy time
My love looks fresh, and Death to me subscribes,
Since, spite of him, I'll live in this poor rhyme,
While he insults o'er dull and speechless tribes:
  And thou in this shalt find thy monument,
  When tyrants' crests and tombs of brass are spent." [107]

This analysis which permits the reader to follow the plot and sequence of the story, half told and half concealed in Thorpe's volume, naturally leads to an effort to identify the powerful enchantress—celebrated with such a strange mixture of love and hate—who caused the rift between Shakespeare and Southampton.

That she was dark, that she was married, that she belonged to a world inferior to that of the young patron is proved by the sonnets themselves. Since the early days of the last century there have been three claimants for the credit—or discredit—of having been Shakespeare's mistress. Gerald Massey, the author of *The Secret Drama of the Sonnets,* sustains the attractive idea that the famous Penelope Devereux, Lady Rich, was the siren in question. But the tone in which the dark lady is addressed shows that it could never have been used to Essex' sister even if there were any evidence pointing that way.

Those who wish to think that Mary Fytton, one of the Queen's Maids of Honour, dismissed from court for an unplatonic intrigue with William Herbert, later Earl of Pembroke, was the original dark lady, base their arguments on the work of Professor Tyler and the play of Bernard Shaw. But, here it

is necessary to observe once more that the sonnet treating of
the love episode had been already published in the *Passionate
Pilgrim* a year before the scandal which caused her banishment
from court in 1600, and I might add that Mistress Fytton was
of the popular blonde complexion and notoriously a spinster!

The Jacqueline Field hypothesis, though fragile, is more ten-
able; we have no data concerning the colouring, or the reputation of Richard Field's wife; unless we subscribe to the Anglo-
Saxon dictum, "all French women are dark and many unfaith-
ful"; on the other hand, both Shakespeare and Southampton
undoubtedly frequented Field's printing-house at a date which
could concord with this identification of Jacqueline as a possible
"dark lady." But to erect a theory on such unsubstantial premises
is to build on emptiness, especially when we have a firm base
of serious and oft-repeated testimony.

Many echoes of a scandal which once involved an inn-
keeper's wife, "pretty and witty, wild and yet too gentle," a
young lover called Harry, and the author of the "Rape of
Lucrece," are found in a volume entitled *Willobie His Avisa*
printed in 1594. Suppressed by the censor and republished two
years later, this libel recounts, in vulgar form, the drama of
Shakespeare's sonnets.

This curious pamphlet, signed from Oxford by "Hadrian
Dorell," is without literary merit; but it has a superior interest,
for it contains this very first printed allusion to Shakespeare as
an author: "SHAKESPEARE PAINTS POOR LUCRECE'S RAPE."

It is a curious mixture of prose and blank verse, a venomous
attack made upon an Oxford inn-keeper's wife. This English
Lucrece, as she is called, is courted by a troop of gallants, among
them young Mr. H. W., whose name is Harry. This noble
youth takes love so seriously that he nearly dies of unrequited
passion. His friend, an actor, Mr. W. S., who has passed through

like torments, gives Harry wise counsel founded on experience, as to how this dame may be won. To make the identification of Harry Wriothesley more evident, Mr. H. W. is constantly quoting the Italian aphorisms, which are to be found in his professor's hand-book, Florio's *First Fruits*. The Censor naturally decreed that the personages were too easily recognisable *under their own initials* and consequently suppressed the volume; Shakespeare's name, together with his player's quality, having been printed in full, the subject of his identity does not even admit of discussion.

Now the hostelry owned by the Davenants is inscribed at the date of *Willobie His Avisa* under the appellation *Golden Cross* or ensign of *Saint-George*. The dwelling is indicated in the verses of the travesty thus:

"See yonder house where hangs the badge of England's Saint."[4]

The next fact to establish before connecting Mrs. Davenant with the heroine of the Sonnets is whether she could have known both poet and patron before 1594.

Southampton had accompanied Queen Elizabeth to Oxford in 1592, remaining throughout the jousts and comedies given to honor her progress. He is described in the College records as having appeared like "one of King Arthur's Knights, so handsome and so debonnair." Shakespeare at the same epoch was on a provincial tour and, as his troupe was attached to the Court, it is not unreasonable to suppose that he had his rôle in the Oxford pomps and pageants, and therefore that the three principal personages concerned were simultaneously on the scene of action.

A study of sources always leads us back through Beeston, Betterton and Oldys, to that inn afterwards known as the

---

[4]Charles Hughes and Doctor Harrison see the stage of the sonnet drama at Cerne Abbas in Dorset.

Crown as the veritable stage of the romantic love drama of William Shakespeare.

Sober history hints at the same story as the Oxford libel. The life of Sir William Davenant, playwright and poet laureate under Charles II, is thus condensed from the *Athenæ Oxonienses:*

"This poet's mother was a very beautiful woman, of good wit and conversation very agreeable; in which she was imitated by none of her children but this William. The father, who was a very grave and discreet citizen (yet an admirer and lover of plays and playmakers, especially Shakespeare, who frequented his house in his journies between Warwickshire and London) was of a melancholic disposition and was seldom or never seen to laugh; in which he was imitated by none of his children, but by Robert his eldest son.

"It is probable that he (Shakespeare) stood sponsor for this William. He appears to have been very much attached to Children, and particularly so to the son of Mine Host of the *Crown,* Robert, afterwards Fellow of St John's College, and a reverend Doctor of Divinity."

When Shakespeare's godson, William Davenant, tried to prove his descent from an ancient Norman family and inserted an apostrophe in his spelling of the name, a contemporary wit remarked: "Useless! Everybody knows that d'Avonant comes from Avon."

Oldys, in his *Choice Notes,* recalls an anecdote told by Betterton to Pope over which Oxford wagged its head knowingly:

"Young Will Davenant was then a little school boy in the town, seven or eight years old, and so fond of Shakespeare that whenever he heard of his arrival, he would fly from school to see him. One day, an old townsman, observing him running homeward, asked him whither he was posting in all that hurry. He answered: To see his godfather, Shakespeare. 'There's a good boy,' said the other; 'but have a care how you take the name of God in vain.' "

Aubrey, in his *Brief Lives, Chiefly of Contemporaries,* says: "Now Sir William (d'Avenant) would sometimes, when pleasant over a glass of wine with his most intimate friends, say that it seemed to him that he writ with the very spirit of Shakespeare, and seemed willing enough to be thought his son. He would tell the story as above, in which way his mother had a very light report."

In sustaining the Shakespeare-Southampton-Davenant theory of the Sonnets, I am far from wishing to suggest that the scandal concerning Mistress Davenant was justified by the facts, especially as her son William who wrote the charming ode "In Remembrance of Master William Shakespeare" was born in 1603, too late to fit into the Sonnet period. That the Oxford hostess was beautiful and admired by the guests of her husband's tavern and that Shakespeare's plays were produced in the inn yard whenever his troupe passed, was enough to set tongues wagging. We know that "scandal's mark is ever yet the fair," and that the ornament of beauty is always an object of suspicion.

I have done no more than collect certain written chronicles and tried to expose them impartially, knowing full well that calumny is not evidence, and that no one has ever yet heard the dark lady's own defence. Certainly I have *invented* nothing to smirch the reputation of the poet, it is he who brings against himself the accusation of marital infidelity and judges his case with more severity than a twentieth-century biographer could ever dare!

That Southampton's offence was light upon his conscience is

indicated by the fact that he and his wife jested about Mistress Davenant under the sobriquet of "Dame Pint-Pot."

It still remains a matter of wonder that our age so eagerly swallows Oscar Wilde's invention of Willy Hughes, an inexistent boy-actor, as the rich and powerful patron to whom Shakespeare owed his first success in the world of London letters. Wilde himself presented his *Portrait of Mr. W. H.* as fiction not as fact.

Those who refuse to recognise Harry Wriothesley Earl of Southampton, as the "only begetter" of the Sonnets in praise of the fair youth and who endeavour to substitute for him William Herbert, Earl of Pembroke, do so in spite of reason, dates and historical possibility, since Herbert came into the poet's life only after the verses alluding to the romance of love and jealousy had been printed. But, as Sir Henry Irving said, these critics *do not read Shakespeare's work as a whole,* but merely to seek a few lines which may be used as confirmation for a preconceived idea.

Most certainly they never read "A Lover's Complaint" where the three personages involved are the poet who listens sympathetically to the tale of love and sorrow confided by Elizabeth Vernon when to the eyes of the Court she appeared abandoned by her lover. Reference to contemporary correspondence shows that point for point the "Complaint" merely repeats what gossips were saying about Southampton's irresistible charm and the girl's despair at his departure. Perhaps it was Shakespeare's poetic plea which brought the young man back from Paris in such hot haste to acknowledge the secret marriage which Essex, the girl's guardian, favoured.

This union, type of the perfect

> . . . "Marriage of true minds
> That looks on tempests and is never shaken"

came as the fruition of Shakespeare's repeated appeals which were voiced in "Venus and Adonis," "The Sonnets," and "A Lover's Complaint." Even "Lucrece" was an admonition to straying youth in its devastating picture of the results of illicit passion.

CHAPTER EIGHT

WHO MR. W. H. REALLY WAS

THE DEDICATION PAGE which accompanied Thorpe's volume containing "Shakespeare's Sonnets" and "A Lover's Complaint," has caused endless controversy and speculation since the last half of the nineteenth century. The question was clarified more than sixty years ago, however, when Charles Edmonds found another dedication in the same form set up by the same printer and composed by the same Mr. W. H. who figures in Thorpe's volume.

It may be remembered that although brief, the composition of the Sonnet-Dedication page is rendered obscure by the fact that it contains no punctuation, but only ornamental dots separating each word.

Two interpretations can be given to the lines, but the usual reading is that Thomas Thorpe wishes prosperity to him who had inspired these Sonnets or to him who had procured them for press, and also the eternity of fame promised by the immortal poet.

In order to impose this meaning it should be said that eighty editions of Shakespeare's Sonnets offer to their readers a false transcription of the dedication page adding punctuation to support their claim and even placing the initials "Mr. W. H." on a line by themselves and in a central position which necessarily designates him as the subject of the Sonnets. All sorts of extravagant suppositions have been advanced as to the identity of Mr. W. H. One eminent German critic, for example, declares that W. H. stands for "William himself." François Victor-Hugo made a better guess in deciding that the manuscript monogram had been so made that the printer misread it and, as it was perfectly obvious that Henry Wriothesley was the Sonnet patron, had reversed the order of the initials "W. H." instead of "H. W." Before taking cognisance of another contemporary dedication where Mr. W. H. appears as the editor of the volume, which I will describe later, I sustained the reasonable solution offered in 1856 by François Victor-Hugo.

Even if, for the sake of argument, we should abandon the idea that Henry Wriothesley was the "fair youth" of Shakespeare's Sonnets, he would remain the recognised patron of their author between 1590 and 1595, through the twice repeated dedications offered by Shakespeare to young Southampton in "Venus and Adonis" and "The Rape of Lucrece" (1593 and 1594). It would therefore be obvious that the reasonable place to search for the owner of the initials "W. H." would be in the recusant coterie which revolved about young Southampton and favoured the Poet of Avon in London, and it is there that we find him in the person of William Hervey, a soldier, sailor and man of letters who had been with Essex on the Spanish campaign and was instrumental later in getting two of the day's "best sellers" into the hands of the printer Eld, friend of the Cloptons and Carews and who counted Thomas Bodley among his intimates. In the "declared accounts, audit Number 1690/35, his diet and board wages, when serving under the charge of Lord Thomas Hardy, are found."[1]

[1]"Sir William Hervey, Knight, for his diet serving Her Majesty as Capten of her highness shippe the *Garland,* by the space of twenty-one daies, begonne the 15th day of August, 1599 and ended the 15th of September following at eleven shillings, sevenpence per diem, and for the wages of a master and the rest of the said shippe's company serving in herborewe from the second of July till the tenth of Auguste aforesaid, and at Sea from the eleventh of the same month till the eleventh of September, aforesaid." The total came to one hundred and eighty-five pounds, three shillings and eightpence, and seems reasonable enough in our day.

But Hervey formed a more important connection with the poet when, in 1598, he became the third husband of Harry Southampton's mother, and fell heir, at her death, to all her books and papers. Needless to say he belonged to precisely the same political camp as his stepson and was a firm supporter of James Stuart's right to the throne of England; certain correspondence shows him in the light of a bold adventurer and political opportunist. There is one addressed to "My verie good Lord the Lord treasurer of England"; it is dated from Lisbon, April 22, 1591, where he was prepared to turn adverse circumstances and secure ransom by conveying useful intelligence verbally.

"Ryght honorable, the bearer hereof canne by now deliver you that which at this present I cannot wryte for dyvers occasions. These papers enclosed and others Recandos, our counsel here at Lisbone, and John Taylor, my verry frende gave me to see conveyed unto you, perhaps you wyle discover by them things for your purpose. I am dealing and hope hyt will take effect for my ransome, and promysed owte of the Galleys one of myne own company to go back pr. the delivery of a Spanyshe captain in my place. Hyt will not be longe I hope before this take effecte. In the meanetyme I passe heare some misery. I beseech your Lordship that when my frende shall arrive you procure him speedy dispatche, for hyt is now fifteen monethes that I was taken at the Ilands and, by one John Jones,—a Bristow man that passed heare for a Scot I procured my dispatche and remove for Lisbone. Of other affairs this bearer my very frende, shall inform you, to whome I praye you shewe al favor you may, for he goeth as you may see, by his patentes upon suertyes for his ransom. This mutche in haste, owte of the castel in Lisbone, this twenty-second of April, 1591, Your Lordship's ever assured servant, William Harvye."

As partisan of King James when that monarch achieved the

English throne, Hervey helped to celebrate that event by lend-
ing a large canvas awning to Robert Cecil for the reception of
His Majesty on his way down from Scotland.

"Savoy, May 3rd., 1603. Right Honorable. The hale you writte
for I have not, but I have sent you a double Tent of more rome
than the hale was, wishinge it may be useful unto you. If there
be anythinge els in my powre which may doe you service, That
it may please you to command. My desyne is rather by performans than by letter to make you know your interest in me
which I assure you is much more than I make shew of as by
any good occasione you shall have Testymony and for this time
I leave remaininge ever ready to do you service.

Willm. Harvye."

"To the right Honorable Sir Robert Cecill, Knight, principall
secrytary and Councellor of estate unto his Ma^te/ At Theo-
bald's." (*See Plate VII, at end of volume.*)

Before submitting new evidence as to the part William
Hervey took in getting Shakespeare's Sonnets and other poetical
works printed, it is essential to recall conditions then prevailing
in the censorship of the London book trade in Elizabeth's time.

Among injunctions given by Her Majesty, which were pro-
mulgated as a corollary to the Edicts of 1559, it was forbidden
to print "any book or paper of what sort, nature or in what
language soever it be, except the same be liscensed by her Majesty or six of her Privy Council or by two at least of a certain
list of officials." The Archbishop of Canterbury, censor cen-
sorum, might, however, act alone.

Editions of Latin and Greek classics were exempted from
these drastic measures, but they affected the London publishing
trade in all its branches and their application became more
severe as time went on.

In 1566, the Star-Chamber issued an *Ordinance for the reformation of divers disorders in the printing and uttering of*

books. Heavy fines and imprisonment were decreed against all who printed or brought into the realm "any book against the form and meaning of any Statutes, or Law, or Injunction passed by the Queen's authority." A series of Royal proclamations reiterated the prohibition still more sternly, so that the status of all Catholic books was reduced to that of *Traitorous and Seditious libels.*

In 1586, the penalties already imposed upon printer and importer of unauthorised books were extended to all who "sold, stitched or bound them." With the exception of *one single press* at Oxford and *one* at Cambridge, the establishment of any printing whatsoever outside of London was forbidden and, if existing already, was ordered broken up and destroyed.

Literary offenses came under the jurisdiction of the Bishop's court or that of an ordinary Justice of the Peace; but when the Government found it advisable to act rapidly and with rigour the crown lawyers invoked some clause of the penal code to secure conviction at the Assizes for *felony* and *treason.* Catholic suspects were endlessly harassed by denunciations and searching, often conducted by most ignorant men. They reported that the historian John Stowe must be "a great favourere of Papistry" on the strength of finding the Venerable Bede's *Church History of England,* which they took to be seditious, listed among the works therein contained. Often the incursions were abused and faked. Self-styled officials sprang up, produced false search-warrants, and threatened to make arrests and seizures if money was not immediately offered to buy them off. How often this trick was successfully accomplished cannot be estimated, for many who had allowed themselves to be taken in by false warrants feared to make complaint lest it might lead to bona fide investigations. According to Thomas Nash there is no doubt that good letters were supposed to be the special belonging of the Catholic camp. Poetry and romance were regarded by the

Elizabethan Puritan as "devised by the devil, authorised by the Pope, printed in Hell, bound by hobgoblins, and dispersed that men might be kept from reading of the Scriptures." A curious proof of this may be found in a pamphlet published in 1622, of a kind so popular at that time. The writer, Thomas Robinson, gives out therein, that for many years he served in the English nunnery at Lisbon, and declares that if the grace of God had not prevented, he might have grown as old in wickedness as the oldest among them:

> "They do indeed fair chastity profess,
> Obedience, poverty and seem no less,
> But God doth know, and Robinson can tell,
> All is a beastly falsehood in this cell."

The Shakespearean scholar is not so much interested in the truth or falsehood of the author's assertions as in his statement that the daughters of Sir Anthony Brown, Viscount Montague, aunts of Shakespeare's patron, and Cicely Arundel were among the sisterhood, and more especially his accusation—for want of a better—that when the confessor was "merrily disposed after supper, it is usual for him to read a little of 'Venus and Adonis,' 'The Jestes of George Peel,' or some such scurrilous book, for there are few idle pamphlets printed in England that he hath not in the house," and this again recalls the Puritan accusation, "as the lapwing with her busy cry draws men away from her nest, so the Popish generation by these fabulous devices draw men from the scriptures."

In spite of such complaint, the demand for poetry and Catholic literature went on increasing, throughout these times of persecution. Booksellers' stalls and back-shops were crowded with semi-religious volumes and those of "Popish" origin. Father Parsons's book of *Christian Resolution* and Leicester's *Commonwealth* had a phenomenal output; works from Douay,

Rheims, Antwerp and Rouen came pouring into England in defiance of the Queen's repeated proclamations. Even the execution of certain printers and booksellers, both Catholic and Puritan, did little to check this influx.

Among the most paradoxical things connected with the question is the astonishing fact that it was the Archbishop of Canterbury himself who authorised the impression not only of William Shakespeare's poem "Venus and Adonis," which by strict ecclesiastical standards must have been deemed "lascivious," but another sort of volume the sole possession of which might suffice to condemn the reader or seller to death, namely: *Saint Peter's Complaint* and *Mary Magdalen's Funeral Tears,* by the Jesuit priest Robert Southwell.

Even if the influence of a then powerful man like Southampton sufficed to make the Archbishop close his eyes to the "lewdness" of Shakespeare's verse, the conscious or unconscious connivance of those in authority, when it came to publishing the works of Robert Southwell, is more difficult of explanation.

When I reflected that the same man who as Bishop of Worcester issued young Shakespeare's marriage license bond in 1582, and, elevated to the dignity of Archbishop of Canterbury in the early nineties, was setting his satisfecit upon Shakespeare's poems and even on those of Southwell, I began to believe that strong and recondite influences were at work in the very heart of the Anglican church. Bishop Whitgift's taste for literature is recalled by John Stowe's declaration that the prelate's great love and entire affection for all good letters was so "great and singular" that all inclined thereto "did justly claim him as their particular patron."

I became still more convinced that it was no mistake to assert that John Whitgift was but a lukewarm enemy to the Church of Rome, on finding proof in the State papers that Richard Topcliff, the Queen's chief Intelligencer, evidently held this same view, when he denounced Whitgift as a traitor and declared his earnest wish "to hang him with five hundred others of the same kind."

Not only was the desire expressed, steps were taken to carry it into at least partial effect. There was at that time a priest under indictment whose name was John Portmort or Pormort, but who went sometimes by the alias of Whitgift. Topcliff visited him in prison with the tempting offer of immediate liberty and emolument if he would only swear that his expenses at the Overseas Seminary had been defrayed by the Archbishop of Canterbury upon whom he looked as a father.[2] Portmort indignantly repulsed the lure, and reported the conversation to the Privy Council. As a result, the spy was himself sent to the Tower, as punishment for libelling the Queen so grossly that only a portion of what the Council listened to can be printed.[3]

The Stationers' Register at the date November 8, 1593, shows this astonishing inscription:

"Under the hand of the Lord Archbishop of Canterbury, a book intitulated Mary Magdalen's Funeral Tears." The asker was Gabriel Cawood,—the same whose house two years later brought out Shakespeare's "Venus and Adonis." After Cawood's death, the house passed to Thomas Leake who made a specialty of "suspected books" and who continued to be associated in Shakespearean publication.

[2]"A copy of certaine Notes written by Mr. Pormort, priest and martyr of certain speeches used by Top. Unto him while he was prisoner in the house and in custody of the said Topcliff. The which notes were since delivered to Wade one of the clarcks of the counsel and by him shewed to the Co in Nov last (1593).

"Item. Whitgift of Canterbury was godfather unto this Mr. Pormort Topcliff offered this priest his liberty yf he would say that he was a bastard of the Archbishop's that the Archbishop had maintayned him beyond the seas. That the Archbishop was a fitter counsellor in the kitchen among wenches than in a prince's court and that he would hang the Archbishop and fifty more yf they were in his hands. . . ."

[3]". . . That he is so familiar with her majestie . . . that she gave him for a favour a whyte linen hose wrought with silke when he pleaseth to speake with her he may take her away from any company . . . that he did not care for the counsel for that he had his authoritie from her majestie."

Although Robert Southwell, the young Jesuit author of "Tears," was then hiding in peril of his life, although he was, by the time Shakespeare's book came out, brought to torture and execution, yet permission was granted and the work speedily went into print. A second edition appeared in 1594, another in 1596 and successively in 1602, 1607, 1609, 1620, 1630 and 1634, besides the two editions published in Douai in 1616 and 1629, a better seller than the phenomenal "Venus and Adonis" or "The Rape of Lucrece"!

It was William Shakespeare's cousin, fellow-poet and near neighbor, in the shire, John Trussel of Billesley, who had the temerity to publish Southwell's *Triumph over Death* in 1596.

These magnificent pages were written by way of condolence for the death of Lady Margaret Howard, daughter of Thomas Duke of Norfolk (beheaded in 1572), and were dedicated to her beloved brother Philip Howard, Earl of Arundel, imprisoned for his faith in the Tower of London from 1585 to his death in 1595.

Trussel's reprint bears the sub-title:

A consolatory Epistle for afflicted Minds in the effects of dying friends, first written for the Consolation of One, but now published for the general good of all.

So little pains were taken to disguise the authorship of the volume that the verses which accompany the *Dedicatory Epistle* form an acrostic which when read vertically spells Robert Southwell.

R Read with regard what here with true regard
O Our second Ciceronian Southwell sent;
B By whose persuasive pithy argument
E Each well disposed eye may be prepared,
R Respectively their grief for friend's decease
T To moderate without all vain excess.

S   Sithence the work is worthy of your view,
O   Obtract not him which for your good it penn'd
U   Unkind are you if you it reprehend
T   That for your profit it presented you;
H   He penn'd I publish, this to pleasure all,
E   Esteem of both then as we merit shall.
W Weigh his work's worth, accept of my goodwill
E   Else is his labour lost, mine crossed, both to no end
L   Lest then you ill deserve what both intend,
L   Let my goodwill the small defects fulfil . . .

Yet, if perhaps our late sprung sectaries
Or, for a fashion, Bible bearing hypocrites,
Whose hollow hearts do seem most holy-wise
Do, for the author's sake, the work despise
I wish them weight the work, and not who writes.

This is the second instance when volumes from the pens of Southwell and Shakespeare are found printed over the same trade mark, and there is a third whose character is more sensational, where the juxtaposition of the printer's name again occurs. Shakespeare's Sonnets and a posthumous poem attributed to Southwell appeared under the same auspices, even with substantially the same dedication.

In 1606, the *Fourefould Meditation* was printed by George Eld. It is dedicated to a certain Mathew Saunders frequently mentioned in the correspondence of the Southampton family. This dedicatory epistle is in the same form as the one which, three years later, was printed in Thorpe's edition of Shakespeare's Sonnets and, what is still more significant, it is signed with those same initials which have puzzled the readers of Thorpe's Sonnets' publication:—"W. H.," and is printed by the very man who set up Shakespeare's Sonnets, namely, George Eld.

Sir Sidney Lee's conjecture that Mr. W. H. must be identified with *William Hall,* an obscure member of the Stationers' Com-

To the Right Worſhipfull and
Vertuous Gentleman, Mathew
Saunders, Eſquire.
W.H. wiſheth, with long life, a proſperous achieuement of his good deſires.

Ir ; *as I with great deſire apprehended the leaſt opportunity of manifeſting towards your worthy ſelfe my ſincere affeƈtion, ſo ſhould I be very ſory to preſent any thing vnto you, wherein I ſhould growe offenſiue, or willingly breed your leaſt moleſtation: but theſe meditations, being Diuine and Religious (& vpon mine owne knowledge, correſpondent to your zealous inclination) emboldened me to recommend them to your view and cenſure, and therein to make knowne mine owne entire affeƈtion, and ſeruiceable loue towards you. Long haue they lien hidden in obſcuritie, and happily had neuer ſeene the light, had not a meere accident conuayed them to my hands. But, hauing ſeriouſly peruſed them, loath I was that any who are religiouſly affeƈted, ſhould be depriued of ſo great a comfort, as the due conſideration thereof may bring vnto them. As for my ſelfe, Sir, the knowledge you haue of me, I hope will excuſe the coldneſſe and ſterilitie of my conceipts, who couet to illuſtrate my intire affeƈtiõ vnto your worſhip, by reall and approued aƈtions, referring my ſelfe wholly in this, & all other my indeuours, to your fauourable conſtruƈtion, who ſhall euer be of power, in the humbleſt ſeruices to command me.*

Your Worſhips vnfained affeƈtionate
W. H.

pany, is no more than a supposition, although it has been confidently accepted as a fact by those who use the document in support of Lord Vere's authorship of the sonnets. It was only arrived at for lack of a better, *for,* affirmed Sir Sidney, *no other man in the world of letters at that date possessed those initials.*

This is a mistake, as I have shown; there is, in the British Museum, a letter addressed to the Queen, which is signed

TO.THE.ONLIE.BEGETTER.OF.
THESE.INSVING.SONNETS.
Mr. W. H. ALL.HAPPINESSE.
AND.THAT.ETERNITIE.
PROMISED.

BY.

OVR.EVER-LIVING.POET.

WISHETH.

THE.WELL-WISHING.
ADVENTVRER.IN.
SETTING.
FORTH.

T. T.

merely with the letters W. H.[4] and Mrs. Carmichael Stopes makes no doubt that this epistle was written by William Hervey

[4] The letter of W. H. to the Queen contains some interesting and confidential advice concerning her affairs both abroad and at home. It clearly indicates that as was suggested by Mrs. Stopes in her *Life of Lord Southhampton,* his future stepfather in early days had belonged to those military and political adventurers who turned their knowledge and aptitudes toward secret-service. W. H. described himself as a *man of judgment and action neither decrepit in body or in mind and whose present necessities crave to be provided for.* He hints that he has been set on the black book of proscription by many superior to him in rank. His advice to the Queen is practical, the keys of Flushing should be in the hands of her Majesty's governor and a sufficient

175

whom she also plausibly identifies with the *W. H.* of Thorpe's Sonnets, arguing that as stepfather of Shakespeare's young patron, William Hervey was more apt to have "The Lover's Complaint," and the "Sonnets" of Shakespeare fall into his hands, than an obscure member of the Stationers' Company like William Hall.

Mrs. Stopes in this instance made no discovery, for, as I said, over sixty years ago, Charles Edmonds, in issuing a reprint of the poetical meditations ascribed to Robert Southwell, reproduced a facsimile of the original prefatory epistle which is signed "W. H." and, in giving it, made the following comment:

"I have always presumed this 'W. H.' to be the same who gave Shakespeare's Sonnets to the world, from the press of the same printer George Eld." Thus Edmonds recognised, from the form itself in which the dedication-page of Shakespeare's Sonnets is composed—constituting as it does a complete parallel with his recommendation of Southwell's poetical meditations to read-

---

garrison should be installed to quell the civil mutinies to which the townsmen were inclined. He recommends that Sir Thomas Cecil should obtain possession of Meesland Sluice and Delphs Haven as important keys to the whole river and also of the key and bridal of all North Holland and the navy belonging thereto. He cites certain Papists who are nevertheless good patriots and suggests a plan by which the Governor of a low country may be surprised on a hunting party or boating excursion. He offers to effect a *coup de main* on Calais and seems fully assured of his capacity to succeed in this attempt, as the townsfolk have grown over-secure by wealthiness. He takes up the criticism against the Queen for her alliance with a Mohammedan Sovereign against the Christian King which, to the eyes of Europe, was one of the most serious charges against her Government. "Your Majesty is not arming a Barbarian against the Christian, but against the most dangerous Barbarian of any age, Usurper of Kingdoms and subverter of real religion." He adds "that by hindering his fishing in New Foundland and the Bay of Biskay, she may starve out his navy which is their chief strength, and recommends the planting of colonies in Virginia under discreet governors, capable of constructing boats on the American coast as the surest way to possess King Philip's purse and ruin the Usurers depending upon him, who have been the purses of unjust wars in Christendom for many years past."

The letter which is dated the 20th of December 1585, is subscribed: "Your Majesty's loyal and devoted true servant, W. H."

The postscript adds: "It may please your Majesty to make a salamander of my papers and observations for I have none to behold and trust to but yourself, nor after your life any assurance on earth to build upon. Be good to me therefore in time, least I perish by necessity. *In fidens et sedulus site princeps propensior quem in ceteris.*"

ers who were "piously inclined"—that Mr. "W. H." was the man who was presenting the work just as he had done three years before with Southwell's poems.

When Sir Sidney Lee took up this question, he had his own reasons for ignoring Edmonds's conclusion, and, like Professor Tyler, persisted in viewing Mr. W. H. as the man to whom Shakespeare's Sonnets were dedicated and not the man who was presenting the poems, so he hit upon William Hall as the most satisfactory candidate in the printing world.

Considering the important part he played during Elizabeth's reign, few traces of William Hervey's existence have come down to us, and I searched many years before obtaining sight of a letter which bears the full signature of Lady Southampton's third husband. The lack of documentary knowledge may be explained by the fact that even in his missive to the Queen, which bears only the initials "W. H.," there is a suggestive request that Her Majesty "make a salamander of these, my papers" and this, added to the fact that those who belonged to the recusant world were not apt to leave many written documents behind them, accounts, perhaps, for scarcity of papers concerning his personality. All that I have been able to retrieve is herein given, but meantime I must return to the thread of my argument concerning his literary activities, first reminding the reader that the two "best sellers" in London, either in prose or verse, were Shakespeare and Robert Southwell, and that the young priest acted as confessor to all the Montague connection.

Even as prisoner in the Tower, through the jailer's connivance, Southwell had overseen Philip Arundel's literary work. Arundel's dog plied constantly between their cells: "to get or to carry a blessing" as the turnkey remarked, and the best critics today are agreed that the "Fourfould Meditation," although printed under Southwell's name, was, in reality the work of Arundel and only proof-read by the greater poet. However this may be, these verses, after Southwell's execution and Arundel's death in the Tower, naturally came back into the hands of the Arundel family and, consequently, into those of the old Countess of Southampton, whose daughter married Thomas Arundel. Her third husband, Mr. "W. H.," was not the man to let slip an occasion of turning an honest penny, and, considering the vogue Southwell's name possessed in the world of letters, the manuscript must have tempted him sorely. His marriage to the dowager did not take place without a good deal of talk, criticism and obstruction, notably an exchange of letters between Essex and the Countess concerning her intentions, and finally a missive from court from that indefatigable correspondent Sir Dudley Carleton affirms that: "Lady Southampton's marriage to Sir William Hervey, which hath so long been smouldering, comes to be published."

Seven years later he gives another piece of news: "The old Countess of Southampton is dead. She hath left the best part of her stuff to her son, and the most part to her husband."

From her will it is easy to see that the testatrix was anxious to reconcile the maintenance of the Southamptons' family dignity with the endeavour to help her husband,[5] who was in permanent need of money. With this end in view, her executors were charged to see her buried in Tichfield Church, beside her first husband, the second Earl of Southampton "Inhibiting them to use any superfluous charges at or about my funeral, neither more blacks (mourning outfits) to be bestowed than on my household servants."

"I leave to my Honourable and dear son Henry, Earl of Southampton, ten pieces of hanging tapestries of the story of Cyrus Six pieces of hanging in which the months are described. Two

---

[5]It is significant that almost immediately after the Countess's death the "Fourfould Meditation" saw the light, and that it emanated from some member of the family into which Mary Wriothesley had married, is as natural as that her stepfather should have carried it to the printer.

pieces of hanging with gold wrought in them and Sir Thomas Heneage's arms. A scarlet bed with gold lace with all the furniture, stools, chairs and cushions and all other furnitures. Two of my best downe beds with bolsters pillows and blankets. Four of my best Turkey carpets whereof one in silk. Two of my best and fairest ewers and basins of silver with four pots of silver belonging to them. Six of my best and greatest candlesticks of silver. A ring of gold with a fair table diamond in it which Sir Thomas Heneage had of Sir Walter Raleigh. Sixteen loose diamonds which my desire is that my said dear son should set in a George of gold and wear in memory of me his loving mother. Also I give to my good and loving daughter-in-law Elizabeth Countess of Southampton, my double rope of round pearls which myself did accustom to wear around my neck. My best tissue kirtle and six pairs of my finest sheets with twelve pillow beers.

"To my good daughter the Lady Arundell wife unto lord Arundell my jewel of gold set with diamond called a Jesus.

"All the rest of my goods and chattels household stuff and estate to my dear and well beloved husband Sir William Hervey whom I make sole executor of my last will and testament praying him as an argument of his love to me that he will be careful of my page Robert Jones and, at his discretion, at my request to provide for him that he may be able to live and know that I had a care for him.

"I have set my hand and seal to this on 22 April 1607.

M. SOUTHAMPTON.

"Memorandum. I leave my dear son all the pictures in the little gallery at Copthall."

"Probatum fuit 14th of November 1607 by Sir William Hervey."

It is obvious that the W. H. who recommends Southwell's verse as *divine, religious and likely to bring moral comfort to those who are piously inclined,* cannot be remotely associated with Will Hall, for the books we know which issued from Hall's infrequent press show that this printer's tastes were sectarian and protestant: *"The Sermons of John Tynley,"* a violent anti-Catholic preacher, and a tract *"Jhesuiterie Described as Babylon's Policy"* are sufficient proof that Hall could neither recommend Southwell's work in glowing terms nor yet select the pious tutor Saunders as dedicatee of the volume; on the other hand, whoever was the W. H. who carried the *"Meditations"* to Eld, he may be safely identified with the same intermediary who brought him the Sonnet book three years later, for the two are couched in the same form.

The "Worshipful Mathew Saunders," to whom the book is dedicated, figures in the Southampton familiar letters as a man of great learning and piety to whom many catholics confided the religious instruction of their children.

A glance at the Epistle shows a strong resemblance with that contained in Thorpe's sonnet-book. But instead of: *to the onlie begetter of these ensuing sonnets,* in this case it is: *to the Right Worshipful and Virtuous Gentleman, Mathew Saunders, Esquire,* that W. H. wisheth, *with long life, a prosperous achievement of his good desires.*

The milieu for which these religious meditations were destined was that of recusant London. Saunders, to whom the book was dedicated, was strong in the old faith—consequently the editor, even if not belonging strictly to the communion, may be supposed to have counted, at least, among sympathisers.

William Hervey fits perfectly into the picture as editor of Southwell's verse. It is still more natural to connect him with the publication of the sonnets addressed to his step-son, in which he seems to have played exactly the part of what today would be called literary agent.

For if, laying aside any preconceived ideas as to the natural reading of the sonnet dedication page, we look at it as though for the first time, it appears quite clearly that Mr. W. H. is not the *object* of Thorpe's address, but that, on the contrary, he is uniting with Thorpe to present the poems to the public and, at the same time, offers a compliment to the "only begetter" by repeating the poet's promise of immortality.

The place occupied by these initials W. H. at the commencement of the second line, the spacing with double-leads which divides the paragraphs into two distinct groups, showing "wisheth" as the key word, indicate Mr. W. H. as the "editor" of the poems in the true sense of that term, *i.e.,* the man who is presenting the work.

It is not "To the begetter of the ensuing sonnets Mr. W. H." that we must read, but, on the contrary, that "Mr. W. H. wisheth happiness to the only begetter of the ensuing sonnets to whom the ever-living poet promised eternity."

In quite a new paragraph, the printer affirms that his intentions in venturing money to publish the volume are entirely benevolent.

Thus, we find William Hervey acting not as the purveyor of stolen goods to a pirate-publisher, but operating with full authority to place in the hands of the printer George Eld—with whom he had already been in negotiation over Southwell's verse—a volume even more likely to be profitable.

As money must always be laid out before a book begins making any financial return, in this case it was Thomas Thorpe who, by his own signed declaration, provided the cash for the venture.

In thus adding his signature, T. T., to the dedication of Mr. W. H., Thorpe shows William Hervey acting with full authority through his wife's will, as head of young Southampton's family, to bring out the sonnet volume; that he also had the author's consent and encouragement so to do is more than probable, for not only do many of these poems contain the recognition of their literary merit, but the author repeatedly asserts, as in number 81, that it is *by* the Sonnets that Southampton will be famous in the centuries to come, which certainly could not be the case had they not been printed.

> "Your monument shall be my gentle verse,
> Which eyes, not yet created, shall o'er-read,
> And tongues-to-be your being shall rehearse,
> When all the breathers of this world are dead;
> You still shall live,—such virtue hath my pen—
> Where breath most breathes, even in the mouths of men."

John Benson, who re-edited the Sonnets in 1640, declared that Shakespeare himself when living, "avouched their proportionable glory" with the rest of his immortal works. This, in itself, is a sufficient reason to conclude that Thorpe's volume was not produced in 1609 without the author's consent. There is a weightier testimony upon this point, however, which emanates from Thomas Heywood, so often associated with the greater poet that his word is of extreme importance.

It was Heywood who wrote about the familiarity, bordering on disrespect, which incites the English to remember their great men by a nickname: Marlowe became Kit, Beaumont Frank, and Jonson—though he dipped his pen in the Castalian spring, was universally called Ben. Even

> Mellifluous Shakespeare, whose enchanting quill
> Could move to mirth and passion, was but Will.

Many of the poets cited were dead when these lines were printed in the *Hierarchie of Blessed Angels* (1635), but Thomas Heywood said something more interesting when his celebrated friend was still alive. In the concluding epistle to "My approved good friend Mr. Nicholas Okes" Heywood in 1612 referred to the fact that William Jaggard had printed a certain number of Shakespeare's poems in "The Passionate Pilgrim" without authorisation (1599) and, "Much offended that Mr. Jaggard presumed to make so bold with his name, hath, to do himself right, *since published them in his own name.*" This passage in the *Apologie for Actors* can only refer to the publication of Shakespeare's Sonnets by Thorpe, two years previously, and indicates that the author himself had furnished the true copy.

Commentators since Furnival quote and requote that portion of Heywood's statement which recalls his peevishness with Jaggard, and implies that Shakespeare was still more aggrieved, but they omit the far more important context which states that it was *Shakespeare* himself who caused the complete collection of his "Sonnets" and "A Lover's Complaint" to be published in order to "do himself right," a most natural proceeding under the circumstances. To my knowledge, Mr. Marion Spielmann is the only modern critic who draws the conclusion logically imposed by a careful reading of Heywood's assertion, *i.e.,* that Shakespeare himself instigated Thorpe's publication to set right the status of his lyric poems and show that he was in no way responsible for some of the verses which Jaggard had attributed to his authorship in the second edition of *The Passionate Pilgrim*—a fragment of which is preserved in the Folger Shakespeare Library (the third edition was brought out by Jaggard in 1612).

The initials of Mr. W. H., whose identity was well known at that time, was proof enough that the whole volume was written by Shakespeare and that there was nothing clandestine about its appearance.

Mr. J. A. Fort, although not aware how nearly William Hervey might be connected with the Sonnet publication, arrived at a parallel conclusion when he wrote: "either Southampton himself or a *close friend* of his who had permission to act, secured the publication of these delightful poems. Thorpe no doubt would have published them without authority if he could have obtained them, but Southampton was a powerful person in 1609 and I do not believe that anyone would have ventured to give up letters belonging to him for publication at that date without the Earl's express permission."

I suggested long ago that Shakespeare himself alludes to the fact that he had passed on the manuscript. The one hundred and twenty-second sonnet is an apology for having made bold to give away his own copy of these poems: as they stand "full-charactered" in the author's memory it would implicate forget-fulness on his part if he should keep a table-book containing them.[6]

There is every reason to suppose that Sir Sidney Lee before his death had adopted this theory; for when he learned from Mr. Spielmann of our findings his comment thereon was sim-ply: that he might be obliged to rewrite three or four chapters in his *Life of Shakespeare*.

It seems curious that, with this simple solution at hand, such fruitless controversy should have obscured the whole question, and for many years I hesitated to offer what I believed to be the true reason, which caused so much ink to flow. I am, how-ever, convinced that when the historical test, so called, began

[6]"Thy gift, thy tables, are within my brain,
Full-charactered with lasting memory,
Which shall above that idle rank remain,
Beyond all date, even to eternity.
Or, at the least, so long as brain and heart
Have faculty by nature to subsist
Till each to razed oblivion yield his part
Of thee, thy record never can be missed
That poor retention could not so much hold,
Nor need I tallies thy dear love to score,
Therefore to give them from me was I bold
To trust these tables that receive thee more
To keep an adjunct to remember thee
Were to import forgetfulness in me."

to be seriously applied to Shakespearean criticism, the Victorian with preconceived ideas as to what sort of man Shakespeare *ought* to have selected for an intimate friend, received a shock, for the youthful patron to whom the "first fruit of his poetic invention" was dedicated, turned out, upon investigation, to be another kind of hero from what Professor Tyler desired to find. Instead of the supple-kneed courtier, devoted to the Queen and zealous for her policy, history shows Lord Southampton as the moving spirit in a clan which, for the sake of religious liberty, joined with certain Puritan elements under the Earl of Essex, who pursued a like ideal in open revolt against the established powers. The closer special pleaders scrutinised the malcontent world of Montagues, Arundels, Copleys, Blounts, and Southampton, the more urgent it appeared to find a supporter of the recently established church as Shakespeare's official protector. Although it was impossible to eliminate the signed dedications to Henry Wriothesley, it was easy to declare that Shakespeare's first choice had been an error of early days, and to furnish him thenceforth with a literary protector whose political and religious opinions were more in conformity with National ideals.

Thus it is that ever since Professor Tyler's day, the patronage of Papistical Henry Wriothesley, Earl of Southampton and Baron Tichfield, to whom the poet in 1593 had consecrated all that he had done and had still to do, was put aside, and Protestant William Herbert, Earl of Pembroke, to whom the 1623 folio of Shakespeare's works was dedicated by the publishers thirty years later, reigned in his stead as patron of Shakespeare's "sug'red sonnets" in spite of written testimony, date and reason.

There is no real incompatibility between the so-called Southampton and Pembroke theories, though each is usually sustained to the detriment of the other. If Shakespeare had his own reasons for choosing in 1593, as his special patron, the young man who gave his pen "both skill and argument," his publishers had equally good cause in 1623 for presenting their comrade's collected plays to the "MOST NOBLE AND INCOMPARABLE PAIR OF BRETHREN WILLIAM EARL OF PEMBROKE LORD CHAMBER-LAIN, AND PHILIP EARL OF MONTGOMERY, GENTLEMEN OF HIS MAJESTIES BEDCHAMBER."

Pembroke's special functions at court placed all theatrical productions under his direction. He loved the theatre and cared so much for certain players that after the death of Burbage in 1618 he could not bear to see another man act his part without shedding tears. So when the great in-folio appeared in 1623, accompanied by numerous epistles and lauda-tory verses, Shakespeare's comrades declared themselves em-boldened thereto by the favours the Lord Chamberlain had shown "to the author and his works when living. . . . We have but collected them and done an office to the dead in procuring his orphan's guardians: without ambition either of self profit or fame; only to keep the memory of so worthy a friend and fellow alive, as was our Shakespeare."

Moreover, during the last ten years of the poet's life South-ampton was either in the Isle of Wight or absorbed in the colonial enterprise to which the "Tempest" owed its being, and died when about to realise his dream of military honours in the Low Countries. Lady Southampton survived many years, dis-tinguished for the cult of "her dead lord's" memory and loyalty to King Charles who in 1647 took refuge in her "noble seat" at Tichfield.

She carried out her husband's promise by bestowing his fine library on the College of St. John's at Cambridge, together with a magnificent portrait of the donor by Van Dyck. The books having been indiscriminately mixed with others and the portrait removed from the library to one of the residential buildings, no trace remains of this memorial, but we may be authorised to suppose that the volumes particularly dear to Shakespeare's first patron are still there, just as at Oxford we can imagine that the sum of one hundred pounds which Lord Southampton subscribed to help form the Bodleian collection may have gone, in part, to purchase the books by Shakespeare of which there are still good store.

CHAPTER NINE

SHAKESPEARE'S SCOTTISH PATRON

HIGH MILITARY command may lead more swiftly to political disgrace than any other path, as the Earl of Essex learned to his cost in 1599. Honours of every sort were showered upon him; he was made Chief Admiral of the Fleet, Supreme Commander of all Land Forces and Lord Deputy of Ireland with residence at Dublin. Already the darling of the multitude at home, his initial success, with Lord Southampton heading the cavalry, raised a storm of applause which Shakespeare was quick to take advantage of in his patriotic drama "Henry V," for, as Gerard Langbaine asserted: "This play was writ during the time that Essex was General in Ireland, as you may see in the beginning of the first Act where our poet, by a pretty turn, compliments Essex and seems to foretell victory to Her Majesty's forces against the rebels:

'. . . But now behold
In the quick forge and working-house of thought
How London doth throw out her citizens;
The Mayor, and all his brethren, in best sort
Like to the Senators of antique Rome,
With the plebeians swarming at their heels,
Go forth and fetch their conquering Cæsar in;
As by a lower but loving likelihood
Were now the General of our gracious Empress

188

(As in good time he may) from Ireland coming,
Bringing Rebellion broachéd on his sword,
How many would the peaceful city quit
To welcome him! . . .' "

The return was not what Shakespeare foreshadowed. Essex
did not come bearing "Rebellion broachéd on his sword"; the
political conditions at home made his position untenable in
Ireland, by the Queen's refusal to confirm the Viceroy's military
appointments. This threw the army into chaos and brought
her ex-favourite back post-haste to protest. The scene which
took place in the Queen's boudoir need not be recalled. Dexterously played on by her ministers, the royal rage brought
Essex before the Star-Chamber, accused of a new crime called
Contempt which was defined as lack of proper respect for regal
authority. Stripped of wealth after the Irish fiasco and relegated
to close confinement under the Lord Chancellor's supervision,
Essex languished for many months in prison. "Let the Queen
hold her Bothwell while she hath him. He will ever be the
canker to her estate and safety. If you take it for good counsel
to relent toward this tyrant, you will repent it when it shall be
too late . . ." wrote Sir Walter Raleigh to Cecil, who needed
no encouragement to act with rigour.

Southampton, with Sir Christopher Blount, the brothers
Danvers and other partisans, decided to force the Queen to
"hear reason" and name her eventual heir instead of insisting
that to speak of the royal succession constituted a crime of high
treason. Their slogan at Drury House, where the conspiracy
was fomented was, *"Long live the Queen and after her Long
live King James of Scotland, only legitimate heir to the English
throne."* And, in order to work up popular sympathy, they
again had recourse to the novel method already utilised in
"Henry V," namely theatrical propaganda. The troupe of the
Globe was invited to revive Shakespeare's "Richard II." Deal-

ing, as it does, with the tragedy of a sovereign become the prey of evil councillors, the play had, indeed, a direct bearing on the situation. The Queen herself complained:

"Know that I am Richard II !"

adding that it had been many times acted in squares and public places to stir up discontent, and it is significant that neither of the contemporary editions of the printed quarto (1597 and 1598) dared include the abdication scene.

On the eve of the day selected for the outbreak, Shakespeare's play was presented at the Globe where all the conspirators assisted. Each actor's pay was doubled for the occasion and Augustine Phillips, manager and dean of the Company, received forty shillings in gold. These facts were used in the trial of Essex and Southampton as positive proof of premeditated violence.

"The afternoon before the rebellion, Merricke, with a great company of others, that afterwards were all in the action, had procured to be played before them the play of deposing King Richard the Second. Neither was it casual, but a play bespoken by Merricke, and not so only, but when it was told him by one of the players that the play was old and that they should have loss in playing it because so few would come to it, there was forty shillings extraordinary given to play it, and so thereupon played it was. So earnest he was to satisfy his eyes with the sight of that tragedy which he thought soon after his lord should bring from the stage to the State."

A more dispassionate observer of events, William Camden, states, that proof of premeditation on the conspirators' part rested solely on their choice of this play. *"Quod ab eo factum interpretati sunt Juris Consulti quasi illud pridie in scena agi spectarent quod postridie in Elizabetha abdicanda agendum."*

Bacon used the argument of treasonable intent furnished by

Richard the Second, so dexterously that on February 18th, Augustine Phillips, dean of the troupe which presented the subversive drama, was summoned to explain matters to the Privy Council. That the author of a play which was held responsible for so much bloodshed[1] should have escaped scot-free is highly improbable.

As it was, the presentation of "Richard II," brought forward to show that the two Earls had in mind the Queen's forcible removal, was given as a justification of the death-sentence passed on both. Without that, Southampton's plea that the arming of his friends was legitimate self-defence might have been listened to; shortly before the rising, an attempt was made to assassinate him in open street when only his superior swordsmanship and the devotion of his page frustrated the enemy faction.

The doom passed upon him became a life-sentence—close confinement in the Tower—but this did not help his partisans nor render it easier for the friends who relied on his patronage to make a living in the capital. As a matter of fact the Lord Chamberlain's servants did not appear there for more than a year. What happened to them during this interval?

The Stratford records show that on May 1, 1602, William Shakespeare purchased from William and John Combe, one hundred and seven acres of arable land near Stratford upon Avon for the sum of £320; and yet, though it was customary on such occasions for the purchaser to be present in person, the conveyance was sealed and delivered to Gilbert Shakespeare, "to the use of the said within-named William Shakespeare."

This fact alone serves as presumptive evidence that the dramatist was far away. If the author of "Richard II" was neither in London, at Stratford, nor yet touring the English provinces

---

[1]Christopher Blount, Sir Charles Danvers, Sir Giles Merricke and the great Greek scholar Richard Cuffe, who had negotiated with the actors, were hanged or decapitated.

with the Lord Chamberlain's servants, it is logical to search for him in a money-making position which might explain the extraordinary favours James of Scotland showered upon author and troupe from the very moment his reign began in the sister-kingdom. The solution to this problem is all the more important because it gives a reasonable explanation as to why the name of Lawrence Fletcher, who had been known only as an actor favoured by King James in 1599, should suddenly appear as the first and principal personage of Shakespeare's troupe.

Mrs. Carmichael Stopes, who was more conversant with these affairs than any one of her generation, was convinced that Shakespeare got into trouble over the presentation of "Richard II"—trouble serious enough to cause his flight from England, and notes that from the failure of the conspiracy there is no record of his presence or that of any of his troupe from March, 1601, to December, 1602. She says:

"There is no doubt he must have trembled at the time of Essex's conspiracy, not only for his friend Southampton's life, but even for his own. Phillips, the manager of his company, was called before the Privy Council to account for the performance of the obnoxious play of 'Richard the Second.' The danger passed, they hastened from the metropolis, some of his company went to play in Scotland as far North as Aberdeen. I am inclined to think that Shakespeare went with them. The scenery in 'Macbeth' suggests visual impressions and the favour of James VI must have been secured before his accession to the throne of England, for almost the first act the king did, on his arrival at the metropolis, May 7, 1603, was to execute a series of acts that practically gave his company a monopoly."

I believe that Mrs. Stopes was right in her assumption that "Macbeth" had as much political bearing on the situation when King James came to the throne as "Richard II" had had as propaganda for his right of succession. Evidently the King's descent from Banquo was made much of from the first. A short interlude in Latin written by Florio's *alter ego* Mathias Gwynn was shown during James's visit to Oxford. Her argument of the King's utilisation of theatrical propaganda may be completed by another. The censor who had treated "Richard II" so rigorously that the Parliament scene was cut from the quartos of 1597 and 1598 permitted it to reappear as a chief attraction announced on the title page in the edition of 1608.[2]

Mrs. Stopes bases part of her argument that Shakespeare certainly visited the Highlands on points of local colour and even speech: "How far is't called to Forres?" is a Scottish turn which she thinks the poet heard himself when taking the road there, as he must have done in visiting Inverness. But she gives literary reasons which seem to me stronger, to show that the information Shakespeare used in drawing the character of Lady Macbeth was obtained on Scottish soil and probably from the King himself. Certainly the dramatist had another source of information than Holinshed. The English chronicler gives only one short line to describe his wife's influence over the thane of Glamis and Cawdor:

> She burned with unquenchable desire
> To bear the name of Queen.

The source from which the history and character of Lady Macbeth were drawn was Master William Stewart's poetical translation of Boece, "Stewart's Chroniclies" written with the intention of flattering Banquo's line. Terminated in 1535 Stewart's work was not printed for three centuries,[3] but manuscript copies were numerous and no one was more certain to

[2]The/Tragedie of King/Richard the Second/With New Additions to the Parliament Sceane, and the deposing/of King Richard/as it hath been lately acted by the Kinges/Maiesties Seruentes, at the Globe. By William Shakes-speare/at London/ printed by W. W. for Mathew Law and are to/be sold at his shop in Paules Churchyard/—at the signe of the Foxe 1608.

[3]"Stewart's Chroniclies" was first printed in the Rolls Series 1858.

possess one than the erudite King James "apprentice in the divine art of poesy." Stewart tells the tale differently from Holinshed, but wherever a divergency exists Shakespeare follows the Scotch and not the English chronicler. He gives a very full picture of Lady Macbeth, herself heiress to the throne of Scotland, and whose first husband with their children was burned alive in the castle from which she escaped through the snow with one infant son, Luloch, sole survivor of the ancient Scottish line. Macbeth gave her shelter and subsequently married her, thus consolidating the rather slight claim he might himself have to the throne after the king's murder which she incites him to in Stewart by calling him a "coward" and telling him to "look up clear and leave the rest to her." It is Stewart who introduces into the story of Banquo the idea that his race shall reign "til the warldis end."

But if we read the story of Macbeth's encounter with the Witches and the prophecy made to him and Banquo, we shall see that neither Holinshed nor yet Stewart had anything to do with the weird sisters as Shakespeare pictured them. Here are the lines as given in Mrs. Stopes's book *Shakespeare's Industry*, p. 338; in quoting I modernise the spelling:

> In Forres town where that this king Duncan
> Happened to be with many noblemen,
> Where Macabey and Banquo ain ae day
> Passeth at morn right early for to play
> The hand-for-hand intil a forest green,
> Three women met that wisely were beseen
> In their clothing which was of eldritch hue
> And what they were was nane of them that knew
> The first of them that Macabey came to
> "The thane of Glames, good morn to him" said scho.
> The second said, withouten any scorn
> "The thane of Cawdor, sir, give you good morn."

The hindmost with a pleasant voice benyng
"God save you, sir, of Scotland shall be king!" . . .
Then Banquo said: "Abide a little wee,
Ye give him all, what ordain ye for me?" . . .

"Thou, Banquo, take good tent unto this thing:
Thou thine own self shalt ne'er be prince or king
But of thy seed shall lineally descend
Shall wear the crown until the warldis end."
When this was said, they bade all three good night
Syne suddenly they vanished out of sight,
And where away? whether to heaven or hell
Or what they were, was no man yet can tell.

Let us compare this with the passage as it appears in the
1623 Folio: The stage direction of Scene III indicates a heath—
Thunder. Enter three Witches. After their weird dialogue
wherein all the gruesome properties of sorcery are mentioned:
toads, sieves, and tom-cats, in the midst of a spell-binding
dance, Macbeth and Banquo enter, their soldiers remaining at
a respectful distance.

Banquo: How far is't called to Forres?—What are these
So withered and so wild in their attire,
That look not like the inhabitants o' the earth
And yet are on't?—Live you or are you aught
That man may question? You seem to understand me
By each at once her choppy finger laying
Upon her skinny lips— You should be women
And yet your beards forbid me to interpret
That you are so.

Macbeth: Speak if you can.—What are you?
1st Witch: All hail, Macbeth! hail to thee, thane of Glamis!
2d Witch: All hail, Macbeth! hail to thee, thane of Cawdor!
3d Witch: All hail, Macbeth! That shalt be king hereafter!
Banquo: If you can look into the seeds of time,

And say which grain shall grow and which will not,
Speak then to me who neither beg nor fear
Your favours nor your hate.

1st Witch: . . . Lesser than Macbeth and greater!

2d Witch: Not so happy, yet much happier!

3d Witch: Thou shalt get kings though thou be none!
So all hail, Macbeth and Banquo!

Macbeth: Stay, you imperfect speakers, tell me more.
By Sinel's death I know I am thane of Glamis,
But how of Cawdor? The thane of Cawdor lives,
A prosperous gentleman: and to be king
Stands not within the prospect of belief,
No more than to be Cawdor. Say from whence
You owe this strange intelligence? or why
Upon this blasted heath you stop our way
With such prophetic greeting. Speak, I charge you!

(Witches vanish)

Now it is evident that Shakespeare's picture of three super-annuated witches dancing on a blasted heath owed nothing to Stewart's description of a "forest green and benign nymphs," nor yet to Holinshed where a rough woodcut of the encounter represents three women, young and fair, in renaissance garb, with jewelled girdles.

The source followed by Shakespeare was the King's own description. It is hardly necessary to repeat that James, besides being no mean poet, was an eager student of the occult. His highly erudite study *Dæmonology,* in which the royal author observes that Satan always finds his most crafty proselytes among old women, was useful to the dramatist who introduced bearded witches on his stage. In another publication called *News from Scotland*[4] the King's warning against holding

[4]Dæmonologye, in form of a dialogue, Edinburgh, printed by Robert Walde-grave, 1579. "Newes from Scotland declaring the damnable life and death of Doctor Fian a notable sorcerer who was burned at Edinbvrgh on January last 1591 with true examinations of the said doctor and witches as they were uttered then in the presence of the Scottish king." London, printed for William Wright.

commerce with the Evil One through witches or sorcerers, is bitterly repeated by Macbeth:

> Be these juggling fiends no more believed
> That keep the word of promise to the ear
> And break it to the hope.

In his curious book the King describes the confession made before himself and the Council by Agnis Tomson, "who sent by sea with a whole concourse of sister-witches, each one riding in a riddle or sieve very substantially, to the kirk of North Berwick in Lothian. There they took hands and danced a reel, singing all in one voice while the sorcerer, Giles Duncan, played upon a jew's trump."

"These confessions made the king in a wonderful admiration, and sent for ye said Geillis Duncane, who upon the like trump did playe the said dance before the king's maiestie, who in respect of the strangeness of these matters tooke great delight to be present at their examination. Agnis Tomson confessed that she took a blacke toad and did hang the same up by the heels and collected the venome as it dropped in an oister shell. . . ." She took a cat and christened it which caused such a tempest that the vessel "wherein was sundrye Jewelles and riche gifts which should have been presented to the now Queen of Scotland perished."

I do not contend that because Shakespeare followed King James's description so closely he necessarily received this documentation on Scottish soil, but atmosphere in the case of Macbeth is more striking than documentation acquired by book and once more I agree with Mrs. Stopes that the author of this essentially Scottish drama had sojourned in the North and even become acquainted with the Highlands. I need not point out how, on so many occasions, Shakespeare shows himself a discreet propagandist in voicing the King's sentiments or excusing his behaviour. One instance will suffice: the portrait in "Measure for Measure" of the serious-minded and reflective sovereign with all the horror of popular demonstrations which were so dreaded by the son of Mary Stuart.

> . . . I love the people
> But do not like to stage me to their eyes,
> Though it do well I do not relish well
> Their loud applause and aves vehement. ·
> Nor do I think the man of safe discretion
> That does affect it.

"Hamlet," to my mind, contains a reference to the Scottish journey which was well understood at the time. The Jacobean audience was perfectly aware that Shakespeare's company had been superseded. The rival troupe, the children of the chapel, were performing Ben Jonson's "Cynthia's Revels," so that the conversation between Hamlet and Rosencrantz (Act II, Scene II) formed an amusing topical allusion.

To the Prince's inquiry why the tragedians of the city should chance to travel since they could earn more at home, Rosencrantz replies "That *perhaps* their inhibition is caused by the recent innovation and that the boy actors carry all before them even Hercules and his load"—this palpable allusion to the Globe and Shakespeare's comrades has been often noted.

I believe myself that the *inhibition* referred to was the suspension of their patent as punishment for the representation of "Richard II," but the object of the dialogue being, aside from a desire to cause a laugh, to draw in Hamlet's remark on changing fashions, the author naturally dwelt on the "late innovation" which made his uncle popular as King of Denmark.[5]

[5]George Wyndham argued along these lines forty years ago in his introduction to the poems of Shakespeare. He attached much importance to the title page of the first quarto of Hamlet which reads: "As it has beene divers times acted by his highnesse's servants in the Cittie of London: as also in the two Universities of Cambridge and Oxford and elsewhere." This word *elsewhere* was considered by Mr. Wyndham as significant.

Such considerations should. be kept in mind as we follow the argument of Charles Knight—the first to assume that Shakespeare visited Scotland with Lawrence Fletcher when the sister-kingdom "became too hot to hold him"—and Charlotte Carmichael Stopes the latest exponent of the theory.

There is nothing particularly daring in the assumption that certain Essex partisans who desired to keep out of political trouble should have hastened North from Elizabeth's court. Even before the storm broke, Giovanni Florio was in Edinburgh (as is shown by the Calendar of State papers) where a letter addressed to him in Scotland, August 10, 1600, from Niccolo Molina, speaks of certain correspondence sent to him by order of Robert Cecil and asks for a receipt.

Arthur Acheson, the first person to call attention to this missive, drew the uncertain conclusion that Southampton's old tutor was in Cecil's pay and that his presence in Scotland meant "miching Milecho" to all concerned in Essex's designs. But was there really any treasonable intention on Florio's part? From the time the whole Essex faction passed under a cloud, London must have become a difficult place for the pedant to make a living and if he sought the rising sun farther North his daring was recompensed, for he was found soon thereafter writing himself "Gentleman of the Chamber to the Imperial Maiestie of the highest born Princesse Anna of Denmarke by God's permission crowned Queene of England Scotland and Ireland."

Certainly the King's favour toward Southampton preceded his departure. The last thing he did on leaving Holyrood, April 5, was to order the young man's release and inform the Privy Council of his decision.[6]

6". . . we are now resolved, as well in regard of the great and honest affection borne unto us by the Erle of Southampton as in respect of his good parts enabling him for ye service of us, and ye state, to extend our grace and favour towards him, whome we perceive also ye late Queene our sister, notwithstanding his fault towards her, was moved to exempt from the stroke of justice nevertheless because we would be loathe in

Little time was lost: Southampton left the Tower April 10, to take horse, gallop northward, join the King at Huntingdon and thenceforth carry the sword of State before the monarch in his progress, and the first reception given in a private house to Queen Anne when she arrived at London was a performance of "Love's Labour's Lost" at Southampton House.[7] Moreover, when this entertainment was being prepared and the question of an appropriate play came up between Burbage and Sir Walter Cope then Master of Revels, the former stated that her Majesty was acquainted with all the players' recent repertoire, but that an old Comedy just revived was certain to please. No one seems to have inquired where and when King James's consort had become so familiarised with the repertoire of Shakespeare's company if not in Scotland?

The Venetian ambassador noted that while journeying down to London the King already destined the Earl of Southampton "to great rewards" and remarked that the King had personally invested him with the Order of the Garter (adding a post worth 6000 crowns a year). A contemporary[8] observed that for some time there was every appearance that Shakespeare's patron

---

such a case as this wherein the peeres of our Realme have proceeded in the honorable formes used in lyke cases, to take any such course as maie not stand with our greatnes and the gravity fitt to be observed in such matters, we have thoughte meet to give you notice of our pleasure (though ye same be to be executed by our owne regal power) which is only this: Because the place is unwholesome and dolorous to hym to whose bodye and mynde we would give present comforte, intending unto him much further grace and favour, we have written to ye Lieutenant of ye Tower to deliver him out of prison presently to goe to any such place as he shall choose in or neare our cytye of London. . . ."—*Third Earl of Southampton*, p. 259.

[7]"Burbage ys come & sayes ther ys no new playe that the Quene hath not seene, but that they have revyved an olde one, cawled Loves Labore Lost, which for wytt and mirthe he sayes will please her excedingly." (Hatfield MSS.)

"It seems we shall have Christmas all the yeare. . . . Last night's revels were kept at my Lord of Cranborne's where the Q with the Duke of Holst with a great part of the court were feasted, and the like two nights before at my Lord of Southamptons." (Letter from Dudley Carleton to John Chamberlain, State Papers, Dom. Jac. I XII 13.)

[8]The Court and character/of/K./James/written and taken by Sir A. W. (Anthony Weldon) being an eye and ear witness London . . . sold by John Wright at the King's-head in the Old-Baily MDCL.

would be his Majesty's chief councillor and favourite but that Robert Cecil "not liking that any of the Essex faction should come into play destroyed his chance by putting some jealousies into the King's head."

Queen Anne was indeed on excellent terms, from the first, with Shakespeare's patron and took into her service another poet who vied with Shakespeare in singing Southampton's praises; this was Samuel Daniel, John Florio's brother-in-law, who was also elevated to the rank of Gentleman of her Chamber.

If Florio's clan did so well for themselves under the new régime, and the King, even before leaving Scotland, acknowledged his debt to the "Great and honest affection of Henry Wriothesley," need we feel unduly astonished at the suggestion that the troupe who had presented "Richard II" at his political instigation should have taken shelter in Scotland when the horizon in London clouded and the dean of the company was arrested for complicity in the Essex affair?

The cumulative evidence which I can bring forward to show that the company from England led by Lawrence Fletcher in 1601 was the very same who had prepared the King's advent to the throne with Essex and Southampton, is weighty enough for serious discussion and explains why Fletcher's name should suddenly appear closely associated with actors who, up to that time, admitted no outsiders.

In 1599 Lawrence Fletcher had already acted in Scotland with a certain Martyn Slater; but, in 1601, all that is known from local Scottish documents is that players, whom Fletcher had pressed into service at the King's request, were numerous and that they were "Inglishe men."

The King's solicitude for these actors is shown by an order preserved at Edinburgh to despatch twelve feather-beds to Dunfermline for their use.

An objection which might at first sound relevant would be:

Why is there no trace in the Scottish Archives and royal accounts of the presence of Shakespeare's troupe in the North? The answer to this is simple, although not generally known: All national records were removed by Oliver Cromwell and carried to London to be placed with the English rolls in the Tower. This act of the Lord Protector was like a thorn in the side of every good Scotchman and at the time of the restoration of King Charles one of the first demands made to him by his subjects in the North was that their archives might be returned to Edinburgh or Stirling. The King at once consented and the documents were shipped, but, as Stow's *Chronicles* observe: "Pity it was they were, for the vessel that carried them was wrecked on its voyage on the coast of Holy Isle." Thus all traces of what Fletcher's troupe did for the King are effaced from the national memory.

That James I immediately on his arrival in England should have been occupied with the affairs of the theatre and keen to create a monopoly for the particular troupe of Fletcher, Shakespeare, Burbage and their comrades, making them Grooms of the King's Privy Chamber as well, would indeed have been incredible had he not possessed previous knowledge of the men and their repertoire. This patent is drawn up in such a way as to indicate that the sovereign acted on personal initiative backed by experience, for he expressly declared that it was bestowed *"of our special grace certaine knowledge and mere motion."*

The whole document is so important that I shall include it without abridgment, recommending special attention to the last four lines and asking whether they could have been inspired by anything but personal friendship and gratitude on the part of the sovereign who wrote them:

PRO LORENTIO FLETCHER ET WILLIELMO SHAKESPEARE ET ALIIS

"James, by the grace of God, etc., to all Justices, maiors,

sheriffs, constables, hedboroughs and other our officers and lov-
inge subjects Greetinge. Knowe that wee, of our special grace,
certeine knowledge and mere motion have licenced and authorised, and by these presents do licence and authorise theise our
Servaunts Lawrence Fletcher, William Shakespeare, Richard
Burbage, Augustyne Philipps, John Heminge, Henry Condell,
William Sly, Robert Armyn, Richard Cowly and the rest of
their associates freely to use and exercise the Arts and Facultie
of playing Comedies, Tragedies, Histories, Enterludes, Morals,
Pastoralls, Stage-Plaies and such other like as they have already
studied or hereafter shall use or study as well for the Recrea-
tion of our loveinge Subjects as for our Solace and Pleasure
when wee shall thinke goode to see them during our pleasure;
and the said Comedies, Tragedies, Histories, Enterludes,
Morals, Pastoralls, Stage-Playes and such like to shewe and
exercise publiquely to their best Commodity when the Infec-
tion of the Plague shall decrease, as well within their now
usuall House called the Globe within our Countie of Surrey as
also within anie Toune Halls or Moute Halls or other convenient Places within the liberties and freedom of any other
cittie, Universitie, Toune or Boroughe whatsoever within our
said Realm and Dominions.

"Willing and Commanding you and everie of you as you
tender our Pleasure, not onlie to permit and suffer them herein,
without anie your Letts, Hindrances or Molestations during
our saied Pleasure but also to be aiding and assistinge to them
if anie Wrong be to them offered and to allow them such
former Curtesies as hath been given to men of their place and
qualitie; and also WHAT FURTHER FAVOUR YOU SHALL SHEWE TO
THEISE OUR SERVAUNTS FOR OUR SAKE WEE SHALL TAKE KINDLY AT
OUR HANDES. WITNESSE OURSELFE AT WESTMINSTER THE NYNE-
TENTH DAY OF MAYE, PER BREVE DE PRIVATO SIGILLO."

The extraordinary favour, shown by James to the players'

quality, did not always meet with the approval of his subjects, as is evidenced by this palpable hit from the pen of Gilbert Dugdale: "King James gave not only to those worthy of honour, but to the mean gave grace as taking unto him the Lord Chamberlain's servants now the King's actors."

On the Coronation account of Sir George Holmes, Master of the Great Wardrobe, for March 15, 1604, William Shakespeare is named first among the grooms of the Chamber to receive four yards of red cloth "against His Majesty's royal proceedings through the city of London." Augustine Phillips, Lawrence Fletcher, John Heminge, Richard Burbage, William Slye, Robert Armin, Henry Cundall and Richard Cowley are down for the same gift.

So great was the sovereign's partiality for these particular men that when it was decided to make a great solemnity of the reception of an Ambassador Extraordinary from Spain who came with seven high dignitaries to sign a final treaty of peace and was received at Somerset House, who should be appointed to "wait and attend" on the Constable of Castile during his three weeks' stay but this same troupe of actors, clad in scarlet liveries for their service as grooms of His Majesty's chamber?

The fact that Augustine Phillips in his will dated 1605 left to "my fellowe William Shakespeare" "a thirtie shillings in gould" and to "my fellowe Lawrence Fletcher twenty shillings" indicates that Shakespeare, in his comrade's eyes, remained the most important personage of the troupe, although Fletcher had first place on the letters patent because his acquaintance with King James antedated that of the other players.

In solemn procession they accompanied the envoy from Somerset House to Whitehall where a magnificent banquet was served, the Earls of Southampton and Pembroke acting as high stewards. The Lord Chamberlain paid out twenty-one pounds to the players for their services and the Constable bestowed a personal gift upon each. Sir Sidney Lee observes that during the first twelve years of James's reign Shakespeare's company received fees for no less than 150 performances at court. Shakespeare, in Sonnet 125, alludes to the procession where he and his fellows carried the royal dais:

"Were't ought to me I bore the canopie,
  With my extern the outward honouring . . ."

Now I think that a legitimate argument may be drawn from this totally unprecedented favour. Why should King James accord such an important rôle to mere players on an occasion of great weight and moment if he knew nothing about their personalities? The answer is simple—if King James thought that these men could be counted on to create a better impression than his ordinary palace staff it was because he had already employed them in a similar manner while still in Scotland.

The personal letter which James sent to Provost Cullen to ask special privileges for Lawrence Fletcher's English troupe has disappeared, but its record exists at Aberdeen and shows that the King held these actors in exactly the same esteem and utilised their personable appearance and good manners in the same way, as later when he made them Grooms of the Chamber to attend on the Ambassador from Spain.[9] The Aberdeen visit has faded into oblivion. I believe that I am the first person who can show the inscription on the municipal records of the royal borough, proving not only that, at the King's recommendation, the provost and his council listened to the plays presented by Fletcher's troupe, but also that they were rewarded with a

[9]The mention of this letter reminds me of the tradition several times recalled that Sir William Davenant had in his hands an amicable letter from King James to Shakespeare which disappeared after Sir William's death. The publisher Lintot, who reprinted Shakespeare's poems, recalls the fact and adds that a credible witness whom he knew had seen it. It occurs to me now as an interesting suggestion that possibly this may have been the very letter introducing Shakespeare to the Provost and "bailisses."

"soper" in the "Toon House," and the freedom of the city was conferred on their impresario Lawrence Fletcher.

In September, 1935, I was most hospitably received by the Provost of Aberdeen who put the services of his Charter Room at my disposal. Thanks to the Town Clerk and Mr. Forster who helped me in the search for these records, and Miss Margaret Melvyn, who transcribed them and saw to their photographic reproduction, I am now able to reproduce the report of this entertainment showing that the actors were ceremoniously attached during the journey northward to attend a foreigner of mark who was then making a tour of Scotland.

This fact will plainly appear in the following "Ordinance" drawn up when Alexander Cullen was Provost of Aberdeen.

Ordinance of the Dean of Gild.   Nono Octobris, 1601.

The Samen day the Prouest, Bailleis, and Counsall ordanis the svne of threttie twa merkis to be gevin to the Kingis Seruandes presently in this burcht quha playes comedeis and staige playes Be reasoun they are recommendit be his majesties speciall letter and hes played sum of their comedies in this burcht and ordanis the said svme to be payit to tham be the dean of gold quhilk salbe allowit in his comptis.[10]

There follows on another page and undated among the payments and receipts recorded between Michaelmas 1601 and Michaelmas 1602 an entry by David Cargill, Dean of the Guild as follows:

DISCHARGE

Item, to the stage playeris, Inglischman,   XXXII lib
Item, for the stage playaris suppor that
    nicht thaye plaiid to the towne,   iii lib

[10]Extract from Council Register of Aberdeen, Vol. 40, folio 210.

Curis Ballivorum Burgi de Abriden Conventa . . .
Vegisimo tertio die mensis Octobris anno Dom. 1601.

. . . .

Persones maid Burgesses.

The Quhilk day Sir Francis Hospital off Hantzie knycht frentch-
men being reccomendit be his Matie to the prest Baillzies and Counsell off this bur^h to be favourablie Intertenit with the gentillmen his
ma^tis seruandis efter speit. quha war direct to this bur^h be his ma^tie
to accompanie the said frencheman being ane nobillman of france
coming onlie to this bur^h to sie the toune and contrey, the said
frencheman with the ~~gentillmen~~ [deleted] knychts and gentillmen
folowing war all messaint and addmitted Burgesses of gild of the
bur^h quha gave thair aithes in commun forme.

Followes the names off thame that war admitted Burgesses

Sir Francis Hospitall off Halzie knycht

Sir Claud Hamilton of Schawfield kny^t

Sir John Grahame off Orkill kny^t

Sir John Ramsey off Ester Baisine kny^t

James Hay   James Auchterlony   Robert Ker   James Schaw
Thomas Foster   James Gregorie   David Drummond   servitors
to his ma^tie

Monsieur de Scheyne, Monsieur la Bone servitors to the said Sir
Francis

James Law

James Hamilton servitor to the said Sir Claud

Archibald Sym, trumpeter

Laurence Fletcher comedien servitor to his ma^tie

Mr David Wod

John Brouder Stains

(*See Plate IV, at end of volume.*)

On the 30th of May, 1602, Lawrence Fletcher, presumably
on his way down from Scotland with his troupe, gave a performance at Ipswich calling himself and his company "His
Majesty's players." Sir Sidney Lee in quoting this adds that the

title was "irresponsibly assumed." May it not prove on the contrary that James VI of Scotland had already conferred the privilege of this appellation on Fletcher and his new comrades when he sent them to Aberdeen, and simply confirmed a favour which had been already granted by the patent issued to them on May 7, 1603? Certain it is that as soon as the Queen and court were installed at Wilton, the troupe of Fletcher, Shakespeare and Burbage journeyed from Mortlake to Salisbury and were given thirty pounds reward by his Majesty. At Christmas when the sovereigns moved to Hampton Court, the same players gave six performances between Christmas and New Year and again in February, and from that time received from the sovereigns favours which had never been bestowed on their "Qualitie."

PART 3

❧❧

DOCUMENTARY STUDIES

CHAPTER TEN

THE PHŒNIX AND THE TURTLE

WHEN SIR E. K. CHAMBERS, in his *William Shakespeare,* consecrated a chapter to The Blackfriars' Gate-House, he dwelt on the suspicions constantly cast on this building as a refuge and hiding place for proscribed priests and proved that they were well founded. The connection thus established with Shakespeare is only implicit, for this side of the question forms no part of his book any more than it did in that of Sir Sidney Lee. Perhaps, however, I have brought out enough facts in the preceding pages to show that the Puritan horror for the theatre was largely an outgrowth of the supposed connection between the giving of stage-plays and Papist plots. Lady Bacon protested loudly when her son, Anthony, took lodgings near the Bull Play-House. She lived in constant fear of the Catholic connections he might form when his secretaryship for Essex kept him in touch with so many British exiles. There is, therefore, nothing particularly daring in the assumption that Shakespeare, living in the very portion of the Essex world most tainted with recusancy, should have occasionally been in touch with graduates from the Overseas Seminary, particularly those who came from his own region.

The vicinity of the theatre is denounced by the spy Anthony Munday, in his *English Romayne Life,* as the special haunt of priests "who, sometimes under the habits of gentlemen, serving men, or what apparel they might imagine convenient to their purpose, daily resort there to say mass and hear confessions before and after the plays." And the Lord Mayor of London denounced such houses as "ordinary places of meeting for all vagrant persons and masterless men that hang about the city, thieves, horse-stealers, whoremongers, cozeners, conycatching persons, practicers of treason, and such other like, where they consort and make their matches to the great displeasure of almighty God and the hurt and annoyance of her Majesty's people." Thomas Nash wrote in 1596, of how the players were piteously persecuted by the Lord Mayor, adding that through the Lord Chamberlain's intervention on their behalf they had supposed their "state settled" and it is noticeable that after Lord Hunsdon's death July 22, 1596, acting was no longer tolerated "in London proper."

The Princeton University Press has already published an article by Doctor T. W. Baldwin called "William Shakespeare adapts a hanging," which shows how this local colour of Holy-well (where the theatre was situated), utilised in the last scene of the "Comedy of Errors," was taken circumstantially from the tragic end of a Warwickshire neighbour denounced by Sir Thomas Lucy as commissioner to put down abuses in religion. This was William Hartley of Rowington who met a traitor's death at the theatre October 5, 1588, and as it was Walsingham's policy to set the place of execution as near as possible to the scene of his victim's activities, we may conclude that Hartley was the priest most often at the theatre. An equally plausible connection may be established between the dramatist and three other Warwickshire neighbours: William Freeman, John Ingraam and Robert Dibdale (for reasons hereafter specified) and whose studies like those of William Hartley were made in Cardinal Allen's overseas seminary during the period of its establishment at Reims.

Just at the time young Shakespeare got into trouble at Strat-

ford, Robert Dibdale, a lad from Shottery who had gone overseas, returned with the perilous mission whose ranks had already begun to thin. The hamlet of Shottery was too small for
the few inhabitants to ignore each other and it is impossible
to doubt that Shakespeare knew something of his wife's neighbour. With the friendliness prevailing among yeomen's children
the large brood of Hathaways and Dibdales must have inter-
mingled, and as there was no place there where a boy might
be educated we may infer, without putting any strain upon
imagination, that young Robert Dibdale daily trudged to the
Stratford Grammar School and sat under Simon Hunt, until
the rigour of anti-Catholic legislation forced both pupil and
teacher into exile. It is a noteworthy point that the Stratford
schoolmaster finished his days in the Overseas College.

The proof of friendship between the three families—Shakespeares, Hathaways and Dibdales—is to be found in a record
of monetary indebtedness. Two bonds, subscribed by John
Shakespeare, show that he had come to the aid of Richard
Hathaway financially, and this same Hathaway acknowledged
in his will that he owed a small debt to his neighbour John Pace
who had married Robert Dibdale's sister. This fact appears in
the public records where a letter, written by Robert, while
a student at Reims, gives a list of tiny presents contained in it,
together with a Roman antique coin for his brother-in-law
John Pace. This letter, though it never reached its true destina-
tion, fell into the hands of Walsingham's spy service when the
bearer, Father Lawrence Cottam, was arrested.[1] But it still
enables us to form an idea of the yeoman's family.

"Aftere most humble and dutifull wyse ryght welbeloved
parents, I have me commended unto you, desyring of you,

---

[1] Father Cottam, who left Reims shortly before Dibdale received ordination, took his
degree of Bachelor of Arts at Brasenose, Oxford, the very year before the Statutes began
to be enforced. After that he taught school in London some time before the period of
exile at Reims and upon his arrival as missionary was hanged, May 14, 1582.

your dayly blessing, trusting in God that you are also in healthe with my brothers and sisters. The cause of my wryting unto you ys to lett you understand that I am in healthe commending unto you my especiall friend Mr. Cottame, who hathe bene unto me the to-halfe of my life. I cannot sufficiently commend unto you his loving kyndnesse showed and bestowed uppon me. Wherefore I beseech you to take consayle of hyme in matters of great wayt. I have sent unto you certain tokens to be divided amongst you, a gylte crucifyxe and medall unto my father, and ye payre of bedes unto my sister Johne, the other payre of bedes unto my mother, the sylver romayne peyce of coyne unto my sister Agnes, and ye other peyce of French coyne unto my brother Rychard. The two stringes of graynes to be divided amongst you. I have sent unto my brother John Pace the peice of French coyne wrapped by ytselfe. Thus briefly I ceasse to troble you any ffurther. Desyring Almyghty God to preserve you in long lyffe and prosperity and send us a mery meting. Fare you well, the fourth day of June, ffrome Reimes. Youre obedient son, Robert Debdall."

In the volume of State papers (Eliz. Vol. CLM 65) this serious indictment may be read, showing that the folk at Shottery were suspected of the grave offense of "relieving a priest":

"Sent to Robert Dibdale from his father, the third day of November a letter and two cheeses, a lof of bread and V shillings in money brought by William Greenway the carrier."[2]

During the brief period Robert Dibdale exercised his ministry near London, a curious adventure brought him into indirect conflict with Sir Thomas Lucy, through the knight's

[2]The London prisons were not supposed to furnish food to their inmates, this was the affair of private charity. Many London tradesmen made generous bequests to this effect, as may be seen in Stow's *Chronicles,* but in some cases there is a proviso that money so left must not be spent to feed either "atheists or papists," so that these latter categories were obliged to look to their friends and relations for the means of life, but the fact that such charity was apt to bring the donor into trouble was not an encouragement to practise it.

former tutor John Foxe, whose marriage was celebrated at Charlecote. Dibdale specialised in occult study, and conjured the devil out of persons demoniacally possessed, to the terror and admiration of all who witnessed his exorcisms. Mr. Foxe, who claimed to possess the same gifts, had undertaken the cure of a certain "young Mr. Bridges student of the Middle Temple, violently possessed of Satan."

A contemporary account tells how Mr. Foxe's prayers and efforts were widely advertised by the preacher's friends but, according to the adverse party, "the young gentleman grew rapidly worse and Mr. Foxe becoming the prey of a strange agitation was declared to be himself possessed." Then, to the consternation of one part of London but the satisfaction of the other, the devil that agitated the student of the Middle Temple definitely abandoned his prey through Dibdale's intervention.

An eye-witness describes how two of the housemaids being bewitched, at Sir George Peckham's near Uxbridge, were relieved by the exorcism practised by the young priest from Shottery, and tells how, "in the house of old Lord Vaux, who then lived in London, many persons of distinction met—with great profit to their souls—to see and hear things far exceeding the forces of human nature accomplished by the martyr Dibdale."

Such anecdotes formed the staple of conversation in Shakespeare's world. His characters constantly refer to visions, spectral apparitions and occult practices as belonging to the common things of human existence and any news of the duel between the tutor from Charlecote and the priest from Shottery, to prove which side best prevailed against the artifices of the Demon, certainly commanded the poet's respectful attention.

"So have I heard, and do in part believe it," says his soldier in similar circumstances, acknowledging like the Prince that there are more things in heaven and earth than sceptical philosophy consents to take into account. "Such things as dreams are made on" are part of the local colour without which we cannot attempt any reconstitution of a period.

Dibdale's success brought too much publicity for him to keep hidden from the army of spies and informers who lived on the rewards and premiums earned by their "catch." Part of the tale was told in a manuscript at Douay by a fellow missionary, Father Thomson:

"I left Mr. Dibdale upon Ascension Eve, and, coming up to London, was myself apprehended by two pursuivants, Newal and Worsley, and sent to the counter in Wood Street. Two gentlemen were taken with me, a third who had brought me a missal, escaped by giving the pursuivants three pounds."

Stow's *Official Chronicle* of October 8, 1586, concludes the story:

"*John Lowe, J. Adams and R. Dibdale before condemned for treason in being made priests by the authority of the Bishop of Rome, were drawn to Tyburn, and there hanged. . . .*"

Another Warwickshire priest, John Ingram, has several suggestive connections with Shakespeare. He was born at Warwick, concluded his studies at Worcester and was a poet of special gifts, with a turn that was both homely and humorous, although the vehicle of his verse, which was Latin, does not often lend itself to Shakespearean wit. The first thing in the records which called my attention to Ingram as a person who moved in the same world as the poet's family was the fact that his expenses at Reims were paid by Sir Francis Englefield of Fulbrook Park, shown to have been William Shakespeare's happy hunting ground in the days when it was free to all and the scene of his punishment when it became, through seizure, the property of Sir Thomas Lucy. A more mysterious fact connects John Ingram with the players' company where the dramatist's whole career was made. When the priest from Worcester was incarcerated an offer to buy his life and freedom at the price of a thousand crowns was made by the Lord Chamberlain, Shakespeare's titular patron.

Reason enough to seek further data! But, alas, all that is known of the priest's existence was set down by his own hand and the information is slender. On the walls of the Beauchamp Tower where Philip Howard, Earl of Arundel, inscribed his pious resignation, Ingram, with a knife blunted by the jailer to prevent his captives from suicide, summarised his life in Latin odes, epigrams, and sapphics. They are now effaced by damp and time, but were happily preserved by his comrade Father Holtby and transcribed by Father Christopher Grene in his *Collectanea,* for there are high lights of dramatic intensity and familiar touches of humour and pathos which foreshadow the work of Burns; but no better than Shakespeare, could Ingram free himself from Ovid's influence. He calls "Pallas," Phœbus and Phœbe to witness his devotion to the Muses.

Several letters exchanged between Burleigh and the Earl of Huntingdon discuss the identity of a mysterious Scotchman called Byrne and decide that he must be "syfted."[3] But although the sifting which Ingram underwent in the North as well as at the Tower was exceptionally severe it gave no result. Ingram remains wrapped in mystery like the man with the iron mask.[4]

Not much more is known of William Freeman than that he

[3]"Whatsoever he be for birth and gentrie he is not Scottish borne I may affirme for soe he confesseth . . . and I thinke he will not saye much more that is fitt her Majestie should knowe until he see or feel the racke . . . To this goal I durst not send him for that I heare verie confidentially of some liberall offers for his enlargement which moved me to think him more fitt for the Towre where he might be in more safetie and better syfted than here he could be. He will not tell with whom, in whose houses or in what place in Scotland he hath been."

[4]Twenty-one odes and epigrams composed by Ingram in the tower may be found in the publications of the Catholic Record Society, Volume V, *English Martyrs, 1584–1693,* pages 270–286.

was educated at Magdalen College, Oxford, was ordained in 1587 and that his mission on returning to England was exercised exclusively in the region of Worcester and Warwick, at which latter place he was hanged on August 13, 1594, having by his saintly behaviour enlisted the sympathy of a large part of the town. But the interesting point in this case is that again we find him arrested and judged through the zeal of Thomas Lucy of Charlecote. I have already shown the many literary links which exist between Shakespeare's poems and the muse of Robert Southwell, whose "Burning Babe," that little masterpiece, Jonson declared he would willingly sacrifice all his own work to have written.[5] At present I pass to more positive evidence showing that the key to Shakespeare's most enigmatic poem may be found at Tyburn when the last victims of the Essex conspiracy met there, on the "triple tree."

The discovery made in the Public Record Office by Mr. Leslie Hotson, whose scent for important documents had already brought him praise as a light-giver, bade fair, when he found William Shakespeare's name as taking part in an affray against the Queen's peace, to create a sensation which was far from pleasant. So much so indeed, that a veil has been drawn over the whole affair, and the world which long complained of knowing "too little" about the poet's life seems afraid of learning too much.

Mr. Hotson's discovery, published in the *Atlantic Monthly*, was developed more fully in a volume printed by the Nonesuch Press, *Shakespeare versus Shallow,* when a photographic facsimile displays a plea for *Sureties of the Peace* or pecuniary guarantee against aggression, taken out by William Wayte, stepson of the Southwark Justice of the Peace, William Gardiner, because he had been threatened with danger to life and limb by

---

[5]Jonson, it will be remembered, joined the Catholic Church in 1599 when he was for a time prisoner in Newgate. He abjured the faith twelve years later.

William Shakespeare, Francis Langley, owner of the Swan Theatre in Southwark, and two women, Dorothy Soer and Anne Lee.

The finder of the paper was almost apologetic for thus exhibiting the poet in what he terms "a raw incident of London life" and does not pretend to guess what the trouble was all about. But to one who has explored the untrodden ways of Elizabethan research the incident bears all the characteristic signs of a priest-hunt which had become one of the common sights in the London suburbs and sooner or later brought out the Watch.

When the supposed connection of actors with the idea of "papistry and plots" caused all play-houses to be relegated to the Surrey side of the Thames and Shakespeare's troupe had been obliged to dismantle the famous theatre in Shoreditch, he himself removed from Bishopsgate to lodgings in Southwark near the Bear Garden in close proximity to Langley's new theatre called the Swan, constructed in the precincts of Paris Garden.

Wayte's plea, which couples the names of Shakespeare and Langley, points to the conclusion: that author and manager were professionally associated at this time.

The entry of a petition for *Sureties of the Peace* translated from the quaint legal Latin in which it is couched runs as follows:

"Be it known that William Wayte craves sureties of the peace from William Shakespeare, Francis Langley, Dorothy Soer and Ann Lee for fear of death, etc." It is dated on the last day of Michaelmas Term—that is November 27, 1596.

But not the least important part of Mr. Hotson's discovery is the establishment of a hitherto unsuspected association between Shakespeare and the proprietor of the Swan Theatre in November, 1596, indicating that "Hamlet" was produced at

Langley's Swan, a fact strongly corroborated by Dekker's parody *Satiromastix,* where the actor, who comes from Paris Garden, is given the name of Hamlet—Revenge.

Mr. Hotson says: "Hitherto it has been supposed that Shakespeare's company used the theatre in Shoreditch until 1597, but if so why did Shakespeare move from Bishopsgate, a district within easy reach of Burbage's theatre, to the Bank side in or before November, 1596, and give himself a gratuitous daily journey of more than two miles each way over the water and through London to the playing place in Shoreditch? I wish to suggest that Shakespeare went to the Bank side because he and his fellow-actors had shifted their chief center of operations from the theatre in the autumn of 1596 and established themselves for a time in Langley's new Playhouse, the Swan in Paris Garden, described as the largest and fairest of all the playhouses. . . . Although the Swan must have been finished by the middle of 1595, it has not been known what company of players used it before 1597. Professor Wallace discovered that in February of the latter year a newly formed group of actors 'Servants to the Right Honorable the Earl of Pembroke' contracted with Langley to play at the Swan for one year following. But we also learn that these were not the first actors at the Swan, for they later testified, in a suit against Langley, that the house had been used for plays 'lately afore' February, 1597." (*Shakespeare versus Shallow,* pages 16–18.)

The petition also furnishes an interesting indication that the traditional enmity of the Stratford Justice continued active in the metropolis through the collaboration of Sir Thomas Lucy's Southwark relatives. William Wayte was the son of Frances Lucy and through his mother's second marriage to Judge William Gardiner, had become stepson to the Southwark Justice of the Peace.

William Gardiner—like his Warwickshire associate—grew

rich upon fines and seizures from Catholic neighbours, and enlisted the services of his stepson Wayte in his favourite sport of priest-hunting.

The State papers show Gardiner of Southwark presiding at Paris Garden over a "search for a notorious person of Papistry." He found eight Papist books hidden in sundry places of the house, certain papers and one crucifix and further states in his report: "Though we watched the house with a strong watch, the owner would not suffer us to come in but kept the door, having his weapon in his hand and 'stale' away in the night for fear he should be taken."

Mr. Hotson regrets that nothing can be found about the true cause of the dispute wherein danger to life and limb seems to have been threatened on both sides. But apart from Francis Langley's declaration that the Southwark judge was "a false perjured knave, and his henchman Wayte, a loose person of no reckoning or value," he could discover no trace of Shakespeare's female companions except that a certain Soer lived near Paris Garden. Of Anne Lee no echo from the past came back to him.

Convinced that Mr. Hotson was following a wrong trail, I decided to prosecute a search over ground where the "standardised" student seldom or never sets foot and was more fortunate in finding some lost links and a plausible identification of Anne Lee.

Remembering how zealous Wayte's uncle, Sir Thomas Lucy, had always been in reinforcing legislation until it became a capital offence for any civilian to shelter or relieve the wants of a Romish priest, I realised that here was a practical illustration of how the new measures were working.

If the affair began with a priest-hunt, it only remained to find out which particular one the entry refers to. There are scores of such raids recorded between 1586 and 1600.

One incident tallies with the Shakespeare-Wayte episode as to place and personages. Ranged on one side we find William Wayte with the forces of law and order, on the other a band of pious gentlewomen—among them Mistress Anne Lyne, later hanged for harbouring; Mistress Lee and her whole house-staff, and, above in the chapel, the famous Jesuit John Gerard with his devoted servant John Lilly. I can only think that the Shakespeare-Wayte incident was directly connected with one of the most dramatic escapes of those dramatic times, recounted in his autobiography by Gerard himself. The dates are more difficult to control—nothing shows how long after the threats to "life and limb" had been made William Wayte turned in his plea for *Sureties,* nor is Father Gerard's narrative ever precise on such points. To me, at least, "the fourth or fifth day of the Spiritual Exercises of Saint Ignatius" conveys no positive clue. But in the *Condition of English Catholics under Elizabeth and James* may be found this narration which, though slightly abridged, is transcribed in John Gerard's own words:

"I did not wish to be without a place in London where I could safely admit some of my principal friends and perhaps house a priest from time to time. I therefore joined with a prudent and pious gentleman, Roger Lee, who had a wife of similar character, in renting a large and spacious house between us in which I had a fair chapel, well provided and ornamented. Hither I resorted from time to time when I came to London."

The narrative goes on to say that the ladies, assembled in Mistress Lee's parlour, "although fasting, had set cakes and wine on the table so that if molested they might declare they had gathered for friendly gossip and to hear the talk of the town." Father Gerard was vesting himself upstairs when a call from below warned him that the Watch was making a forcible search and that he must hide himself quickly.

"The Mistress of the house who had great presence of mind

stood on the bottom step in the searchers' way, purposely oc-
cupying the whole width of the staircase. One of them thrust
his head past her in hopes of seeing what was going on above
stairs. Indeed, he almost caught sight of me as I passed along
to the hiding-place. For, as soon as I heard the lady's words
of warning, I opened the door and with the least possible
noise mounted from a stool to the hiding-place which was
arranged in a secret gable of the roof. When I had mounted,
I bade John Lilly to come up also, but he, more careful of me
than of himself, refused to follow, saying: "No, Father, I shall
not come. There must be some one to own the books and
papers in your room, otherwise, upon finding them, they will
never rest till they have found you too . . . I acquiesced re-
luctantly and closed the small trap-door. Scarcely had he removed the stool by which I had mounted and gone back to
the room and shut the door, when the two chiefs of the searching party knocked violently, ready to break the door. The
intrepid soldier of Christ threw it open and presented himself
undaunted to the persecutors. They found there, on a table, my
breviary and many Catholic books, and, what grieved me most
to lose, my manuscript sermons and notes which I had been
writing or compiling for the past ten years."

Convinced that they had caught a priest, they locked and
sealed the chapel door and, taking John by the arm, went
downstairs and delivered him into custody.

Now, when he entered with his captors into the room where
the ladies were, he, who at other times was wont to conduct
himself with humility and stand uncovered in such company,
covered himself and sat down, assuming a sort of authority.
He said to the Justice: "These are noble ladies, it is your duty
to treat them with consideration. . . ." And here a touch of
nature is brought in: the ladies could scarcely refrain from
laughing at the excellence of the servant's impersonation.

"The magistrates took away John Lilly. The ladies represented that they had only come to pay an after dinner visit, not knowing a priest was there, so they were let off on bail to appear when summoned. The same favour was ultimately shown to Roger Lee, though it was with great difficulty that the justices could be persuaded he was only a visitor . . . I removed that very night lest the searchers discovered their error and returned."

Father Gerard was not always so successful in avoiding the pursuivants, but when he was consigned to the Tower this same John Lilly appeared as the hero of a more sensational rescue which was effected in the company of no less a person than William Shakespeare's cousin, Francis Arden who, it may be remembered, was imprisoned as accessory in the Arden-Somerville affair.

With the help of a ferryman on the Thames the faithful serving-man succeeded in throwing a rope on the roof of the Cradle Tower and aided Gerard and Arden to descend thence, and cross the moat in safety; a news-letter dated 1599 mentions that "One John Lilly is taken to the Tower on suspicion of having helped Gerard the Jesuit out of the same."

The rest is silence.

But one discovery among documents of this sort leads to another and, though I could find no more about John Lilly or Roger Lee and his wife, who in 1596 had been co-proprietors of Father Gerard's house, in compensation I learned a great deal about one of the women who had been present to hear Mass. This was Anne Higham, widow of Roger Lyne.

Under the sobriquet of Mistress Martha she presided successively over three different houses consecrated to the proscribed clergy; among Anne Lyne's lodgers many were notable: William Alabaster, the poet and classical scholar who had been chaplain during Essex's Spanish voyage; John Pones, a Franciscan, hanged in 1598; Robert Drury, who met the same fate at Tyburn, February 26, 1607; Francis Page; Father Garnet, and many others who, for a time, baffled the pursuivants.

Her employer, himself, gives this sketch of Anne Lyne in a report (1609) addressed to the Roman authority (*Narratio P. Joannis Gerardi de rebus a se in Anglia*) which records her devoted service:

"She was just the sort of person I wanted as head of the house, to manage the money matters, take care of the guests, and meet the enquiries of strangers. She had a good store of charity and wariness, and in great patience she possessed her soul. She was nearly always ill from one or other of many divers diseases, which purified her and made her ready for heaven. She used often to say to me, 'Though I desire above all things to die for Christ I dare not hope to die by the hand of the executioner, but perhaps the Lord will let me be taken some time in the same house with a priest and then be thrown into a chill and filthy dungeon where I shall not be able to last out long in this wretched life.' Her delight was in the Lord, and the Lord granted her the desire of her heart."

A *Brief Life of Anne Lyne* recently compiled by G. L. Whitfield establishes the main facts concerning her,[6] but for the circumstances of her death I prefer to return to the quaint language of the contemporary report:

"On Candlemas day the pursuivants, having some intelligence or suspecting Mrs. Lyne entertained a priest, beset her

[6]Anne's parents were William Higham of Dunmow in Essex and Anne Allen his wife, who had profited on the spoils of a convent dissolved under Henry VIII and naturally brought up their children as members of the church as by law established. Anne, "qualified in every point that an educated lady can be, dwelt for a long time with the family of a lord attached to the court and her brother William was well versed in Latin and touched the harp admirably. Both at an early age were 'reconciled' to the Catholic church and turned out of their parents' house."

Anne married a certain Roger Lyne, who shared the faith which he had embraced with apostolic fervour and it is probable that his arrest was brought about by the Mass said at their marriage, for both he and Anne's brother when officially examined by

house at the very time Mass was actually beginning; however, as the door was strongly barred and fastened, they were forced to wait some time before they could come in, and in the meantime the priest, Mr. Francis Page, had leisure to unvest himself and make his escape. After they broke in, they searched every corner of the house, and seized upon everything that they imagined to savour of popery, but could find no priest.[7] However, they hurried away Mrs. Lyne to prison, and with her Mrs. Gage (daughter to Baron Copley) whom they found in the house. Mrs. Gage, by the interest of a certain nobleman was, some time after, set at liberty, but Mrs. Lyne was brought upon her trial at the Old Bailey before the Lord Chief Justice Popham. She was carried to her trial in a chair, being at that time so weak and ill that she could not walk. The evidence against her was very slender. One Marriot deposed that he saw a man in her house, dressed in white, who, as he would have it, was certainly a priest. However, any proof, it seems, was strong enough with Mr. Popham against a Papist; and the jury, by him directed, brought in Mrs. Lyne guilty of the indictment, viz., of having harboured and entertained a Seminary priest. According to which verdict, the judge pronounced sentence of death upon the prisoner and sent her back to Newgate

---

Mr. Justice Young were described as "gentlemen under nineteen years." Higham was consigned to Bridewell and placed with vagrants under the lash toiling at the tread-mill. He died as a lay brother at Valladolid, where he went after his sister's execution. Roger Lyne remained long in Newgate refusing the great estate of Ringwood offered by his uncle conditionally upon recantation; he was deported and died in Flanders. His widow, left destitute, was cared for by the family of John Wiseman, whose daughters were Brigitine nuns in Rouen in 1593; she herself from that moment consecrated her life to the service of the oppressed Catholic clergy. On the 30th of January, 1593, she was denounced as being present with Mrs. Shelley at Masses in the Earl of Worcester's house. Stow's *Annals* report "on the last day of February, 1601, Mark Bosworth and T. Silcox priests executed, a gentlewoman a widow Mrs. Anne Liue executed for relieving a priest. Woodhouse, Merricke, Knight and Cuff, gent. were hanged for assisting Essex."

[7]*Memoirs of Mission priests as well secular as regular and of other Catholics of both sexes that have suffered death in England on religious accounts from the year of our Lord 1577 to 1684.*

to prepare herself for execution. When her keeper acquainted her with the death warrant being signed, and when afterwards she was carried out to execution, she showed not the least commotion or change in her countenance. At Tyburn she declared to the standers-by with a loud voice: 'I am sentenced to death for harbouring a Catholic priest, and so far I am from repenting for having so done, that I wish, with all my soul, that where I have entertained one, I could have entertained a thousand' . . .

"The day was so bitterly cold that it seemed, for a time, Anne might 'cheat the gallows.'[8]

"With Anne Lyne perished Mark Barkworth of Lincolnshire.[9] At the foot of the gibbet where Anne had just suffered, the priest embraced her dead body whilst it was still hanging, exclaiming, 'Oh, blessed art thou, Mistress Lyne, who has now happily received thy reward; thou art gone before us, but we shall quickly follow thee to bliss . . .' "

Instead of being set up on London Bridge, according to the

[8]A Catholic bystander bribed the hangman for the sleeve of her gown and a stocking as relics, and noticed that her limbs "were no bigger than the rope about her neck."

[9]An eye-witness to Barkworth's trial at the Old Bailey shows the priest who belonged to the Benedictine Order calmly countering the interrogations of the Bench point for point:

"The clerk bade him hold up his hands:—'For what crime?'—'For the crime of priesthood and treason'—'Can any one maintain that to be a priest is treason? Was not our Saviour a priest according to the Order of Melchisedech?'—'By whom wilt thou be tried?'—'By God and the Saints in Heaven.'—'Not so, you must say, "By God and my country." '—'What, my Lord? These poor men of the Jury? I will never let my blood lie at their door, for you will oblige them to bring in their verdict against me right or wrong, or lay so heavy a fine upon them in the Star Chamber that they will be scarcely able to pay it in their whole lives.'—'I see that thou art a priest.'—'If you can prove it I am a dead man.'—'If thou wilt not confess thyself to be a priest, what art thou?'—'A Catholic, but were I worthy to be a priest I should look upon myself as placed in a dignity not inferior to that of angels, for priests have a power given them of remitting sins in God's name which was never given to angels.' "

With that the company all laughed, and the question was again put to him as before: By whom would he be tried?

When ordered to request trial by the Jury which had been impanelled he answered

common practice, Barkworth's head was bought from the hangman by an agent of the Jesuit Order in England, whose dangerous duty required him to be present at every Catholic execution.

The body of Anne Lyne, acquired by the same method, was carried off by her friends, who, in nocturnal procession, under the dark London skies and falling snow, bore the relics of Anne to an unmarked grave, and the priest's head to the Benedictine convent.

The heroic conduct of these two last victims, who for political reasons figured as participants in the Essex conspiracy, may have suggested Shakespeare's mysterious allegory, "The Phœnix and the Turtle," where the poet appears in 1601 as "chorus to their tragic scene."

"The Phœnix and the Turtle" first appeared in a collection by Robert Chester in 1601, under the following descriptive title:

"Love's Martyr; or Rosalin's Complaint. Allegorically shadowing the truth of Love in the constant Fate of the Phœnix

---

firmly: "My Lord Justice, I do not desire to be judged by these unlearned artisans for I was born a gentleman, bred a scholar and have taken my degrees among the wise."— The Justice sneeringly replied: "Will you call for a Jury of priests?"—"Your Lordship knows that there are double the number required at your bidding in Wisbeach prison." Upon which retort Justice Popham was so angered that without taking any deposition from witnesses, nor even waiting for the verdict, he pronounced sentence for high treason against the prisoner. He received the sentence of death with a joyful and smiling countenance and began a hymn of joy after which, addressing a discourse to the standers-by, he exhorted them to show forth by their works what they confessed in their words, not fearing what the world can do against them since "to die for the cause of justice and truth is a Christian's greatest gain."

He was sent back to Newgate and walked through the streets fettered as he was, with that air of magnanimity that the crowd enquired whether he was not one of the ringleaders of the Earl of Essex's riot: "No," said Mr. Barkworth, "but I am a soldier of Christ who am to die for his faith."

Tradition, as has been said above, always linked "The Phœnix and the Turtle" with an obscure event of the Essex conspiracy, and the crowd's persistent desire to connect the priest's condemnation with the revolt which cost the Ringleader's life may be the justification for the appearance of Mark Barkworth in Shakespeare's allegory.

and the Turtle. A poem enterlaced with much varietie and, raritie; now first translated out of the venerable Italian Tor- quato Cæliano by Robert Chester. With the true legend of famous King Arthur, the last of the nine Worthies, being the first essay of a new British poet; collected out of diverse authen- tical Records. To these are added some new compositions, of several modern writers whose names are subscribed to their several works, upon the first subject: viz., the Phœnix and the Turtle."

The following title prefaces these new compositions:

"Hereafter/ follow diverse/ Poeticall Essaies on the former sub-/ ject; viz. the *Turtle* and *Phœnix. Done by the best and chiefest of our/* moderne writers with their names sub-/ scribed to their particular works:/ *never before extant:/* And (now first) consecrated by them all generally, / *to the love and merit of the* true-noble Knight,/ Sir John Salisburie/ *Dignum laude viram Musa vitat mori.* MDCI."

Sir Israel Gollancz comments thus on Chester's volume:

"The genuineness of the contribution with Shakespeare's name subscribed is now generally admitted, though no suc- cessful attempt has yet been made to explain the allegory, nor is any light thrown upon it by the other poems in the collec- tion; among the contributors, in addition to Shakespeare, were Jonson, Chapman, and Marston. In all probability the occasion and subject of the whole collection, which has so long baffled patient research, will some day be discovered, and Shakespeare's meaning will be clear. It would seem from the title-page that the private family history of Sir John Salisbury ought to yield the necessary clue to the events. There is not much to be said in favour of the view that the Phœnix shadows forth Queen Elizabeth, and the Turtle-dove typifies 'the brilliant but im- petuous, the greatly dowered but rash, the illustrious but unhappy Robert Devereux, Earl of Essex.'[10] On the other hand, the problem is not settled by describing the allegory as 'the delineation of spiritual union,' and refusing to recognise the personal allegory."[11]

Emerson's words,[12] uttered some sixty years ago, may well bear repetition: "I should like to have the Academy of Letters propose a prize for an essay on Shakespeare's poem, 'Let the Bird of Loudest Lay,' and the 'Threnos' with which it closes, the aim of the essay being to explain, by a historical research into the poetic myths and tendencies of the age in which it was written, the frame and allusions of the poem."

> "Now yield your aids . . . light my weaker eye . . .
> That whilst of this same Metaphysical;
> God, man, nor woman, but elir'd of all,
> My labouring thoughts with strained ardour sing,
> My muse may mount with an uncommon wing."

If we would reach a satisfactory solution of the enigma we must proceed according to the maxim of Sherlock Holmes: eliminate the impossible and see what can be done with what is left. One thing seems to me clear enough: each "modern pen" which took up the subject which Robert Chester pretended that he translated from the Italian of Torquato Cæliano followed an individual idea, selecting as prototype of Love and Constancy the special instance which best befitted his particular theme, for though all commentators—including those who have recently taken part in a *Times Literary Supplement* Debate on this subject—seem to think that Shakespeare and Jonson were treating the same episode. I doubt this very much. Jonson's contribution is almost in a comic vein. Nor do I be-

---

[10]Cp. Dr. Grossart's edition of *Love's Martyr* (*New Shak. Soc.* 1878); *vide* also the same scholar's remarks in his privately printed scarce Elizabethan books, *Manchester,* 1880, etc.; cp. Transactions of *New Shak. Soc.*

[11]Cp. Halliwell-Phillipps, *Outlines,* Vol. I, 191.   [12]Preface to *Parnassus,* 1875.

lieve that the dedication to Sir John Salisburie has any direct connection with the subject of the verses. The volume challenges censorship[13] and the address to Sir John may represent a blind.

The tradition that it alludes in some remote manner to the Essex conspiracy, is too persistent not to contain some germs of truth. The only tragic event which I can connect with the name of Salisbury which has not hitherto been examined, is that a Captain Owen Salisbury was killed in defence of Essex's house the day of the revolt. Shakespeare's poem, however, deals with the simultaneous deaths of two persons and there is undoubtedly some Catholic allusion or the words "Requiem" and "Anthem" would not figure nor would the "priest in surplice white" appear:

> "Let the priest in surplice white,
> That defunctive music can,
> Be the death-divining swan
> Lest the requiem lack his rite."

In taking up the short allegorical poem contributed by Shakespeare we shall find that certain symbolic birds representing high and noble beings are summoned to commune after a tragic scene where the emblems of love and constancy have perished. These five characters may each be connected with a historical personage of Shakespeare's world, for although tyrants are warned to keep aloof, the royal Eagle is summoned:

> "From this session interdict
> Every fowl of tyrant wing,
> Save the eagle feathered king:
> Keep the obsequy so strict."

This fits King James, who had pledged himself with Essex that should the revolt place him on the English throne, he

[13]The volume seems never to have been inscribed in the Stationers' Register.

would tolerate the practice of the Catholic religion. A report contained in the State Papers, February 15, 1601, goes so far as to declare that "Essex is in reality a Catholic, but conceals the fact by policy in order to draw both puritans and protestants to take his part," and in confirmation of this theory adds that 35 recusants imprisoned in York rejoiced exceedingly at a report that the Earl's affair was like to prosper. When the sovereign came to the throne without bloodshed two years later Catesby considered King James's promise as still binding and it was the indignation and disappointment among many leading Catholic families when they perceived that the Supremacy Act was still rigorously enforced, which caused the outbreak of the Gunpowder Plot.

The author also makes an exception for another magnate:

> "And thou treble-dated crow
> That thy sable gender makest
> With the breath thou giv'st and takest
> 'Mongst our mourners shalt thou go."

The "treble-dated crow" may well represent the aged John Whitgift, archbishop of Canterbury, whom the Queen playfully called "my little black husband" and whom Richard Topcliff considered a Catholic sympathiser and denounced as such. If the poet merely referred to the old fable mentioned by Pliny, of how the crow was supposed to reproduce his species, there would be no symbolic fitness in the couplet:

> "That thy sable gender makest
> With the breath thou givest and takest"

Whereas the allegorical meaning is evident when we recall that, in the ordination of Deacons, the presiding prelate draws his authority from heaven and transmits it to his clergy which is thus perpetuated by breath from above. We may remember that Whitgift twice befriended Shakespeare and was known as the patron of good-letters, which also constituted a reason for his entrée among the mourners.

The ill-omened screech-owl, warned to remain far away, may be equally well identified with Popham, the "hanging justice." It was he who condemned Anne Lyne and on whom the ladies at Court "turned their backs or stormed at" for having sentenced a gentlewoman to be hanged. The allusion might also apply to Richard Topcliff:

> "But thou shrieking harbinger,
> Foul precursor of the fiend,
> Augur of the fever's end,
> To this troop come thou not near."

In proposing Anne Lyne with her self-imposed vows of chastity, poverty and obedience as the Phœnix, it seems to me that a chaste martyr—a being who leaves no posterity and yet by her death quickens the faith which causes a new martyr to arise—concords with Shakespeare's lines, and also with the tragic scene of her execution.[14]

> "Death is now the Phœnix' nest;
> And the turtle's loyal breast
> To eternity doth rest,
>
> Leaving no posterity:
> 'Twas not their infirmity,
> It was married chastity."

[14]Anne's history shows her as indeed the very emblem of devoted abnegation. Father Garnet's letter sent to Rome with a description of her death makes this portrait of her:

"She was indeed a holy woman, and for the last fourteen years had to bear most patiently the persecution of her former friends, great poverty and extreme sickness, and those who knew her carefully can testify that she lived as though dying daily. She had made a vow of chastity and poverty, and I believe also of obedience although no one was found willing to receive her vows." . . .

The allegorical union between constancy and faith as exemplified by the priest's embrace of Anne Lyne's dead body
may well explain the beautiful and mysterious verses:

> "So they loved, as love in twain
> Had the essence but in one;
> Two distincts, division none:
> Number there in love was slain.
>
> Reason, in itself confounded,
> Saw division grow together
> To themselves yet either neither,
> Simple were so well compounded;
>
> That it cried, 'How true a twain
> Seemeth this concordant one!
> Love hath reason, Reason none,
> If what parts can so remain.'
>
> Whereupon it made this threne
> To the phœnix and the dove,
> Co-supreme and stars of love,
> As chorus to their tragic scene."

Though making no claim to the prize suggested by Ralph
Waldo Emerson, for a "reasonable" solution of this most interesting of Shakespearean enigmas, I do contend that, in the
absence of any hypothesis whatever which fits in with the dates
and historical events, this one should command serious attention.

It is useless to beg the question by suggesting that "perhaps
Shakespeare was not the real author of "The Phœnix and the
Turtle."

No work published under his name carries with it so complete a certificate of authenticity. For the printer's device on

"Love's Martyr" is that of Richard Field, the poet's comrade in Stratford and his first publisher in London. I need hardly repeat that "Venus and Adonis" and "The Rape of Lucrece" were brought out in 1593 and 1594 respectively by this same Richard Field. Both were accompanied by signed and dated epistles inscribing the poet's work to the young Earl of Southampton.

If there was one printer in the world who was fully qualified to know a poem of William Shakespeare when he saw it, that man was Richard Field, the Stratford tanner's son.

CHAPTER ELEVEN

SHAKESPEARE'S OWN COPY
OF HOLINSHED'S "CHRONICLES"

SINCE THE EARLY DAYS, when Langbaine, Rowe, and Malone began seeking the sources of Shakespeare's lyric and dramatic plots in Ovid, Plutarch, Belforest, and Boccaccio, scholars have acknowledged how large a debt the playwright owed to an old British historian, Raphael Holinshed.

Except for the changes rendered necessary when prose is transformed into blank verse, the dramatist's work now and then is almost word for word transcription. Not only does he follow Holinshed's historical facts, he is influenced by the political philosophy of the man who wrote them, and impressed by his literary style. He agrees with the historian's predilections and espouses his political hatreds. It is rare to find such complete acquiescence in another writer's point of view unless there is more than a literary link between the man who wrote and the reader who followed his writings. Shakespeare seems almost to have occupied the position of a disciple towards the sage who penned Britain's history. Without personal admiration to aid his cult, it is hard to suppose that Holinshed's precepts would have been followed so blindly.

Until recently it was impossible to establish whether the young poet could have had individual contact with Ralph Holinshed, or listened as a child to the stories of Macbeth and his wicked Queen, King Lear and his Cordelia, or the trials of

236

Cymbeline and his patient daughter. When W. G. Boswell Stone published his work on Shakespeare's Holinshed he was obliged to confess that nothing is known about the great historian *save what his will reveals;*[1] to this Mr. Allardyce Nicoll added that the family probably came from Cheshire.[2]

Today many things may be contributed to this meagre information, thanks to my discovery at Somerset House not only of William Holinshed's testament, which his son Ralph, as executor, presented for probate (July 5, 1519), but also to that of Robert Burdett of Bromecote to the parents of whom the historian confided, at his death in 1580, all his worldly goods. Thanks also to the efforts of the indefatigable searcher Leslie Hotson it is now definitely established that Raphael Holinshed served as estate manager at Packwood, where dwelt the Christopher Shakespeares, close kin to John the poet's father. Christopher and John shared the same political disfavour and both were denounced, as suspects, to the all-powerful Leicester by the county commissioner, Sir Thomas Lucy, and, later, to the Queen's Privy Council. Packwood was the very centre of what were termed in the papers of those times "obstinate and malitious papists."[3] It is only necessary to read Holinshed's *Chronicles* to realise how his old-fashioned point of view conforms

[1]London, Chatto and Windus, MCMVII.

[2]The text of Ralph Holinshed's will was published by Edmund Malone and recently examined by Leslie Hotson, who gleaned new information through a Chancery suit which shows that he lived near the Christopher Shakespeares and the man he terms "My master Thomas Burdett of Bromecote." Now Robert Burdett's will, made on March 21, 1602, may help to define the place exactly, for he instructs "John Barwell of Seckington Warwickshire, clerk, to sell the Capital Messuage lands, etc., called THE MITH because my debts be greate that I can hardly pay them sodainely and prouide for my children as I would gladly have done."

That the testator's family stood high in several counties for learning and philanthropy is indicated in the Patent Rolls of Edward VI, where a grant to Macclesfield, in the parish of Prestbury of a free grammar school ordains that fourteen of the best townsmen shall be governors and possessors of said school—and among them Hugh Hollynshede. William's testament enlightens us on his religious connection with Norfolk, the birthplace of "Emmot," his first wife and Ralph's mother.

[3]Like John Shakespeare in his spiritual testament, William Holinshed bequeaths

throughout to the Roman tradition. He believed in the old standards, the old nobility, and the old church. He believed in auguries and portents—that when nature was let loose in storms, earthquakes and tempests, her perturbations boded ill to the citizens of the realm where such things happened. He believed that "murder will out" and proves it many times in the course of his *Chronicles,* but, like Shakespeare, he believed also that a sovereign, however wicked, when once duly anointed by proper ecclesiastical authority, might not, without sacrilege, have violent hands laid upon him or her,—in short, it is not exaggerated to declare that most of the moral and political maxims in Shakespeare's historical plays, together with all the descriptions of nature in her relation to man, and the hand she takes in framing what is monstrous, were noted by the historian before they were put into dramatic form by the poet. One example may serve to illustrate hundreds of others.

At the conclusion of the last act in "Henry VI," Part 3, the imprisoned sovereign reproaches his would-be assassin with his physical monstrosity, mystically linked to moral turpitude:

> "The owl shrieked at thy birth, an evil sign,
> The night crow cried, aboding luckless time,
> Dogs howled, and hideous tempests shook down trees!
> The raven rook'd her on the chimney's top,
> And chattering pies in dismal discords sung."

---

his soul to "our Lady St. Mary and all the company of hevyn" and directs "that there shall be song for my sowle four trentalles in the Chapell at the Cleve of the ege above the holinshede" when the work of construction undertaken by the neighbours shall have been completed. A number of small legacies to the service of the high altar in each church where during his career he sojourned any length of time indicates that this William was given to roving about the country, and also lends colour to the most recent findings, which place his son Ralph in the centre of Warwickshire recusancy: Packwood. "I will have a secular prest to syng for my soule in St. Martyn chirche in new Bokynham and for my wif soule my fader soule and my moder soule and all my good frendis Soule and all Xpen Soules the space of half a yere"—a suggestive reminiscence of Ophelia's "God ha mercy on his soul, and on all christian souls I pray God" of the first "Hamlet" quarto.

Then comes the astonishing parallel:

> "Thy mother felt more than a mother's pain,
> And yet brought forth less than a mother's hope;
> To wit an indigest deforméd lump,
> Not like the fruit of such a goodly tree.
> Teeth had'st thou in thy head when thou wast born,
> To signify thou cam'st to bite the world . . ."

The rest is cut short by the assassin's knife and Richard himself takes up the narrative:

> "Indeed 'tis true that Henry told me of,
> For I have often heard my mother say
> I came into the world with my legs forward,
> The midwife wondered, and the women cried . . .
> 'O! Jesus bless us! he is born with teeth!' . . .
>
> Then, since the heavens have shaped my body so,
> Let hell make crook'd my mind to answer it."

In Holinshed, you may read at page 712, Vol. III: "It is for truth reported that the Duchess, his mother, had so great ado in her travail, that she could not be delivered of him uncut; and that he came into the world with the feet forward . . . and, as the fame runneth also, not untoothed. Whether men of hatred report above the truth or else nature changed her course in his beginning, for in the course of his life many things unnaturally committed, so that the full confluence of these qualities, with the defects of favour and amiable proportion gave proof of this rule of physiognomie, 'distortio vultum, sequitur distortio morum.'"

This striking parallel has been noted by many of Shakespeare's editors as proof positive that Shakespeare followed the historian's text very closely in composing "Henry VI," but with what rhythmic genius dull prose has been clarified and vivified when set to the music of his rhythm! Well might jealous rivals curse the facility with which this "upstart crow could bombast out blank verse till he thought himself the only 'Shake-scene' of the country."

When, through an extraordinary series of coincidences, I came to identify a copy of Holinshed's *Chronicles* as the very one used by Shakespeare when composing "Henry VI," I was not surprised to find the passage above quoted marked with a double cross and heavily underscored, and further observed that every passage so designated throughout the same volume leaves its trace on one of Shakespeare's plays of the historical period.

There is more matter for astonishment in the fact that no-body ever appears to have looked into the *second* edition of Holinshed for traces of Shakespeare's ownership. This fact may perhaps be explained, however, when it is remembered that until very recently scholars have always taken for granted that when the dramatist was working up his historical plays he must have gone for exact data to Holinshed's first edition of the *Chronicles of England,* which was published in 1577; consequently, ever since serious study of Shakespeare's sources was instituted by such early commentators as Langbaine, Winstanley, and Rowe, it is this first edition which has been investigated in public and private libraries, but without result. Another reason which kept searchers off the scent was that, among bibliophiles, the *editio princeps* 1577 is technically known as the "Shakespeare Edition."

It is indeed curious that with so many scholars searching far afield to discover the actual source of Shakespeare's historical learning, and combing the collections of Europe for some of the books belonging to the poet's original library, this precious relic was to be seen for the asking so near his familiar haunts, mid-way, that is, from his birthplace in Henley Street and the "prattie house in brick and timber" called New Place where he finished his days, and in close proximity to the Grammar School where, without too much strain on the imagination, we can see old Ralph Holinshed dropping in now and then from Packwood to find out how the neighbouring Stratford youth was learning its history.

However that may be, it is more to the purpose just now to examine this particular volume which had lain so long unnoticed, how its importance was revealed to one so far from the beaten tracks of Shakespearean criticism as myself.

In tracing the circumstances which led up to the discovery, it must be admitted that my wandering in the untrodden ways of research—exemplified in the foregoing chapters—was precisely what brought about the find and leads me to echo the exclamation which Hamlet himself took from Montaigne: "There's a divinity that shapes our ends, rough-hew them as we will."

When J. B. Lippincott decided to bring out an edition of my historical novel in England, the printing of *My Shakespeare, Rise* was entrusted to the Shakespeare Press of Stratford-on-Avon. I already knew Mr. Jaggard through his monumental bibliography, which is so useful to Shakespeare scholars, but had some doubts as to whether he would enjoy printing certain passages in my Shakespeare story which place some of the old Warwickshire families in a not too favourable light. I could not help recalling Sir Walter Scott's prefatory remark in *Kenilworth* that scandal about Queen Elizabeth is not much relished even today. In this I was right. As proof-correction proceeded, Mr. Jaggard checked up severely on certain of my findings and seriously questioned, among other points, whether I did not exaggerate the rôle played by the

Elizabethan censor in Shakespeare's time. What texts had I to prove Edmund Tilney's hostile attitude toward the plays? After quoting Stowe's *London,* I reminded Mr. Jaggard that such a purely historical work as Holinshed's *Chronicles* had been threatened with suppression, if a certain number of pages were not removed. I cited a report of the Queen's Privy Council as evidence. Much interested, Mr. Jaggard replied that he had on hand a copy of this second edition of the *Chronicles* (begun in 1585 and completed in 1587) and that he would check over his two volumes page by page to see what portions the authorities might have found objectionable. I may say at once that they concerned the Earl of Leicester, but this was not the important point his search brought out.—In turning the pages over methodically, he noticed several marginal annotations which led him to surmise that this particular set which had come into his possession nine years before in regular descent from the original owners—all Warwickshire people —had been in Shakespeare's own possession. But I must confess that when, after a thorough examination of the third volume which, without my suggestion, would have continued to lie in oblivion as it had done for the last three hundred years, he told me that certain marginal inscriptions looked like Shakespeare's writing, I was sceptical. It seemed too good to be true, and overmuch luck to come my way. I wired for a photograph of the writing and he at once despatched several amateur prints to Paris. It may well be believed that I lost no time in flying to Stratford to investigate the discovery for myself.

There is nothing particularly significant in the external appearance of the set. The first two volumes bound together in blackish Victorian leather showed nothing of special interest inside or out, but the third tome, inside at least, proved passionately interesting. On the blanks of the index several lines of writing closely resembling Shakespeare's signatures in the formation of each individual letter attracted attention. There were also a quantity of marginal notes in the middle of the volume, six ornamental monograms of the letters "W.S." on the colophon page and a great deal of writing besides. Three distinct hands may be noted. I shall naturally speak only of the writing which resembles that of Shakespeare and undoubtedly is of his period. Together with Doctor G. B. Harrison I went systematically through the volume in London and subsequently had the privilege of studying it for six months under my own roof with the assistance of some of the best experts from the Ecole des Chartes, Bibliothèque Nationale, Archives and Affaires Etrangères. The internal evidence presented by the notes in the section on the reign of Richard II, more eloquent than similarity of handwriting, divulges a secret of Shakespeare's artistic and literary method.

The set can be traced to three successive owners. Since the date of the first ex-libris, Shakespeare's book remained in the region of his home. The first bookplate is that of Sir Francis Skipwith, Baronet,[4] set in handsome Baskerville type, and inscribed as belonging to the family library at Newbold Revel, Warwickshire (near Rugby). Next is that of Harriet third daughter of Gore-Townsend, Esquire, of Honington Hall. This Harriet married Sir Grey Skipwith, born September, 1771. Her lozenge-shaped ex-libris is found between that of Sir Francis and the next owner, Sir Paton d'Estoteville Skipwith, whose elaborate and many-quartered blazon bears the date 1889. When this Sir Paton died a large part of his library

[4]This baronial family traces its genealogy, according to Dugdale, from Robert d'Estoteville, Baron of Cottingham, companion of William the Conqueror. A first connection may be established with the Shakespeares through Sir John Skipwith, who was knighted by Henry the Seventh for services against the rebels in Cornwall, while it may be remembered that the Shakespeare claim to gentility was founded on similar services to the same King.

(which included a fine 1623 original Shakespeare Folio) was sold, and the Holinshed folio was acquired by a well-known Elizabethan scholar, the late Arthur Henry Bullen of Stratford-on-Avon. Bullen died in 1920 and the Holinshed was taken over with other trade assets by Mr. B. H. Newdigate and was sold by him a few years later to the present owner Captain William Jaggard.

Thus, for more than a hundred and fifty years, this book remained close to the poet's birthplace and passed through only six different hands.

Two solutions of the question how and when it left the hands of Shakespeare's immediate heirs and successors may be offered. The poet's last lineal descendant, who became his direct heir, was Elizabeth Hall, only child of his eldest daughter Suzanna. Elizabeth married Thomas Nash and continued to live with her mother at New Place. A complaint, emanating from a Stratford mercer, Baldwin Brooks, dated 1636, may furnish one explanation of how a number of Shakespeare's books left his library, for we may read in the Public Record Office how Brooks, unable to recover from the estate of the late Doctor John Hall, "now deceased nearly two years, though his will hath not yet been proved by Suzanna Hall and Thomas Nash," sues to enter into his credit. He did so by summoning bailiffs to break into New Place, where they seized—as is certified by the counter-suit of Suzanna Hall and her son-in-law Thomas Nash, in the Court of Chancery—books, boxes, desks, monies, and other goods to the value of £1,000. Readers of Dickens are aware that a suit which goes into Chancery rarely or never comes out, so we need not be surprised at remaining in ignorance of the merits of the case undertaken by Shakespeare's daughter to recover some of Shakespeare's books, etc., but the incident may explain how her father's Holinshed first left New Place. Thomas Nash's wife, Elizabeth

Hall, after her husband's death, moved up somewhat in the social scale by marrying the widower Sir John Bernard of Abington, near Northampton. Tradition says that when she left Stratford (June 5, 1647) to finish her days at Abington Manor, she removed a large number of books and papers.

I have been able to gain contact with only one volume belonging to Shakespeare's granddaughter, a Bible of 1599, handsomely bound, interleaved with extra copperplate engravings and presented to Elizabeth by her second husband who inscribed it: "To my dear wife, Elizabeth Bernard, whom God bless." It remained, forgotten and unrecorded after Elizabeth's death, February 17, 1669, and was sold two centuries after as an item in an "extensive library of well-bound books" and has returned to Stratford. What were the others, and what in the interval became of the Holinshed is a mystery, but when examined it yields a key to many hitherto unexplained enigmas.

On opening the third volume one is struck by the excellent condition of the beginning and the end. Should one consult the early Plantagenet or the late Tudor period, the reader's impression might be that the book had seen little service. When, however, it is opened between the reigns of Richard the Second and Henry the Seventh, it is another matter. The text contains numerous marginal annotations and underscored passages. In some cases pointing fingers are used to indicate an important paragraph and practically all these markings occur at points made use of later in one of the dramatist's historical plays.

That the poet leaned often over the volume, dripped a large amount of ink thereon, and fingered the pages which tell of these reigns, is shown by the fact that the lower portions are worn thin by thumbing. This, in itself, is of interest, for it shows constant usage over a period of years and answers a possible hypothesis that a later hand than Shakespeare's might have marked the allusions in order to detect what part of the *Chronicles* the dramatist had "cribbed." Such detective work could have been done in a month or two, without damaging the book. An important indication that these markings were made in Shakespeare's own day is the ink and handwriting. Both are declared by British Museum and Bibliothèque Nationale experts as prior to 1620. When deciphered, letter by letter, thanks to the alphabet supplied by Doctor W. W. Gregg in the volume entitled, *Shakespeare's Hand in the Play of Sir Thomas More,* we are richer by the possession of nearly a hundred words from his pen, and this new treasure trove may naturally lead to the discovery of others.

In going through the volume page by page, a clear impression can be formed as to why the man who studied it made the pen-marks at the places indicated and to what use he converted them. The proof that the author of the dramas himself inscribed these marginals rests on common sense quite as much as on paleography.

There is nothing particularly significant to my eye in the first 200 pages. The reader seems to have paid particular attention to the origin of certain ancient customs and usages both civil and ecclesiastical; the establishment of the Salisbury ritual is indicated as important on page 15 by the marginal note "secundum usum"; the institution of four terms and the founding of Oxford as a seat of learning are also marked. "The King giveth an abbey" refers to one of the rare good acts of William Rufus; Pope Alexander's consent that Henry the Second should annex Ireland to the Plantagenet dominions is underlined as an important fact. The writer notes that, in case of imminent danger of death, baptism might be administered by any person and in any place. The anti-Jewish riots under Richard Cœur-de-Lion and the King's eagerness to obtain money, no matter how, are also underlined. Marginal writing

again occurs between pages 152 and 212: "Twelve men chosen
to see the assizes kept," "a lieutenant appointed to see missa
demeanours punished." The word "Thunder," sweepingly written, refers to an account of a curious perturbation of the atmosphere during which many domestic animals and barn-
yard fowls took to the woods and became wild. I should not
forget to mention that the annotator throughout is interested
in the game-laws and their application and the early use of
the long bow, which Holinshed credits to William the Conqueror.

Not until the reign of Richard the Second is reached does the
annotator seem to have settled down to systematic work with
a view to literary composition in a series of marginal writings
which refer each and all to the period of Wat Tyler's rebellion.
We read *Wate Tiler, the names of the rebells, the wicked deeds
of the rebels. The wickedness of the Northfolke men destroys
all records* . . . etc. (*See Plate IV, at end of volume.*)

At first this caused me perplexity: for, as the dramatist never
made any use of the riot episode in his drama of "Richard the
Second," why did he indicate this period as though he intended
to quote from it? As I read the marked passages, however,
the sphinx spoke. The old black-letter phrases concerning the
"wicked naughtiness" of the Norfolk men yielded up their
secret and divulged the poet's literary method. The words written in Shakespeare's own hand beside the text are: THE LAWES
OF INGLAND SHOULD COME FORTH FROM ONE CREATURE'S MOUTH.
A like phrase is in Shakespeare, to be sure! but *not* in "Richard
the Second." Nor does he apply Wat Tyler's boast, as recorded
by Holinshed, to the disorders created by that famous rebel.
There is more subtlety in Shakespeare's art, enough to keep
commentators and critics guessing for upwards of three centuries. But how simple it looks when, turning to the scenes
of Jack Cade's riots in "Henry the Sixth" (Part Second), we

perceive that what Shakespeare picked out of Holinshed, concerning the Wat Tyler disorders, he has used to vivify and point up, with a touch of greater realism, the mock trial of the schoolmaster caught setting boys' copies, and Jack Cade's successful occupation of London Stone.

The passage marked in Holinshed reads: "What wickedness was it to compel teachers of children in Grammar schools to sware never to instruct any in their art . . . if any man was found with a penner and ink horn at his side such seldom or never escaped with his life."

Shakespeare makes Jack Cade exclaim:

"Thou hast most traitorously corrupted the youth of the realm in erecting a grammar school . . . away with him, I say! Hang him up with his pen and ink-horn about his neck."

("Henry the Sixth," Part Second, Act IV, Sc. VII.)

It is also made plain why on page 432 in the Holinshed Shakespeare had noted Tyler's threat that all law should be abolished and issued thenceforth by his personal decree, for turning to "Henry the Sixth" once again, we find Dick the butcher apostrophising his leader Jack Cade to this effect:

"*Dick:*   I have a suit unto your lordship!
Cade: Be it a lordship, thou shalt have it for that word!
Dick: Only that the laws of England shall come out of your mouth.
Cade: It shall be so. Away! burn all the records of the realm; my mouth shall be the parliament of England."

(Part Second, Act IV, Sc. VII.)

Who but the author of these scenes could have marked the Holinshed passage and taught modern readers that his study of Richard the Second's reign was primarily utilised in building up his "Henry the Sixth"? This does not mean that the historian's picture of England under Richard of Bordeaux was neglected by the dramatist, on the contrary—John of Gaunt's famous tirade against the scandals created by the sovereign's purchase of Papal Bulls "the better to grievously censure" his personal enemies is based on a long passage whose importance is shown by roughly drawn index fingers, and more writing in the margin shows the spread of luxury among the *unlearned* and *ignorant* had brought effeminacy upon the kingdom.

The statement of Henry the Fifth's claim to France proves still more conclusively Shakespeare's debt to the historian:

Holinshed: "*In terram Salicem Mulieres ne succedant*—that is to say, lette not women succeed in the land Salique, which the French glozers expound to be the land of France, and that this law was made by King Pharamond; whereas their own authors affirm, that the land Salique is in Germany between the rivers of Elbe and Sala and that when Charles the Great had overcome the Saxons, he placed there certain Frenchmen, which, having in disdaine the dishonest manners of the Germain Women made a lawe: that no female should succeede to anye inheritance within their lande, which at this day is called Meisen."

and it is amusing to observe how closely the dramatist renders this passage in blank verse at the same time making his argument more clear.

Shakespeare: In terram Salicam mulieres ne succedant,
No woman shall succeed in Salique land:
Which Salique land the French unjustly gloze
To be the realm of France, and Pharamond
The founder of this law and female bar.
Yet their own authors faithfully affirm,
That the land Salique is in Germany,
Between the floods of Sala and the Elbe:

> Where Charles the Great, having subdued the Saxons,
> There left behind and settled certain French,
> Who, holding in disdain the German women,
> For some dishonest manners of their life,
> Established then this law,—to wit no female
> Should be inheritrix in Salique land;
> Which Salike, (as I said) 'twixt Elbe and Sala
> Is, at this day in Germany called Meisen.

Once more a pointing finger, which indicates King Henry's conduct at the siege of Rouen, shows that the author intended to make use of a phrase he had underlined; and, in fact, at page 567, he notes how the "Goddess of battle, called Bellona, had ever, of necessity attending on her, blood, fire, and famine." Need we recall, in the prologue to "Henry the Fifth," the description of the warlike King:

". . . and at his heels, leashed in like hounds, should famine, sword and fire crouch for employment."

Again, writing in the margin indicates a prophecy made by Henry the Fifth and utilised by Shakespeare in the first part of "Henry the Sixth," concerning the ultimate loss of England's French possessions:

> "And now I fear that fatal prophecy
> Which, in the time of Henry, named the Fifth,
> Was in the mouth of every sucking babe,
> That Henry, born at Monmouth, should win all,
> That Henry, born at Windsor, should lose all."
>
> (Act III, Scene 1.)

On page 612 Holinshed, after describing the recapture of Dieppe and Bois-Vincennes, observes:

"So that here partlie was accomplished the prophesie of Henrie the Fift guien out in the ninth yeare of his reigne when he laie at siege before Meaux, that Henrie of Windsor should lose all that Henrie of Monmouth had gotten (for so they are named according to the place of their nativitie) and this prediction was complet and full by that time the yeares of his regiment had expired."

Curiously enough, Boswell-Stone in his conscientious study of Shakespeare's debt to the old chronicler seems to have missed this passage—as I myself would have done perhaps had it not been for the marginal note in the Skipwith volume, and selected, like him, as the source of Shakespeare's lines a previous paragraph on page 581 where this same prophecy was first noticed.[5]

At page 655 a *Bracket* (the first and last time this form of reference is used) indicates a passage on the horrors of civil discord, remarking that these apples are far more bitter than *coloquintida*. Later, Iago will recall the same word, which once and only once is to be found in Shakespeare:

> "The food that to him now is as luscious as locusts,
> Shall be to him shortly as bitter as coloquintida."
>
> ("Othello," Act I, Scene 3.)

Page 714 inaugurates a series of underlinings which refer, not to historical events, but to moral considerations, such as Holinshed loved to scatter through his writings and the dramatist was not averse to picking up. Holinshed dwells on the unwisdom of trusting a new friend made of an old foe. Can we think "that the kindliness contracted in an hour is deeper

[5] "This yeare at Windsore on the date of St Nicholas in December the quene was deliured of a son named Henrie . . . The King being certified hereof, as he laie at siege before Meaux, gaue God thanks . . . But when he heard reported the place of his natiuitie; were it that he warned by some prophesie, or had some foreknowledge, or else judged himselfe of his sonne's fortune, he said unto the Lord Fitz Hugh his trustie chamberlaine these words: "My Lord, Henrie Borne at Monmouth, shall small time reigne, and much get; and Henrie Borne at Windsore, shall long reigne and all loose; but as God will so be it."

settled in their stomachs than long accustomed malice many years rooted," a theme constantly brought out by Shakespeare in dealing with the Duke of Gloucester's dupes and other "fools of time" throughout his works?

At page 721, the historian begins to foreshadow the catastrophe which awaits Lord Stanley and Lord Hastings and the pen of Shakespeare underlines: *"they wist not what they feared nor wherefore . . . men's hearts, by a secret instinct of nature misgive them as the sea, without wind, swelleth of himself sometimes before a tempest."*

Holinshed refers in this passage to the public feeling prevalent in June, 1483. Shakespeare applies it to much later events in "Richard III," Act III, Scene 3.

Three London burghers meet and discuss the news of Edward IV's death, which is not yet generally known.

> "Truly the hearts of men are full of feare:
> You can not reason almost with a man
> That looks not heavily and full of dread."

> "Before the days of change, still is it so:
> By a divine instinct men's minds mistrust
> Pursuing danger; as, by proof, we see
> The water swell before a boisterous storme."

When the historian dwells still further on the occult influences which cast their shadows over coming events, Shakespeare underscores a long passage:

Holinshed: "The self-same night before his death, the Lord Stanley sent requiring him (Hastings) to rise and ride— aware with him he had so fearful a dreame. He thought a boar with his tusks so razed them both by the heads that the blood ran about both their shoulders. . . . Certain it is also, that riding towards London the same morning in which he was beheaded his horse twice or thrice stumbled, which thing, albeit every man wote well, also happeneth to them to whom no such mischance is toward, yet hath it been of an old rite and custom, observed as a token, notably foregoing some great misfortune."

Hastings's lamentation on going to the scaffold recalls both the dream and his horse's premonition of danger.

"I, too fond, might have prevented this,
Stanley did dream, the boar did raise his helm
But I disdained it, and did scorn to fly,
Three times today my foot-cloth horse did stumble
And started when he looked upon the Tower
As loath to bear me to the slaughter-house."

On page 725 there is an underlined passage telling how the king jestingly termed Shore's wife "equal to three concubines as in three divers properties, she diversely excelled, the merriest, wittiest and holiest harlot in the realm."

Is not this the origin of Richard's contemptuous reference to Edward's mistress?

". . . consorted with the harlot-strumpet, Shore."
                              ("Richard III," Act III, Scene 4.)

On page 726 the marginal reference: *Answer of a chaste and continent lady* is heavily underscored as is also the reply of Lady Grey in the text, when courted by the king: *"as she wist herself too simple to be his wife, so thought herself too good to be his concubine."* Out of this short passage Shakespeare has made an entire scene, at which Richard of Gloucester and his brother Clarence look on ironically, it terminates:

Edward: "Sweet widow, by my state I swear to thee
               I speak no more but what my soul intends
               And that is, to enjoy thee for my love."

Lady Grey: "And that is more than I will yield unto:
I know I am too mean to be your queen
And yet too good to be your concubine."
("Henry VI," Part III, Act III, Scene 2.)

Page 728 shows an underlined passage referring to the king's extortions, *"immersements turn to fines, fines to ransomes, ransomes to misprision, misprision into treason."* These words, though not directly quoted, form the *leitmotiv* of Shakespeare's whole play of "Richard the Third" and I need not again cite the striking parallel passages at the conclusion of "Henry VI" already quoted at the beginning of this chapter.

Page 732 contains the extraordinary description of Gloucester's character and his habit of utilising servile flattery and fawning affection to gain his ends. *"A mind which knoweth itself guilty is in a manner dejected and given to servile flattery."* In presenting the Duke of Gloucester, both before and after his coronation, the dramatist never swerves from the psychology traced by the historian,—of Richard's "servile flattery and deep dissembling."

After the reign of Richard the Third no further markings occur on the text except a few scribblings evidently made by a later pen, and which need not concern us here.

But, before taking up the important inscriptions on the index and colophon, I must recall the evidence this volume brings to help settle the disputed authorship of the "Contention" and the "True Tragedy," and also to more full establish that the "Ill May Day" scene in the censored drama of Sir Thomas More is rightly attributed to the Bard of Avon.

Wat Tyler's rebellion, so serviceable to the author of the "Contention between the houses of York and Lancaster," and other mob-scenes whether in "Henry the Sixth," "Julius Cæsar," or "Coriolanus," proved equally useful in the addition to the book of Sir Thomas More known as the *Ill May Day*.

Referring to the rioters in King Richard's time Holinshed indignantly exclaims:

". . . the wretches had utterly forgotten all law, both divine and humane; otherwise they would have been content to live under law and to do unto others as they would be done unto, as the verie lawe of nature (than which there cannot be a better guide) teacheth."

Now Sheriff More, haranguing the multitude in favour of law, order and Christian charity, utilises the Holinshed suggestion in precisely the same manner already noted in the scene between Jack Cade and Dick the butcher, that is: he takes the main thought expressed in a whole paragraph of Holinshed's history and adapts it to brief dialogue.

After More's appeal for the banished strangers "with babies at their backs plodding to the ports," he suggests that if these same Englishmen who are so cruel to foreigners went abroad to Flanders, France and Portingale the tables might be well turned.

What would you think to be thus used? . . .
This is the strangers' case and this your mountainish inhumanity.

Whereupon the crowd moved emotionally exclaims:

"Faith he says true! Let us do as we would be done by."

Miss Agnes Mott, a writer who has specialised upon recusant questions with particular reference to Shakespeare's patron, called attention, in *The Tablet,* to a point in "Henry VI" which, to my knowledge, has not yet been observed, namely: that the scene which amusingly treats of the fraudulent miracle at St. Albans has for its source the direct narration of Sir Thomas More to his son, printed in the *Dialogues* against Tyndale, Chapter 14, and also in Grafton's *Chronicles.*

255

I note with particular interest Shakespeare's use of this episode in "Henry VI" as an indication of his close study of this special reign, again confirmed by the annotations in the Skipwith *Holinshed*. No less illuminating is the attention paid to a document concerning Sir Thomas More. Here is the passage from More's narration touching the beggar who, pretending to have been born blind and to have miraculously recovered his sight, names black as the colour of his interlocutor's gown.

"Anon the beggar told him also the names of all the colours that could be shown. The Duke then bade him walk faytoure and made him to be set suddenly in the stocks for, though he could have seen by miracle the difference between the divers colours, yet could he not by the sight suddenly tell the names of all these colours, but if he had known them before."

Shakespeare uses the incident in a manner which is strikingly analogous.

After making the pretended blind man name the various colours shown, Duke Humphrey recalls More's phrases thus:
"What's thine own name?

"Saunders Simcox, may it please you, master.

"Then, Saunders, sit there, the lyingest knave in Christendom. If thou had'st been born blind, thou might'st as well have known all our names as thus to name the several colours we do wear. Sight may distinguish of colours; but suddenly to nominate them all, it is impossible." . . .

And here I may be permitted to observe that Shakespeare used exactly this method when he borrowed from Montaigne or from Rabelais in the "Tempest," where pages of material are "boiled down" into a few striking lines; but, as I have elsewhere exhaustively studied this question, it may be well to return to the subject of the Holinshed volume.

A blank space to the right of the ornamental device preceding the Index to Volume III contains a curious recipe for a horse's swollen joints. "What a strange thing for Shakespeare to note down," might be the finder's natural exclamation if it did not so pertinently recall the country lad's first employment at the capital. For there is no reason to doubt Sir William d'Avenant's affirmation that on first arriving in London, totally without other funds than could be coined by his fertile brain, he "turned an honest penny by taking care of the gentlemen's mounts who rode to James Burbage's theatre, until his "pleasant wit" obtained him a place among the actors.

"Blacke Soape, pigge meate and honny mingled together, good for a horses legge swollen." (*See Plate IV, at end of volume.*)

So runs the inscription[6] and this rural recipe is still excellent, I am told, for congested horseflesh! The plant referred to as Blacke Soape is the medicinal soap-wort or Pasque flower whose dark purple blossom is reproduced in Gerard's herbal.

"It groweth wild of itself near to rivers and running brooks, in sunny places," and—it may be noted—flourishes particularly in the Midland districts of England. It is true that there is a certain plant called the "field scabious" pictured and described in Edward Hulme's *Familiar Wild Flowers* which, I learn, is sometimes called "black soap" in the South of England, but it seems more probable that Pasque Flower is meant: as for the word "pigge meate" that is certainly good "Warwickshire" language, for it may be remembered that what in our day would be called feed or fodder is set down as horse-meat in Shakespeare's time, and the bran or wash given to the less noble animal is doubtless indicated here rather than flesh which could not be "mingled with honey."

[6]The inscription is, alas! fragmentary for the nineteenth-century binder sacrificed a full inch of the upper margin where supposedly the source of this information was given. Every word would be precious, for these sixty-eight letters are formed in the same manner as the signature of Shakespeare in Florio's Montaigne, which, I agree with Dr. Tannenbaum, is in the same hand as the official signatures. I must add that the whole inscription recalls the More manuscript as much as the marginalia.

On the last index page and written across from end to end is one of the axiomatic phrases of a kind often borrowed by Shakespeare from Florio's *Golden Sayings* at a period when both poet and pedant were under the direct patronage of Lord Southampton.[7]

"As wealth maketh loftie, soe want maketh lowlie."

This truism is accompanied by the enumeration of the four spiritual virtues, so often pictured together in the designs and illuminations of the Renaissance: "Prudence, Justyce, Fortitude and Temperance."

I should like to attribute this inscription to Shakespeare's pen; æsthetically, it is much more beautiful and harmonious than any of his signatures. The lines of the index page have nothing of the cramped appearance of the official autographs, where lack of space produced constraint just as the thickness of the book stiffened the formation of the marginal inscriptions. But experts may debate over pros and cons while we examine the more important colophon page which yields a "whole alms-basket" of words, pen trials or pen play in a moment of idleness by a hand which obviously could not stay quiet when ink and paper lay close by. The name *Rychard* is thrice repeated, *finished in January* many times and in different kinds of script, *Your right Worship, My very goode friend* . . . (*See Plate V, at end of volume.*)

Also five highly ornamental monograms composed with the initials W.S. of a style called in French "Griffe de Notaire" and formed in such a fashion that the pen never leaves the paper until completion but makes the device in one stroke.

The largest of these W.S. monograms is reminiscent in form of the signature in Montaigne, the W tall and slightly inclined,

---

[7]Florio's proverbs which contain "the piths, the proprieties and the purities of a language" are borrowed thirty times and more in the poet's work. (See *Giovanni Florio, apôtre de la Renaissance au temps de Shakespeare,* where this Italian influence is examined.)

but instead of the ornamental dot characteristic of Shakespeare's signatures a tiny minuscule M nestles in the spacious curve of the capital letter, indicating by the terminal the common abbreviated form of the name William (Wm.). Two more *m*s are placed in the design, but as the ink is slightly lighter in tone they may have been added later by the same hand which has already appeared in the volume and may be seen on the colophon in the word *assueredly* placed beside the printer's device.

A fanciful figure also in lighter ink shows two hearts, one upright, the other reversed, cleverly forming the initial *W,* the spaces between the transverse lines are dotted in one case—for it is twice repeated—with tiny *o*s, in the other with hearts, and *might* have stood for the name William Harte set down to amuse this nephew. But we have enough that is solid as evidence to set aside all that is questionable.

This study of Shakespeare's own copy of Holinshed's *Chronicles* has, I hope, already enabled the reader to form a clearer opinion of the dramatist's method of work than was hitherto possible. But it may do much more than that; for, whereas there were no other samples of his handwriting recognised as authentic except the Record Office signature to the lease of the Blackfriars' property preserved at the Guild Hall and the mortgage deed at the British Museum, together with those on the will, we now possess three-score words from the poet's pen, more than sufficient to prove that Mr. Edmund Maunde Thomson, Doctor W. W. Greg, R. W. Chambers and Dover Wilson —not to mention Richard Simpson, who examined the play of "Sir Thomas More" sixty years ago—were right in attributing a large portion of this drama to Shakespeare and in declaring that at least 147 lines were in his own writing.

But I must not quit the subject without myself naming the one weak point in my case and, at the same time, giving the true answer and explanation, for—like many objections certain to be brought up on any debatable point—what first might strike the critic as a flaw in my argument, on looking closer, reinforces my contention that this is the very volume from which Shakespeare took so much historical material.

Why, if the second edition was used to build up the "Richards" and "Henries," do we not find any markings in the first and second volumes of the same set, containing the early chronicles of England and Ireland with the description and history of Scotland annexed thereto?

To this I reply, that it would be ridiculous to suppose that the poet only learned these stories after his flight from Stratford and waited to buy the edition (which was only terminated in 1587) before making acquaintance with the early Chronicles of Britain. For here the old scholars were perfectly right when they called the *Editio Princeps* the "Shakespeare Edition"; the boys at the grammar school could have known only this edition and perhaps Ralph, the author, himself *orally* commented on the volumes roughly illustrated with archaic woodcuts. I may be able to point out the very one Shakespeare read and which remained in his sister's family long after the poet's death and is now in the Folger Library.

It is stained, discoloured, and mutilated—the pages which should deal with Lear are torn from the coverless volume—but index-fingers point not only to the passages in "Cymbeline" and "Macbeth," but also to the old legend of St. Patrick's purgatory, and the stories of Robin Hood and Little John which the poet—man and child—so dearly loved. The stories of Lear and Cymbeline which set his childish imagination alight were stamped indelibly upon his memory, ready to be utilised in later life without book.

As to the second edition which the editors continued so as to include the proclamations and happenings of 1586, that volume could not have been seen or acquired by Shakespeare until after his arrival in London, as the printing was only achieved a year later. Its use between 1587 and 1600 covers precisely the period of composition when the *contention between the houses of York and Lancaster* saw the light, and the play concerning Sir Thomas More was refused by the censor.

The theme of censorship leads me to examine from another point of view the many discrepancies between the edition of 1577 and the one which was afterwards undertaken in a very different spirit by John Harrison, George Bishop, Ralph Newberie, Henry Denham, and Thomas Woodcocke—a group of Puritan printers who had little in common with the original author, apart from a natural desire to make money on their work and his.

It is with the spirit alone that I shall deal for the purely verbal and typographical variants have been so conscientiously studied by Boswell-Stone that little could be added thereto.

Much may be said however upon the attitude adopted by the editors of 1585-87 toward the *Chronicles* as conceived by their original author.

Ralph Holinshed was a true historian in the sense that he did his best to attain impartiality. His personal habit of mind was old-fashioned devotion to the traditions from which the "Merrie England" of his childhood had sprung. Charitable guilds, almsgiving, sports and Maytime festivals formed part of it. His respect for the scholastic training of her universities was unbounded, so that wherever personal predilections peep through his work, Ralph Holinshed appears as a Conservative, and in no way given to the "innovations and new fangles" of Elizabeth's time.

This was not the case with the editors who undertook to reprint the history and "do over" the latter part, by the same occasion. They worked according to the rules of all literary propagandists and time-servers in twisting the facts of history to suit their personal opinions, but without art enough to conceal their bias.

Old Ralph Holinshed boasted that Edmund Campion had contributed his descriptive history of Ireland to the *Chronicles* —a half truth, since it was Walsingham's spy service that seized the manuscript when the priest's baggage was searched in 1570. Holinshed died before Campion's capture and execution, of which a most bloodthirsty and biased account is given by his editors. This was their right, as they were obviously acting under their own responsibility. It is difficult to demand impartiality toward contemporary events from any but very great minds. But it is another and graver matter to re-edit previous work under an author's own name and tamper with it as they did, a fact which the most cursory comparison between the texts reveals. One striking example will suffice to show this "crooked dealing."

The edition of 1577 written by Holinshed himself includes the end of Mary's reign and begins that of Elizabeth with absolutely no personal comment on the essential differences between Henry the Eighth's two daughters. The condemnation of the Oxford martyrs for heresy is set down as a plain fact and, though we may read between the lines where their fine scholarship is described, the author's regret that such men should die for their opinions, there is no criticism of the sentence passed upon them. The last paragraph[8] of Mary Tudor's

---

[8]"Queene Marie seeing no likelyhoode, nor hauing any hope of the restitution of Calays, and considering also, that most of hir affayres had had but hard successe, conceived an inwarde sorrow of mynde, by reason whereof about September nexte she fell sicke of a hote burning Feuer which sickness was common that yeare through all the Realm, and consumed a marueylous number as well Noblemen, as Bishops, Judges, Knightes, Gentlemen, and Rich Farmours but most of the Clargie and other Ancient and Grave Persons. In which while the Queene lay languishing of a long sickenesse and so continued until the rvij of November betweene the houres of fiue or sixe in the morning and then ended hir life in thys world, at hir house of St James besides

reign recounts her illness and death, sums up the political and religious events, then passes straight on to Elizabeth's accession.

Very different is the presentation of these events as shown by the editors of 1587. What Raphael Holinshed expressed soberly in two columns, the new editors spread out over eight pages. The history of the last years of Mary's reign which he made a conscientious effort to recount without fear or favour, they retold in an entirely different spirit. The marginal titles will give an idea of the contents of these interpolated paragraphs. Here are some of them: NOTE THE UNGODLY LIFE OF THESE CATHOLIKES—MORE ENGLISH BLOUD SPILLED IN QUEEN MARIE'S TYME THAN EVERE WAS IN ANNY KINGES REIGNE BEFORE HIR— QUEENE MARIE NEVER HAD GOOD SUCCESS IN ANNYTHING SHE WENT

Westminster when she had raigned fiue yeares, four monethes and eleuen days and in the rliij yeare of hir bodily age.

"The same evening (or as some have witnessed the next day) dyed Cardinall Poole Legate of the Bishop of Rome, lateafore made Archbishop of Canterbury at his house ouer against Westminster called Lambeth.

"This Cardinall was descended of the House of Clarence, that is to say, one of the younger sons of Margaret Countess of Salisbury, daughter of George Duke of Clarence, brother to King Edward the Fourth.

"The death of this sayde Queene made a maruellous alteration in thys realme, namely in the case of Religion which like as by the death of King Edward the Sixte it suffered a change from the establishment of his time: so by the death of thys Queene it returned unto the former Estate again.

"Of such learned men as had written and did live in hir days there were many of whome no small number ended their lyves also during that shorte tyme of hir raigne, some by fire and other in exile. John Rodgers borne in Lancashire, wrote dyuerse Treatises, translated the Byble into English with notes, and published the same under the name of Thomas Mathew: hee suffered in Smythfielde the fourth of Februarie in the yeare 1555: Nicolas Rydley Bishop first of Rochester and after of London, suffred at Oxford in the sayde yeare 1555, Hugh Latimer borne in Leicestershire some time Bishop of Worcester, a notable preacher and a most reuerend father suffred at the same place and in the same day and yeare with Byshoppe Rydley. John Hoper borne in Somersetshire, bishop first of Gloucester, and after of Worcester suffred at Gloucester anno 1555; John Bradford borne in Manchester, a notable towne in Lancashire, a sober, mylde and discreete learnede man, suffered at London, the first of July in the foresaid yeare 1555; Stephen Gardiner, Bishop of Winchester, borne in the towne of St Edmondes Burie in Suffolk of King Henry the Eighths Counsaile and in King Edward's days committed to ward within the Tower, released by Queene Marie, made Lord of Chancelour, and so dyed a stout champion in defense of the Pope's doctrine and a great enimie to the professors of the Gospell: John Philpot borne in Hampshire son to Sir Peter Philpot knycht was archdeacon of Winchester, ending his lyfe by fire

ABOUT— A GOOD KING ALLWAIES MAKETH A FLOURISHING REALM
—QUEENE MARIE PROSPERED AS LONG AS SHE WENT NOT AGAINST
THE LORD—THE ILL LUCK OF QUEENE MARIE IN HER CHILDBIRTH
—Q. MARIE LEFT DESOLATE OF K. PHILLIP HIR HUSBAND—THE ILL
LUCK OF QUEEN MARIE WITH HIR HUSBAND.

All these pages of extra material naturally lead to a new summing up as follows: "Of Queene Elizabeth which now reigneth among us this we must needs saie which we see, that she in sparing the bloud not onelye of God's servants, but also of God's enemies, hath doubled now the reigne of Queene Marie her sister."

in the year aforesaid 1555, vrviij of December going then on the rliiij yeare of his age. Thomas Cranmer in Nottinghamshire Archbishopp of Canterburie a worthy prelate, in sundry virtues right commendable, suffred at Oxford the rrj of Marche 1556, Richard Morrison Knight borne in Oxfordshire, wrote dyuerse treatises and deceased at Strausburge the rvij of March 1556. John Toynet borne in Kent, bishop of Rochester first and after of Winchester deceased likewise at Strasburgh about the tenth or eleventh of August anno 1556. Robert Recorde, a doctor of phisick and an excellent philosopher in arithmetike, astrologie, cosmographie and geometrie most skilful. He was borne in Wales descended of a good family, and finally departed this life in the days of Queene Marie: Bartholomew Traheron, descended of a worshipful house in the West parts of England, dean of Chichester, departed this lyfe in Germany where he liued in exile, about the later end of Queene Maryes raigne. Cuthbert Tunstall, Bishop first in London and after of Durham, borne in Lancashire of a right worshipfull family excellently learned as by his workes it may appear, doctor of both the laws, departed this life in the yeare 1556. Richard Sampson, byshop of Couentry and Lichfielde, wrote certaine Prefaces and departed this lyfe anno 1555. Lucas Sheparde borne in Colchester in Essex, an English poet: Jane Dudley daughter to Henry Gray duke of Suffolke, wrate diuers things highly to hir commendation of whome ye haue hearde more before here in this historie. William Thomas a Welsh man borne of whome ye haue likewise hearde how he suffred for Treason wrote the Hystorie of Italie and other things very elquently. James Brokes a doctor of diunitie, John Standish a doctor likewise of the same profession, greate defenders of the Pope's doctrine as by their workes appeareth, William Peryne a blacke Frier by Profession and a doctor also of diuinitie wrote in defence of the Mass and preached sermons which were prynted of like stuffe: John Baret, borne in Lynne, a doctor of diuinitie and sometime a Carmelite Frier, but rewolted from the Pope's religion became an earnest setter forth of the Gospell, but etc eftsoones hee fell off and returned to hys former opinions nowe in the days of Queene Marie: Henrie, Lord Stafford sonne to Edward Duke of Buckingham, amongst other things which he wrote, he translated a booke out of the latine into English intituled Vtriusq potestatis differentia, that is The difference betwixt the two powers which book (as some thinke) was first compyled and set forth by Edward IV Bishop of Hereford: John Hopkins translated dyururerse Psalms of the Psalter into English meeter which are to be found amongst those apoynted to be sung in churches."

Having frustrated the original author's effort toward a simple exposition of facts, his editors bring the chapter to conclusion with these words in large type:

"Thus farre the troublesome reigne of Queene Marie the First
of that name (God grant she may be the last of
Her religion) eldest daughter to
Henrie the Eight."

The new chapter opens in the same spirit:

"THE PEACEABLE AND PROSPEROUS
Regiment of blessed Queene Elizabeth
Second daughter of Henrie Eight.

"After all the stormie tempestuous and blustering windie weather of Queene Marie was overblowne, the darksome clouds of discontent dispersed, the palpable fogs and mists of most intolerable miserie consumed and the dashing showers of persecution overpast: it pleased God to send England a calme and quiet season, a clear and lovelie sunshine a quitfest from former broiles of a turbulent estate, and a world of blessings by Good Queene Elizabeth. Unto whose gratious reign we are now to make a happie entrance as followeth."

It is at this point and after having offered an absurd stylistic contribution to the original text that Harrison, Bishop, Newberie, Denham, and Woodcocke return and link up their elucubration to Ralph Holinshed's fine prose:

"When true knowledge was had yt Queene Mary was deceased who left hir life in this world rvij day of Novêber as is before mētioned in the latter end of hir hystori in the tyme of hir Parliament, the Lordes that were assembled in the Upper House, being resolved according to the laws of the land, to declare the Lady Elizabeth sister to the said Queene to be the very true and lawful heir to the crown of England sent immediately to the speaker of the Parliament willing him with the knychtes and burgesses of the Neather House without delay to repayre unto them into the Upper House for their assents in a case of great importance who being come thither after silence made (as the manner is) the Archbishop of York Chancellor of England whose name was Nicolas Heth, doctor in divinity stood up and pronounced in effect these words following: . . ."

Then, in ordinary type, comes the usual proclamation of the Sovereign's death and nomination of Elizabeth as lawful successor.

In justice to the original author whose style contributed so much toward forming Shakespeare's prose, and in the name of historical accuracy I call attention to this major difference between the two editions. The article in the National Biographical Dictionary is calculated to lead readers astray in this regard, for in computing the value of Ralph Holinshed's qualities as a historian the writer observes that he shows an *exaggerated Protestant bias*. This bias was none of Ralph's, but this misapprehension leads me to repeat what a former article foreshadowed: that, although the chronicler did his best to attain objectivity, he was in taste, heart and temperament, essentially a man of the old school.

CHAPTER TWELVE

THE NORTHUMBERLAND MANUSCRIPT

AMONG THE PRECIOUS COLLECTIONS inherited from the Percies and preserved at Alnwick Castle there is a manuscript volume whose origin is mysterious. The fact that it figures on the catalogue made by a nineteenth-century librarian as BACON, *A Conference of Pleasure,* offers no clue to the contents.

For many years I have wondered and guessed vainly at the enigma propounded by these pages with which, thanks to an excellent collotype facsimile and type-transcript edited by Frank G. Burgoyne (Longmans, Green, 1914) I have been familiar. However, it has been my rule when possible personally to examine all originals of which I may be led to write and, owing to the courtesy of her Grace the Duchess of Northumberland, I was able, in the spring of 1936, to study the document itself.

How little the public can compute its prime importance may be judged by the fact that Sir Sidney Lee does not speak of it at all, and Sir E. K. Chambers, in Appendix B of his *William Shakespeare,* places it under the heading *Adam Dyrmonth* and yet, when I say that on the tattered index which once served as a cover to several manuscripts, we find quantities of notes, scribblings and pen-trials of precisely the same character and in the same hand as on the colophon page of Shakespeare's Holinshed, it would appear worth critical notice, especially as the poet's name is repeatedly inscribed both abbreviated and in full.

More than this, a glance at the page suffices to convince any one familiar with the Skipwith Holinshed that book and paper belonged to the same man. The three ornamental monograms representing "W.S." on the Northumberland manuscript which

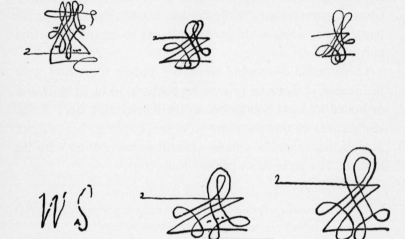

Top Row: Monograms on Holinshed Colophon.
Bottom Row: Monograms on covering page of Northumberland Manuscript.

follow the initials "W.S." plainly written are more individual than a mere signature, and being in two cases identical with two among the six designs of the same letters on the Holinshed colophon page might well indicate Shakespeare as the possessor of both. Happily, however, the monograms do not stand alone, there is a mass of writing on the same page, names, phrases, scraps of verse, and as any inscription which may be attributed to such a pen is interesting in itself, whether or not we can declare just why and wherefore it was set down, I will list all the scribblings. Many were obviously merely trials to see whether the writer's quill worked well or needed trimming, but certain of them clearly refer to his own work. (*See Plate VIII, at end of volume.*)

"Honorificabilitudine," here preserved, is taken up and elongated in "Love's Labour's Lost" becoming "honorificabilitudinitatibus" and we recall how, when poking fun at the pedant for having "stolen scraps from a great feast of languages," Costard marvels that Holofernes has not swallowed the small page, Moth, who would be much easier to mouth than that polysyllable.

There is still a stronger reason to connect the writer with the author of *Lucrece* printed by Richard Field in 1594 and dedicated to Lord Southampton, for the opening lines of the 165th stanza of this poem are set down, but in such a manner as to indicate that the author was still experimenting with his rhymes. The verse in its printed form reads:

> "Revealing day through every cranny spies
> And seems to point her out where she sits weeping;
> To whom she sobbing speaks: O eye of eyes,
> Why pry'st thou through my window? leave thy peeping,
> Mock with thy tickling beam eyes that are sleeping;
> Brand not my forehead with thy piercing light,
> For day hath naught to do what's done by night."

but here, on the Northumberland manuscript, we find:

> "Revealing day through every cranny peeps
> And see . . ."

At this point the line breaks off.

It does not, however, require much art in prosody to divine why the change was made. When the author decided to take as rhymes "weeping," "sleeping" and "peeping" to offset "eyes" and "spies" he could no longer retain "peeps" in the same verse;

an interesting bit of insight into his methods of composition, an indication also of the precise date at which this writing was made, that is to say previous to May 9, 1594.

Let us go farther. Shakespeare's own signature, both abridged and complete, as before remarked, occurs often. The name of "Bacon" is also several times set down but only as author of four articles and an oration, once contained in the folder. The name of "Anthony" and the words "comfort" and "consort" stand out in the beginning.

"Religio fons," "Christ," "as in Christ," "refreshing your-selves," "refusing," "laden with grief and oppression of heart," "your loving friend," "from your service," "more than exter-nally," "many," "and of the hall," "as your," "printed," "others," "yourself among," "divers," "indirectly for profit"—The name of "Anthony Fitzherbert" is noted. This man was a judge who had written wisely on the "Regal Prerogative" under Richard the Second. His grandson, a man of great learn-ing, acted as secretary to Cardinal Allen in Shakespeare's time.

A large space to the left of the index is taken up with the name of the Ambassador to Paris Sir Henry Neville who left his post in time to take part in the Essex conspiracy. Near it figures the play on words which constitutes the surname *ne vile velis* and also a Latin epigram:

> "Multis Annis jam transactis
> Nulla Fides est in pactis
> Mel in ora verba lactis
> Fel in corda fraus in factis."

The importance given to Neville's surname suggests that the contents of the folder were utilised by some one belonging to the Essex faction and this impression is deepened by the fact that the Earl of Arundel's letter to the Queen and *Leycester's Commonwealth* figure in the contents.

Adam is placed rather close to the apparent surname *Dyrmonth,* though I cannot detect connection between the two and the search for a man called Adam Dyrmonth has remained fruitless. One eminent authority digs out a certain Henry Derman or Durman as the possible owner of these papers, but as this personage was not born until 1601 this information appears irrelevant.

What is not at all irrelevant but much to the purpose is the implication revealed by this document that the owner belonged precisely to the recusant world where Neville, Fitzherbert, Arundel were names to conjure with and that this collection as originally listed comprised four manuscripts whose possession could get the owner into serious political trouble or even entail capital punishment.

The index, written on the right-hand side of the cover, reads as follows:

"Mister ffrancis Bacon of tribute or giving what is due.

The praise of the worthiest virtue ⎫
The praise of the worthiest affection ⎪
The praise of the worthiest power ⎬
The praise of the worthiest person ⎭

    Philip against Monsieur—
    Earl of Arundel's letter to the Queen
    Speeches for my Lord of Essex at the Tilt
    Speeches for my Lord of Sussex, Tilt
    Leycester's Commonwealth (Author uncertain)
    Orations at Gray's-Inn Revels by Mr. ffrancis Bacon
    Essays by the same author
    Richard the Second
    Richard the Third
    Asmund and Cornelia
    Ile of Dogs, fragment by Thomas Nash and inferior
      players."

On comparing the original index with the actual contents of the Alnwick collection it will be noticed that four articles by Bacon, not specifically named, are still included:

"Of Magnanimity or heroicall vertue

An advertisement touching private censure

An advertisement touching the controversies of the Church of England

A Letter to a French Gent touching ye procedings in England in ecclesiastical causes.

I take these to be those mentioned under the general heading "Essays by the same Author."

The most striking thing about this list is the fact that four of the items named were highly seditious; two banned plays, "Richard II" and the "Isle of Dogs," one political pamphlet, *Leycester's Commonwealth,* the subversive document *par excellence,* and Philip Arundel's letter to the Queen in which he declares his conversion to Catholicism in 1584, surely not much better!

The hubbub created by the printing of *Leycester's Commonwealth* seems strange to a modern reader, though Queen Elizabeth herself wrote to the magistrates of Cheshire that it was "malitious false and scandalous as none but an incarnate devil could dream to be true . . ." To us these rather boresome pages are but a well reasoned plea for the right of Mary Stuart's son to be declared the legitimate successor of Elizabeth Tudor. As to the revelations about Leycester's private life they were so currently discussed and generally believed that incarnate devils must have been numerous!

Two instances may serve to prove that Shakespeare knew the contents of this seditious document well enough to have borrowed some of its characteristic phrasing both in his dramas and poems. *Quietus* is a peculiar term and probably comes down to us only because the poet used it so effectively. In speaking of temptation towards suicide he makes Hamlet say:

"Who would fardels bear, to grunt and sweat under a weary life
When he himself might his *quietus* make with a bare bodkin."

Again, in Sonnet Number 126 he uses the expression in its standard connection, that of terminating a duly audited account where the words *Quietus est* were commonly placed as endorsement. In speaking of time's conquest over nature, he says:

"Her audit, though delayed, answered must be
And her *quietus* is to render thee."

What suggested this figure? I do not think it was a purely Shakespearean invention, for we may read in *Leycester's Commonwealth,* which was certainly in the author's possession before this Sonnet was composed, that the Queen's favourite is a man "too ambitious suspicious and fearful to allow his particular reckonings to be audited, but would rather stand upon the gross sum and general quietus est by making himself chief auditor and master of all accounts in this life, however he do in the next." Continuing that "he is crafty, subtle to deceive and ingenious to wickedness. As for valour he hath as much as a mouse. His magnanimity is base sordity . . ."

Does it not seem as though Shakespeare had been amused by this phrase and that when composing "Henry IV" he adapted the unexpected epithet of "magnanimous" to the mouse? Falstaff exclaims: "Thou wilt be as valiant as the wrathful dove or most magnanimous mouse!"

General resemblances are equally interesting. One cannot read *Leycester's Commonwealth* without being struck by its influence on Shakespeare's view of certain English kings and their politics. His judgment of Richard III and Richard II seems coloured by this pamphlet quite as much as by the ethical appreciations of Holinshed's *Chronicles.*

To return to the other items on the list which may be classed as subversive: *Sir Philip Sidney's Letter to the Queen,* the copy of which still subsists in the collection, aroused her Majesty's ire though it flattered her too, and caused the writer's banishment from the Court for daring to interfere with the project she so long caressed of marrying the French King's brother. Philip, Earl of Arundel's letter to the Queen was an even less wholesome paper to be found with, for it must be remembered that this great nobleman, who belonged, like Sidney, to the intellectual coterie, had assisted at the famous disputations of Edmund Campion in the Tower and was converted by the priest's eloquence. He openly joined the Church in 1584 to go into voluntary exile with his family; but the Queen's spy services being informed, the boat was stopped and he was sent to the Tower under death sentence. This, the Government dared not carry out and he remained a close prisoner and died in captivity after ten years.

No particular explanation is necessary to show how Shakespeare could have been in possession of his own play "Richard II," for although its performance at the time of the Essex conspiracy caused the death of six men who had "procured it to be acted," it must have been at one time in the author's hands! It was even twice printed in quarto form (1597–98).

It is harder to say why Shakespeare should have handled *Asmund and Cornelia.* For of this work we know absolutely nothing but the title. What became of it? Who wrote it?

Another query opens a wider field for discussion. What was Shakespeare doing with the "Ile of Dogs"? For years no play created so much scandal when first presented. On August 15, 1597, the Privy Council withdrew the licence from the theatre where the "Ile of Dogs" had just been produced and sent Nash, the supposed author, to prison, having advertised Richard Topcliff and four magistrates to this effect, at the same time despatching the incriminating papers which had been seized in the search of the unfortunate actor's lodging:

"Upon information given us of a lewd play that was played in one of the playhouses on the Bankside, containing very seditious and slanderous matter, we caused some of the players to be apprehended and committed to prison, whereof one of them was not only an actor but a maker of the said play . . ."

Nash declared that he himself had written only the "induction" and first act and that then "without my consent or the least guess of my drift, or scope, the players were supplied [with matter] which bred both their trouble and mine too." Nash proceeded to give a full account of this adventure in a pamphlet entitled "Lenten Stuffe" printed in 1599.

"The strange turning of 'The Ile of Dogs' from a comedy to a tragedy two summers past, with the troublesome stir that happened about it, in a general rumour that hath filled all England and such a heavy cross laid upon me as had well near confounded me: I mean not so much in that it sequestered me from my wonted means of maintenance, which is as great a maim to any man's happiness as can be feared from the hands of misery, or the deep pit of despair wherein I was fallen beyond my greatest friend's reach to recover me, but that, in my exile and irksome discontented abandonment, the silliest miller's thumb, or contemptible stickle-back of my enemies, is as busy nibbling about my fame as if I were a dead man thrown among them to feed upon."

Mr. Burgoyne is undoubtedly correct in supposing that Nash's above reference to hostile criticism alludes to Gabriel Harvey's *Trimming of Thomas Nash* (1597), when the pamphleteer exclaimed:

"I cannot but account thee a dog and chide and rate thee."

From these problems we may pass to simpler questions in

examining the other manuscripts listed on the index with the dates on which they were written or appeared in print. It may be noted that all were composed with the same general purpose; to be spoken at revels or masks of an official character. Bacon's *Oration at the Gray's Inn Revels* is known to have been pronounced for the Holiday Celebrations of 1594, but is no longer among the contents; the same is true of the Earl of Essex's *Speech at Ye Tilt. Of Tribute* was written for the Queen's birthday in 1592; the *Speeches* of the *Hermit,* the *Soldier,* the *Secretary* and the *Squire* were spoken in a Mask performed to honor the Queen in 1595[1] and the Earl of Sussex's *Speech at Ye Tilt* belonged to 1596 and was spoken by the youthful Robert Ratcliffe to excuse the absence of Sussex.

I have already observed that the so-called Northumberland Manuscript was certainly a document belonging to a person or persons in close touch with the Essex faction. An unexpected confirmation of this theory has recently come to me. By a curious stroke of luck I have been brought into touch with a folio volume collected and bound up under date Die Veneris Julii primo 1601, by Richard Greene, who was confidential messenger to the Earl of Essex and is mentioned by him in several despatches.

---

[1] A contemporary account in which "My Lord of Essex's device is much commended in his late triumphs" is given in the correspondence of Roland White to Sir Robert Sidney, telling how, when the Earl came, he was met by an old hermit who presented him with a book of meditations, a Secretary of State who brought political discourses, a Soldier who spoke of brave fought battles and the fourth his own attendant. Each naturally attempted to induce him to follow the course recommended by each, and with much flourish of style, but the esquire countered the other three in plain English, saying that his knight "would never forsake his mistress's love whose Virtue made all his thoughts divine, whose Wisdom taught him all true policy, whose Beauty and Worth were at all times able to make him fit to command armies."

We learn also that Toby Mathew acted the squire's part, that the man who played "Pedantiq" at Cambridge was the soldier, Morley the secretary and the hermit the actor who played Giraldy at Cambridge. What a pity, by the way, that he did not give the names of these three players!

Among the forty-three articles therein contained there are two of the lost items of the Northumberland Manuscript, *i.e.*:

A speech at ye Tilt by the Earl of Essex (two pages).

The coppie of Ye Earle of Arundel his letter to the Queen (eight pages).

Thus, at least one precise point may be established in this mysterious case. All these copies were made in the last portion of the sixteenth century by a man working among the Essex faction.

This is easy enough to explain, for Anthony Bacon served the Earl of Essex in the heyday of his success from 1590 to 1597, in the capacity which today would be called under-secretary for Foreign Affairs, and being in those days extremely close to his brother Francis, he naturally made considerable use of the attorney's special knowledge. Mr. Spedding declares that most of the political correspondence received in Anthony Bacon's office passed through his brother Francis' hands before reaching the Earl, and explains that the brothers set up a sort of literary workshop where interesting political documents were copied by hired clerks. Reference to this bureau is frequently made in the correspondence of both brothers. On January 25, 1594, Francis wrote to Anthony: "I have here an idle pen or two—I pray you send me somewhat else for them to write out," and we know that the author of the *Essays* borrowed Richard Topcliff's printed volume of Southwell's *Humble Supplication to Her Majesty* in order to have a transcript made. Another allusion to the clerks who were regularly employed may be found in a letter written by attorney Bacon to Sir Toby Mathew: "My labours are now set to have those works which I had formerly published well translated into Latin by the help of some good pens who forsake me not." We may learn who held one of these pens on the authority of Archbishop Tenison, who declared that "Mr. Benjamin Jonson, that learned and judicious poet and some others I cannot now recall" translated Bacon's *Essays* into the classic tongue.

The suggestion that William Shakespeare might have had an entry to this workshop directed by Anthony Bacon, even more naturally than Ben Jonson, through the protection he enjoyed between 1590 and 1597 from Southampton and Essex himself, is reasonable; and, although we know only the Northumberland manuscript which was analysed so thoroughly by Mr. Spedding in 1860 with a view to proof that Francis Bacon was the real author of Shakespeare's work, the testimony it brings leads to a quite different conclusion. Shakespeare *may* have been hired to write for the attorney's brother Anthony, while both were under the Earl of Essex's direct patronage, but that Francis Bacon worked to establish Shakespeare's glory by composing the works ascribed to the poet does not follow. Quite the contrary!

Even accepting, for the sake of discussion, the idea that the attorney had adopted the name William Shakespeare as a nom de plume, and had arranged the line from "Lucrece" so that it can be made to read *See Bacon,* why is this writing not in Bacon's hand?

The very title, *Mr. ffrancis Bacon   On Tribute or Giving what is dew* is the negation that the author himself set down this text, nor can the obvious signification of this title be twisted into meaning: Give Mr. Francis Bacon his due . . . see Shakespeare" as certain writers argue.

This essay, however, does furnish an interesting link with Shakespeare's *Holinshed.*

In the article on *Tribute,* we are immediately struck with the opening phrase: "My praise shall be dedicated to the noblest of virtues: Prudence to discerne between good and euill, Justice to stand indifferent betweene self loue and Societie, Temperance to deside aright betweene desire and reason. But the vertue of action the vertue of resolucion the vertue of effect is ffortitude . . ." (*See Plate IX, at end of volume.*)

It may be remembered that one of the largest marginal inscriptions noted on the last index page of Shakespeare's *Holinshed* consists in a moral aphorism accompanied by the words:

"Prudence Justice Fortitude and Temperance," as though the reader's attention had just been particularly called to the juxtaposition of these virtues.

It seems strange indeed that I should be the first person to examine seriously into these papers from a new point of view; probably, without the Holinshed, I should never have presumed to do so. That critics on the Shakespearean side of the debate should have neglected the Northumberland manuscript is natural enough. Like many another interesting document, we owe its rediscovery entirely to such partisans of the Baconian theory of authorship as Mr. James Spedding and Sir Edwin Durning-Lawrence, who invoke it as a conclusive proof that Sir Francis Bacon was the real author of Shakespeare's plays. Others in the same camp wrote with so much assurance on this point that the adverse side, who knew little of the matter except what these scholars told them, hesitated to take up arms. Were they not led to believe, by implication, that the scribblings on the index page were in Bacon's hand, though this was never affirmed directly? The Northumberland manuscript was confidently declared to be a portfolio[2] owned by Francis Bacon. This, I believe, has been shown in the above study to be an erroneous conclusion and if my work can bring further light on this mysterious collection I feel certain that it will afford fresh proof of the traditional authorship of Shakespeare of Stratford.

[2] As a matter of fact it is not a portfolio but merely a rejected first draft of the title page to the Essay on tribute which is found repeated but written fair on the next page. The transcriber, dissatisfied with his first attempt, evidently kept it for a scribbling page and general memorandum.

CHAPTER THIRTEEN

THE BOOK OF SIR THOMAS MORE

IT MIGHT SEEM PRESUMPTUOUS for me to reopen the question of the extent of Shakespeare's collaboration in the play of "Sir Thomas More," were it not that the discovery of the dramatist's own copy of Holinshed gives me standards of comparison which were not possessed when the text received such scholarly examination from the leading authorities of Great Britain and the United States. I might still hesitate to add my word to theirs were it not that this new light tends to reconcile all theories.

Doctor Tannenbaum, who fails to recognise Shakespeare's penmanship in the "Ill May Day" scene, now generally attributed to him, declares that the Montaigne autograph is characteristic of all Shakespeare's signatures. This should lead to his acceptance of the Holinshed marginalia as belonging to the same hand and consequently to the acknowledgment that these writings supply the link hitherto missing between Shakespeare's early script, the three pages of "Sir Thomas More" and the official signatures which all belong to the latter years of his life.

In the preceding chapter I pointed out that the passage in Holinshed concerning the mob, telling how the wretches had forgotten all law, order and the golden rule, was carefully marked. The fact that it was utilised to such good advantage in building up the dialogue of the "Ill May Day" is another point in favour of the evidence already brought forward concerning Shakespeare's connection with the censored play.

The book of Sir Thomas More, to use the old English form of the original title, lay for some three centuries in the Harleian collection among papers which the Elizabethan censor, Edmund Tilney, refused to authorise for production and is now exhibited in the Manuscript Room of the British Museum.

The Censor's reasons for refusal are obvious: praise of the great English Chancellor executed for upholding the integrity of his faith could hardly have been pleasing to Henry VIII's daughter, and the representation of a bread-riot in London during hard times seemed a dangerous subject for stage presentation. At any rate we find the Censor scribbling on the flyleaf:

"Leave out insurrection and cause thereof, at your own perills."

A few efforts were ineffectually made to "tone down" the objectionable passages, but it was the subject itself which would not be tolerated in officialdom and the drama was eventually consigned to oblivion.

There it remained until 1844, when Alexander Dyce, one of Shakespeare's most conscientious editors, went through this section of manuscripts and, being thoroughly conversant with the penmanship of the Stratford signatures, observed that part of a scene in "Sir Thomas More" (the one which describes the May Day riot) was, to his eye, in the same handwriting.

Such an announcement hardly caused a ripple of curiosity in those pre-Baconian days. Shakespeare had written so many "Comedies, Histories, and Tragedies" published over his own name that it seemed superfluous to dig up one more detached scene merely because it was "authentic handmade."

So the manuscript, after being carefully transcribed by Dyce, was shelved for thirty-seven more years, at the end of which period it was again examined by an eminent man of letters, Richard Simpson, and again pronounced genuine. Simpson, however, was an ardent Catholic, and inclined to believe that Shakespeare's sympathies lay with the religious party for which Sir Thomas More died and to which Lord Southampton, Shakespeare's declared patron, belonged. His article "Are There Any Extant Manuscripts in Shakespeare's Handwriting?" revived discussion of the categorical declaration made by Shakespeare's first biographer: "He dyed a Papist," and as this theme has always been unpopular, it soon ended, and the document was once more laid to sleep.

Official silence however has now been brought to an end. In view of the attempts to prove that the "Stratfordian" was nothing but a clown or an almost illiterate pawn-broker whose alleged work was done by Bacon, Lord Derby, Lord Rutland or Edward Vere, Earl of Oxford—what a clever pawn-broker he must have been, by the way, to keep these noble noses so constantly on the grindstone for the glory of Shakespeare of Stratford—it was decided that the time had come to have these old papers scientifically and authoritatively investigated. The manuscript was accordingly turned over to the leading experts in different lines of research and submitted to close scrutiny from five different view-points: geographical, historical, literary, philological and philosophic.

Sir Edmund Maunde-Thompson furnished a complete study of the handwriting with facsimiles. He has shown that the capital and small letters which are common to the 147 lines of text and to the Shakespeare signatures in will and leases, are formed in a like manner, and that the peculiarity of Shakespeare's writing is recalled in the sharply accused personality observed in the penmanship of the "May-day" scene. In short Mr. Pollard, Doctor Greg, R. W. Chambers, and Mr. Dover Wilson agree with the expert graphologist and their precursors of fifty and seventy years ago, in declaring that William Shakespeare of Stratford was unquestionably the writer and composer of the text investigated. (*See Plate X, at end of volume.*)

The scene bears the marks of rapid impromptu writing; the few corrections and crossings out are done *currente calamo* and the appearance of the MSS. concords with the description given by Shakespeare's fellow actors of the original "copy" furnished them by the poet.[1]

According to the custom prevalent about 1590, the play was a patchwork collaboration entrusted by the theatrical manager to professional "hack-writers" wherein each author treated the portion best fitted to his special aptitudes. The four other handwritings have been identified as belonging to the Censor himself, to Anthony Munday ("the best constructor of plots" according to Francis Meres), Thomas Dekker and Thomas Heywood. These latter were lifelong admirers of Shakespeare, acknowledged by Heywood as their artistic superior. There is good reason to suppose that they were several times associated in collaboration of this kind before Shakespeare's name was known in the foremost rank, for we find them bracketed together by John Webster, who speaks of "The right happy and copious industry of M. Shakespeare, M. Decker and M. Heywood, wishing that what I write may be read by their light."

Heywood, speaking of his translation of *Helen and Paris* having been mistakenly attributed to Shakespeare, says, "Acknowledge my lines unworthy of his patronage." Later, in an amusing review of the authors who never succeeded in being known, except by their nicknames, he includes Shakespeare with the best:

> "Marlowe, renowned by his rare art and wit,
> Could ne'er attain beyond the name of *Kit;*

[1] "His mind and hand went together; and what he thought he uttered with that easiness that we have scarce received from him a blot on his papers."

Mellifluous Shakespeare, whose enchanting quill
Commanded mirth or passion, was but *Will;*
And famous Jonson, though his learned pen
Was dipped in Castaly, is still but *Ben."*

However this may be, the most difficult scene in the play was
given to Shakespeare, who was obliged to show the citizens'
legitimate grievances, their unreasonable violence and the
oratorical talent of More, who, at the psychological moment,
turned the crowd from their sanguinary purpose, and became
an impassioned advocate with the King for the ringleader's
pardon. Shakespeare, it should be remembered, had already
succeeded in putting immense life and vigour into the Jack
Cade riot scenes in "Henry VI,"[2] which his company had
newly furbished up to the delight of play-goers. We shall see
presently how he again used similar material in "Julius Cæsar"
and "Coriolanus."

But before arguing along these lines it is necessary to establish once for all that it was actually Shakespeare's Company—
Lord Strange's men—that had the hardihood to submit such a
subversive drama as "Sir Thomas More" to the authorities.
This can be done with evidence furnished by the text itself; for
the stage directions read: "Enter T. Goddall, as a messenger"
and the records show that the comedian of this name belonged
like Shakespeare to *Lord Strange's troupe,* where our dramatist,
according to the expression of a jealous rival, worked as "an
absolute Johannes Factotum."

Let us glance over the "Ill May Day" scene, a miniature drama
in itself, with the militant "Doll" as heroine, John Lincoln, a
modest man of the people as hero and victim. Both are con-

---

[2]"A book intituled the firste parte of the Contention of the two famous houses of
York and Lancaster" was thus inscribed March 12, 1593, on the Stationers' Register
and published in the same year. It became the second part of "Henry VI" in the folio
of 1623.

vinced that the high cost of living is due to French and Flemish skilled labour and believe that if they do not wish to "see butter at eleven pence a pound they must cut foreign throats or at least force all aliens back across the Channel."

It is interesting to note here that, just as the "Roman Populace" desires Coriolanus' exile in order to "buy corn at their own price," so, in this drama, Doll and Lincoln decide to chase the foreigners home in order to prevent living expenses in London from going higher.

The difficult episode is treated by the young playwright with consummate art. The spectator's sympathies are first captured by Doll and her army only to be swayed back, like the mob itself, by the eloquent pleading of Sheriff More. It is the attitude found elsewhere in Shakespeare towards mob-rule: humorous comprehension and sympathy for the honest workingman, horror and detestation of tyrannical brute force.

Sir Thomas More's speech begins: "Friends Masters Countrymen." Is it not significant how close this comes to the famous opening of Mark Antony's oration? The interruptions of the rioters are identical with the shouts of the populace against Brutus and Coriolanus and the whole passage abounds with parallels in style and structure with the celebrated Roman dramas.

More's harangue leads through the same reasoning to a conclusion identical with that of Coriolanus expressed in the same half line: "Would feed on one another"; although one orator is represented as loving the people whom he deems "misguided," the other as openly despising them.

More: "Alas, poor things, what is it you have got,
        Although we grant you get the thing you seek!"
Citizen: "Marry, the removing of the strangers which cannot
        choose but
        Much advantage the poor handycrafts of the city!"

More: "Grant them removed and grant that this your noise
Had chid down all the majesty of England,
Imagine that you see the wretched strangers
Their babies at their backs, with their poor luggage
Plodding to th' ports with costs of transportation
And that you sit as kings in your desires
Authority quite silenced by your brawl
And you in ruff of your opinion clothed
What had you got? I'll tell you! You had taught
How insolence and strong hand should prevail,
How order should be quelled, and by this pattern,
Not one of you should live an aged man.
For other ruffians as their fancies wrought
With self-same hand self-reasons and self-right
Would shark on you, and men like rav'nous fishes
Would feed on one another."[3]

Let us look a little farther:

"You shall perceive how horrible a shape
Your innovation bears, first 'tis a sin
Which th' apostle did forwarn us of
Urging obedience to authority
And 'twere no error if I told you all
You were in arms 'gainst God
In doing this. Oh, desperate as you are!—
Wash your foul minds with tears and those same hands
That you like rebels lift against the peace
Lift up for peace, and your unreverent knees
Make them your feet to kneel to be forgiven!—
You'll put down strangers, kill them, cut their throats
Possess their houses and lead the majesty of law in lien
To slip him like a hound . . ."

---

[3]Coriolanus, after insulting the crowd as "disentious rogues" who dare have an opinion of their own, on public matters, and who, like the sick are always craving what would do them most harm, concludes that without the senate which keeps them in awe they all "would feed on one another."

This metaphor of the hound which is suddenly let slip and cheered on its prey, appears again in Coriolanus where Titus Lartius is described as holding Corioli until the word "Rome" is given:

> "Even as a fawning greyhound, in a leash
> To let him slip at will . . ."

Verbal concordances between these lines and the well known dramas are striking. Who but Shakespeare would use such an expression as *self-reason and self-right,* would couple the epithet *stale* with *custom,* speak of *unreverent knees,* call suffering *sufferance* as he does elsewhere twenty-six times, or make a verb out of the noun *shark,* a daring usage which is repeated in "Hamlet"? Can we read More's description of the insolence of success:

> "And you in ruff of your opinion clothed"—

without being reminded of Hamlet:

> "Dressed in a little brief authority"—

Shakespeare's influence on the composition of the play does not cease, to my mind, with the "Ill May Day" scene. His thought and style can be detected in many passages set down by his fellow-workers. There is nothing astonishing in this; Heywood as we have seen publicly acknowledged the immense superiority of Will's talents over his own.

Rhymed couplets are interspersed with blank-verse in liberal proportion characteristic of the poet's early manner, and a scene concludes with a stanza where More laments Lincoln's untimely death in a way which is almost worthy of Portia, regretting that such a monstrous affront to the majesty of law should have shaken Justice and Mercy out of their accustomed serenity to wreak swift chastisement.

"Oh, God, that Mercy, whose majestic brow
Should be unwrinkled, and that awful Justice
Which looketh through a veil of sufferance
Upon the frailty of the multitude
Should, with the clamors of outrageous wrongs
Be stirred and wakened thus to punishment."

Certain commentators, surprised at Shakespeare's unusual verb "to jet" which he uses for "treat insolently" in "Cymbeline" and "Titus Andronicus," have been moved to declare the expression a probable misprint. Here we find the term repeated and the meaning confirmed. Lincoln declares:

"It is hard that Englishmen's patience must be jetted on by strangers."

And we read in "Andronicus":

"How dangerous
It is to jet upon a prince's right."

There is no trait more distinctive of Shakespeare's style than his use—almost an abuse—of the proverbial aphorism or popular saying. All his early comedies bristle with truisms original and borrowed, domestic and foreign. More than thirty are taken from John Florio's *First Fruits* and *Second Fruits* where the author declares:

"Proverbs are the pith, the proprieties, the purities, the elegancies—as the commonest, so the commendablest phrases of a language; to use them is a grace, to understand them a good."

Shakespeare undoubtedly shared this opinion. Numberless references to the wisdom and force of such epigrams are to be observed in his entire work.

" 'Fast bind, fast find,'
A proverb never stale in thrifty mind."
"Like the poor cat in the adage."

288

"I am proverb'd with a grandsire's phrase."
"They sighed forth proverbs."
"Any such proverb so little kind to the purpose."
"I will cap that proverb with 'There's flattery in friendship.' "
"Thereof comes the proverb, 'Blessing on your heart, you brew good
    ale.' "

A score of like utterances might lead to this legitimate conclusion: If Shakespeare had a principal hand in the play
wherein one scene is written by his own pen, the whole, like his
other work, should contain reference to proverbs in general
and several particular examples of them, and, as a matter of
fact neither reference nor example is lacking.

When John Lincoln, the leader of the riot, is about to die
we find him exclaiming:

> "This the old proverb now complete doth make,
>   That Lincoln should be hanged for London's sake."

The clown gets off an English version of *"C'est le premier
pas qui coûte"*—"The first stretch is the worst, methinks." The
Earl of Surrey, speaking of a Frenchman who, after luring away
a London goldsmith's wife, sends her husband a bill for her
board and lodging, remarks ironically:

> "He's ill bested that lends a well-paced horse
>   Unto a man that will not find him meat."

More declares when he is made Chancellor:

> "I now must sleep in court, sound sleep forbear,
>   The chamberlain to state is public care."

and he terminates the passage leading to the dénouement with
the following reflection:

> "My lord, farewell, new days beget new tides,
>   Life turns 'bout fate, then to the grave it slides."

As for Doll, when the poor girl's turn comes to mount the scaffold, she attempts to comfort her husband with the assurance that in paying God the debt which they owe him, all earthly debts will be acquitted. Now this thought figures in Florio's *Golden Sayings* and Shakespeare also makes use of it again in "Henry IV" when Feeble the Tailor, who has been pressed into military service, cries:

"I care not! A man can die but once—we all owe God a death and he that dies this year is quit for the next."

Thus these ninety pages are found to contain half a dozen epigrammatic sayings and one which is borrowed from Florio's collections, just the proportion we would have expected to find in an authentic Shakespearean work.

What date should be ascribed to this drama? Ought we to agree with Professor Pollard and his collaborators that the *Ill May Day* scene was written prior to 1594, with Doctor Tannenbaum, who considers that the true date is 1596, or rather with Doctor Harrison and Mr. D. C. Collins, who bring weighty evidence to prove that the play, like "Richard II," formed part of the political propaganda in favour of the Earl of Essex and was suppressed by the Censor on this account? In view of the new evidence brought forward in the foregoing pages this last hypothesis appears the most reasonable.

CHAPTER FOURTEEN

SHAKESPEARE'S WILL:
NEW STUDY AND AN OLD CONCLUSION

CONTRADICTORY OPINIONS about Shakespeare's Will have been so heatedly discussed since the document was found with its three pages in old English writing, tagged together with a strip of gummed paper, that it might seem well to restate the problem, sum up the arguments which have been made for and against, and arrive at a definite conclusion. In the course of this study many Shakespearean scholars will be found in error and I think no shame to count myself among them for sincerity is always excusable. The only grave reproach that can be addressed to a zealous student is to still claim to be right when he has been proved wrong.

The discovery of the Will was made by Joseph Greene in 1747. The text was printed in the *Biographica Britannica* and later one of the greatest Shakespearean scholars, Edmund Malone, studied the matter and reached a conclusion which is given in his edition of the Poet's works printed in 1790. This conclusion is that the three pages signed "By me William Shakespeare" and endorsed on the first and second leaves with an abridged signature was drawn up by Francis Collins, a Warwickshire lawyer who was born at Stratford and returned there to finish his days.

Malone gives no reason for his statement and the discrepancy between the writing of the Old English text and the fine Italian hand shown in the signature of Francis Collins as first witness to the Will renders the face value of his conclusion questionable.

Nevertheless, for two hundred years his dictum was not controverted. In May, 1882, however, the Athenæum brought out an article by John Cordy Jeffrieson arguing that Shakespeare's Will was a holograph testament after which a long debate ensued.

Meantime the Will of Francis Collins was discovered and declared also to have been written throughout by the lawyer himself.[1] This considerably muddled the question for the writing of this document shows little resemblance to that of Shakespeare's testament.

Sir Sidney Lee still maintained with Malone that Francis Collins was the draftsman in spite of the discrepancy between "Fra. Collins" written in sloping Italian hand and the same name as it appears in Old English script on the last page of the Will:

"I do intreat and appoint the said Thomas Russell and Ffrancis Collins to be overseers hereof."

Sir E. K. Chambers, reluctant to scrap the old theory *in toto,* advanced that the Will text must have been written by Francis Collins' clerk, and further complicated investigations by declaring that the Will of John Combe, which he asserted that Collins made, is catalogued at Somerset House, Wood, 118; whereas in reality it is Rudd 118; this, though it seems a minor detail, represents a day's work lost for the searcher.

But the major objection is that we have no reason to suppose that Francis Collins ever employed a clerk.

Finding myself thus stranded between Malone's statement and Sir E. K. Chambers' theory of an hypothetical clerk, I decided to reopen the case for myself and confess that the

---

[1]Collins' Will (P. C. C. Weldon 101) is dated Sept. 20, 1617. He was buried at Stratford on Sept. 27, 1617.

first dissenting voice raised against Malone's conclusion appeared seductive; even more so when the authorities at Somerset House declared that the so-called holograph testament of Francis Collins was an undoubted copy and presented, as their only sample of the Warwickshire lawyer's handwriting, the draft will of John Combe above referred to and which, to my mind, shows considerable difference from the text of Shakespeare's Will.

At this stage I returned with increased respect to the Athenæum and followed step by step the debate opened fifty years ago.

Mr. John Cordy Jeffrieson develops the theory that *instead of being intended for the will itself, the writing was meant as a rough sketch for the instruction of a competent draughtsman, and that the emergency of illness obliged Shakespeare to sign it before there was time to have it properly set forth* and that it bears enough evidence, external and internal, to prove that the document was written throughout by Shakespeare himself.

Would it be possible, he argues, for a man who was so keen to build up an estate and found a county family, a man who loved outward display as only an actor can, to consecrate this heritage by a slovenly scrap of paper?[2] Would not the omissions, erasures, confusion of terms and un-clerkly blunders, excusable in a minute will, be unpardonable if drawn by a professional? Mr. Jeffrieson observes that before instructing a lawyer to draw up an instrument in proper form, any client would naturally furnish him with a tentative project. He adds that no lawyer would have thought of dating[3] a draft will, but

[2]An attested copy of Shakespeare's will which is also at Somerset House is beautifully engrossed on parchment.

[3]This date is written in combined script, arabic and roman numerals thus: Vicesimo Quinto Die Januarii Anno Regni Dn nri Jacobi nunc RG Anglii &c Decimo quarto & Scotie XLIX° Annoque Dni 1616; it may be translated thus: Twenty-fifth day of January in the fourteenth year of our Sovereign James now King of Scotland and in the year of our Lord 1616.

would have left a blank space for the date until the time of signature.

Mr. Jeffrieson further points out that the difference in penmanship noticed between the body of the text, interlineations and signatures, is only such as is natural. The writing, set down in January, was strong, free and rapid. The alterations made later, including the substitution of *March 25th* for the January date, were inscribed laboriously as though the hand were enfeebled by two months' illness.

To these seemingly reasonable arguments I was prepared to add that even the form of signature might show that the whole text was composed by the man who endorsed it, for after the lines: I have hereunto put my hand the day and year first above written, *By me, William Shakespeare,* is appended.

This form, "by me," was employed by one of the poet's old neighbours, Ralph Holinshed, as an indication of a holograph will. It was probated April 24, 1581, and concludes with this phrase: "In witness whereof I have writtenne this my last will and testament with myne own hands and subscribe my name and putte to my seal the first day of October in the yeare of our Lord God, a thousande five hundred seventie and eight, per me, *Raphaellem Holinshed.*" No proof, but an indication!

In going over Shakespeare's own Will, even in a cursory manner, personal touches which defy imitation[4] may be noted. The master-mind still knew itself and expressed its wishes without hesitation, forgetting no one whose help had gone into the making of his success: childhood friends, his neighbour, Thomas

[4]The first paragraph reads:

I William Shakespeare of Stratford Upon Avon in the county of Warwick gent, in perfect health and memory God be praised do make and ordain this my last will and testament in manner and form following: that is to say First, I commend my soul unto the hands of God my Creator, hoping and assuredly believing through the only merits of Jesus Christ, my saviour, to be made partaker of life everlasting and my body to the earth, whereof it is made . . .

Combe, his actor-comrades, his sister and her boys, his godson and the little grand-daughter whom he calls "my niece, Elizabeth Hall"; the poor of Stratford, too. But first and foremost is displayed his paternal solicitude for Judith, Hamnet's surviving twin, still dwelling under her parents' roof. Preoccupation about Judith's marriage choice is apparent throughout—we may remember that she married Thomas Quinney between the original date of the will and its signing; but Shakespeare's anxiety for his younger child is compensated by evident satisfaction with Susanna's husband, Doctor John Hall, the ideal son-in-law. To them, as co-executors, the care of his widow is confided. No need to mention her—the wife had her legal third in all real and literary estate, but perhaps as a matter of sentiment, or perhaps in recognition that their bedroom furniture was Anne's personal heirloom and ought, in default of direct issue, to return to the Hathaways, he made her a special bequest: "I give my wife my second best bed and furniture." Why not his best one, many critics exclaim. The reason would seem to have been simple.

In a great house like New Place the *best* or state bed was a component part of the guest chamber. This one was used by Queen Henrietta Maria when, high in hope before the Battle of Edge Hill, she spent three weeks with Shakespeare's daughter and held her court at New Place. The *second-best* bed and furniture could alone have had any sentimental associations for Shakespeare's wife, and we may recall, à propos of this, Desdemona's attachment to her wedding-sheets.

In noting the legacy to his friend, Hamnet Sadler, the testator does not spell the Christian name like Sadler himself—who appears as fourth witness to the publishing—but uses the spelling that he himself had made famous, "I gyve and bequeathe to *Hamlett* Sadler xxviij s. viij d. to buy him a Ringe." The manner of referring to Mrs. Harte may be noticed likewise as personal. He mentions her first, in formal style, "my sister, Johane Harte," but the second and third time she is simply styled "my saide sister, Jone"; and the sword, so sweepingly bestowed on Thomas Combe, seems to carry a mark of personal affection.

Certainly the man who wrote the Will did so with emotion, for the word "decease" which figures eight times always stands forth from the context, and on tracing the words "after my decease" (page 3, line 36) the hand holding the pen trembled. This however can be used as an argument on both sides. If Shakespeare wrote the words, his emotion was natural; if Collins was the penman, it was natural too, as the Warwickshire lawyer certainly figured among the poet's intimate friends.

Personally, I went far enough along the lines suggested by Jeffrieson to declare my preference for the holograph theory, keeping my mind open however to examine further evidence should it be forthcoming.

On December 22, I received from Mr. Frederick Welstood, Secretary and Librarian of Shakespeare's birthplace, a facsimile of the writing of Francis Collins made the very year before Shakespeare's Will was drawn up and showing exactly the same disparity between the lawyer's roman hand as witness and the Old English script of the main text. This document is a deed of sale by "John Gibbes of Stratford Upon Avon gent, to Robert Bellamye of the same, for sixty pounds. A messuage etc. inhabited by the said Robert in Elye Street, Stratford-upon-Avon, 23rd March 12 James" (1614–15).

My first impression was that Malone had seen this document when he made his categorical statement, but Mr. Welstood informs me that it was not among the series of corporation records through which he searched when writing his *Life of Shakespeare*. Malone's authority evidently reposes on a study of Collins' handwriting from the Council Minute Book, for between the time of Shakespeare's death and his own he acted during a few months in 1617 as the Stratford Town Clerk.

However this may be, any one who examines the lease together with the last page of Shakespeare's Will can but arrive at Malone's conclusion: there is no shadow of doubt that Francis Collins held the pen when the poet's Will was consigned to paper and any critic who would continue to uphold a contrary opinion formerly expressed must divest himself of all literary probity. Having declared that I have at least brought zeal and sincerity to my work on Shakespeare, and have sought truth at the expense of personal opinion, I can only say *mea culpa* when I remember that in the first flush of conviction that Shakespeare's Will was holograph I expressed that belief in an article written in *Scribner's Magazine,* July, 1936. (*See Plate XII, at end of volume.*)

In re-valuing the evidence that convinced me, it is a certain satisfaction to note that the principal bases on which my theory was formed remain unchanged. I have always been much struck by the personal character of Shakespeare's Will and considered that the evidence of emotion visible in the trembling pen and undoubted signs of illness in the writing were serious indication that the testator himself held it. But on reviewing the case of Francis Collins these remarks are true of him also. A life-long friend of the testator who was to follow Shakespeare to the grave in scarcely a year's time, the scribe was naturally moved as he set down his friend's will, under his own dictation, and was doubtless already suffering from the arthritic trouble which was shortly to end his days. Nor does his intervention take away from the intimate and personal character of the document. How they must have discussed the interesting legal point brought up by the two dates of January 25th and March 25th! As I have pointed out, the original conception of the text envisaged Judith's marriage as a possibility only. On March 25th her marriage to Thomas Quinney had been consummated since

the Stratford records show that it was solemnised on February
10th: "Tho Quinney tow Judith Shakespeare," and according
to the Visitation Book in the Diocesan Registry at Worcester,
the young couple were cited to appear before the Consistory
Court for having been married without a licence. I would like
to suggest that it was only after a good deal of discussion that
the lawyer decided that no change need be made in the Will
itself and that its dispositions were not affected toward Judith
by her marriage during the interval. If the document on the
contrary had been entirely re-written to fit the new circumstances, much time would have been lost and if the original
date on the Will had not been left apparent, all the provisions
regarding his daughter's future would, after the fact, have
appeared foolish and superfluous. Shakespeare's testament remains as it stands, a most moving document confirming all
that is known of his personality, that mingling of pride, ambition, family affection and fidelity to old ties which, though not
considered as the usual accompaniment of artistic talent, are yet
the perquisite of a rare being who united the wisdom of Nestor
and the genius of Socrates to the art of Virgil.

> "Judicio Pylium, Genio Socratem, arte Maronem
> Terra tegit, populus maeret, Olympus habet."

It is often stated as an indisputable fact that some London
man of letters composed this epitaph but it seems a safer assumption that Doctor John Hall being financially responsible
for the poet's monument—for he and his wife Susanna Shakespeare were the direct heirs—was responsible also for the verses
that adorned it.

Hall was a competent Latinist having written his book of
medicine originally in that language. The London editors in
praising their great dramatist dwell first on his high renown
as *marvel of the stage* while the family, on the contrary, seem

to recognise wisdom and philosophy as Shakespeare's most admirable traits.

Whether the poet's doctrine be called stoical or Christian, his essential conception of life seems to have been developed from Montaigne's thought and summed up in the conclusion of King Lear.

> "Men must endure their going hence
> Even as their coming hither.
> Ripeness is all."

"Sortez de ce monde, comme vous y estes entrez. Si vous avez faict vostre proufit de la vie, vous en estes repeu: allez vous en satisfaict."

While these pages were going through the press, Leslie Hotson, so often referred to therein, published a new volume, *I William Shakespeare,* which establishes the identity of Thomas Russell, Esq., appointed as overseer of Shakespeare's will.

The fact that this Warwickshire gentleman, who dwelt at Alderminster, hardly four miles from the poet's home, was a friend of Endymion Porter and connected with the Digges, Sheldons, Grants, Quinneys, Ardens, Bushells, Winters and Catesbys, once more establishes the truth of Nicholas Rowe's evidence concerning the poet's family as "people of figure and fashion in the shire."

It also confirms my own contention that they moved in a political world which had long been tinged with Recusancy.

PLATE I. CONTESTED SIGNATURES OF SHAKESPEARE

(1) and (2), On a manuscript copy of Essex's Apologie. (3), On North's Plutarch [1579]. (4), On North's Plutarch [1612]. (5), On Ovid's *Metamorphoses*. (6), On Albion's *England*.

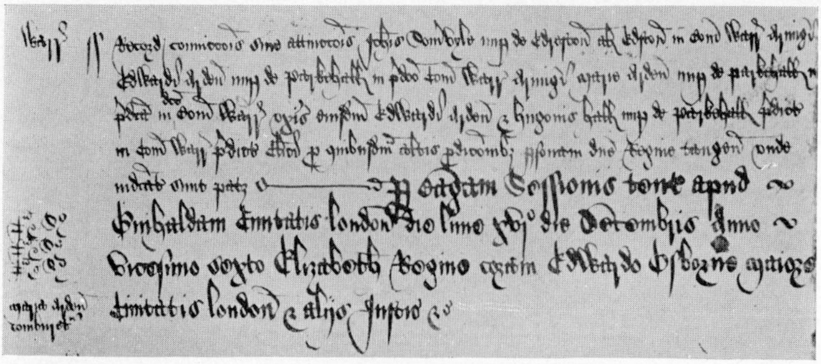

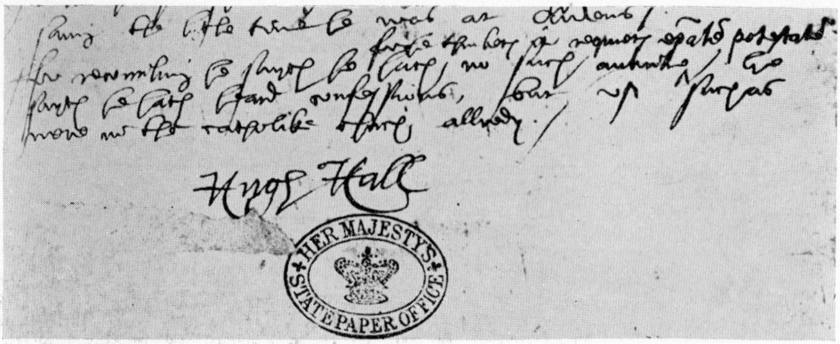

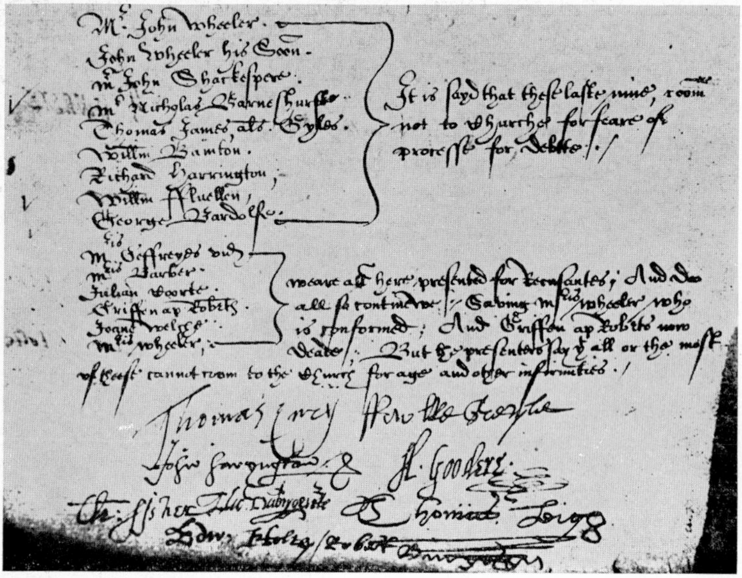

Mr. John Wheeler.
John Wheeler his Soon.
Mr. John Shakespere.
Mr. Nicholas Barneshurste.
Thomas James, als. Gyles.
Willm Bainton.
Richard Harrington,
Willm Fluellen,
George Bardolphe.

It is sayd that these laste nine, coom not to Churche for feare of processe for Debte.

Mrs. Jeffreys wid.
Mrs. Barber.
Julian Coorte.
Griffen ap Roberts.
Joane Welshe.
Mrs. wheeler,

weare all heretofore presented for Recusantes; And doe all so continewe: Saving Mrs. wheeler who is conformed; And Griffen ap Roberts now deade; But the presenters saye that all or the most of theise cannot coom to the Churche for age and other infirmities.

Thomas Lucy

John Harington

H. Goodere

PLATE II. *Top:* Doom of the Ardens, Somerville, and Hugh Hall. The marginal signs indicate that the men are to be hanged and quartered; Mary Arden burned.

Centre: Hugh Hall's examination and signature.

Bottom: Comptrollment roll of Warwickshire signed by Thomas Lucy and his fellow commissioners.

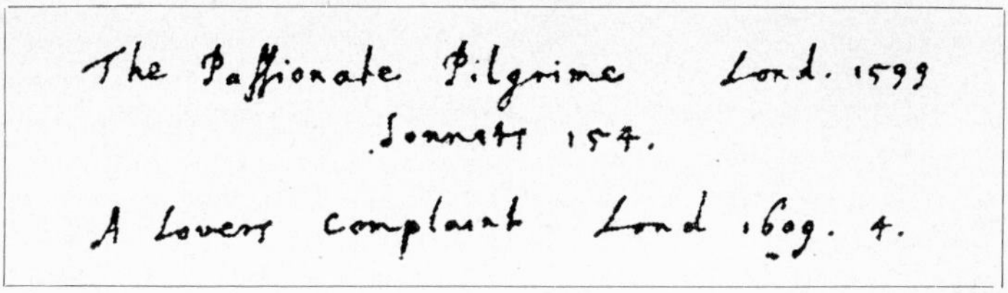
The Passionate Pilgrime Lond. 1599
Sonnets 154.
A Lovers complaint Lond. 1609. 4.

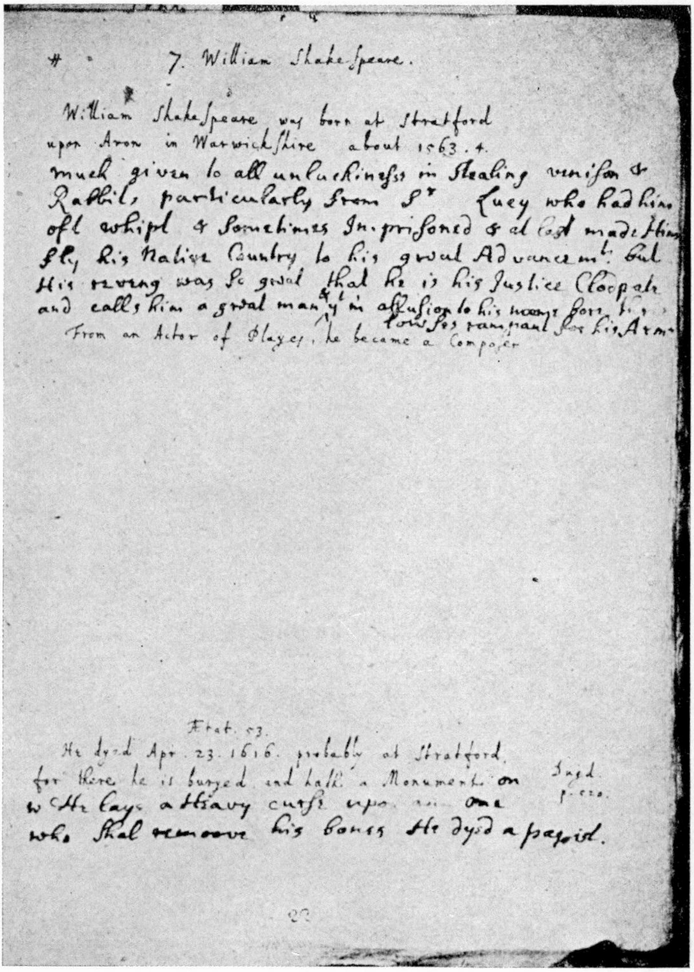
7. William Shakespeare.

William Shakespeare was born at Stratford upon Avon in Warwickshire about 1563.4.
much given to all unluckinesse in stealing venison & Rabbits, particularly from Sr Lucy who had him oft whipt & sometimes Imprisoned & at last made him fly his Native Country to his great Advancement. but His reveng was so great that he is his Justice Clodpate and calls him a great man & yt in allusion to his name bore three lowses rampant for his Arms.
From an Actor of Playes, he became a Composer.

Aetat. 53.
He dyed Apr. 23. 1616. probably at Stratford, for there he is buryed, and hath a Monument on wch He lays a Heavy curse upon any one who shal remoove his bones. He dyed a papist.
Dugd. p. 520.

PLATE III. CORPUS CHRISTI MANUSCRIPT
Fulman-Davies.

rebellion, causing them to be put vnto death, and so by that meanes quieted the countrie. ¶ To recite what was done in euerie part of the realme in time of these wealth troubles, it is not possible: but this is to be considered, that the rage of the commons was vniuersallie such, as it might seeme they had generallie conspired togither, to do what mischeefe they could deuise. As among sundrie other, what wickednesse was it, to compell teachers of children in grammar schooles to sweare neuer to instruct any in their art? Againe, could they haue a more mischeefous meaning, than to burne and destroie all old and ancient monuments, and to murther and dispatch out of the waie all such as were able to commit to memorie, either any new or old records? For it was dangerous

lawes, all things should then be ordered according to the will and disposition of the common people. It was reported in deed, that he should saie with great pride the day before these things chanced, putting his hands to his lips, that within foure daies all the lawes of England should come forth of his mouth. The wretches had vtterlie forgotten all law, both diuine and humane; otherwise they would haue beene content to liue vnder law, and to do vnto others as

king therefore sent vnto them such as declared vnto that sort their fellowes were gone home well satisfied, & from thencefoorth to liue in quiet, and the same forme of peace he was contented to grant to them, if it liked them to accept the same. Herevpon their cheefe capteine Wat Tiler, a verie craftie fellow, and induced with much wit (if he had well applied it) said, that peace indeed he wished, but yet so, as the conditions might be indited to his purpose.

him foorth togither with the lord treasuror, and on the tower hill without reuerence of their estates and degrees, with great noise and fell cries, they stroke off their heads. There were also beheaded at the same time by those rude people, one of the kings seruants that was a sergeant at armes called John Leg, who had vsed himselfe somewhat extremelie in gathering vp of the pole monie, as by one writer it appeareth. Also to make vp the messe, they beheaded a Franciscane Frier, whom they had taken there at the same time, for malice of the duke of Lancaster; bicause he was verie familiar with him. ¶ Some write that this frier was confessor, and other saie that he was physician to the king; but whatsoeuer he was, the commons chopped off his head. To beare the other

rich, for such (saith Polydor) in those daies mounted to preferment. These two appointed to go togither to the court, ech hoping at their comming thither to find some meanes that he might be made abbat of that house. Being thus agreed, to the court they come, and there offer verie largelie to the king to obteine their sute: who perceiuing their greedie desires, and casting his eies about the chamber, espied by chance an other monke (that came to beare them

we did, the same had beene done by his authoritie. Finally, when we had gotten power inough, that we needed not to feare anie force that might be made against vs, we would haue slaine all such noble men, as might either haue giuen counsell, or made anie resistance against vs, speciallie the knights of the Rhodes; and lastlie we would haue killed the king and all men of possessions, with bishops, monks, chanons, and parsons of churches, onelie friers Mendi-

PLATE IV. HOLINSHED'S "CHRONICLES"
MARGINALIA AND INDEX PAGE INSCRIPTION

(1), Wickedness of Northfolk men [de]stroye all [reco]rds. (2), So the lawes of [England] should [com]e forth of one [crea]turs mouth. (3), Wate tiler. (4), The wicked[eeds] of rebell. (5), The Kinge giveth a[n] abbyae. (6), The intent of the rebels.

Finished in Ianuarie 1587, and the 29 of the Queenes
Maiesties reigne, with the full continuation of the
former yeares, at the expenses of Iohn Hari-
son, George Bishop, Rafe Newberie,
Henrie Denham, and Tho-
mas Woodcocke.

AT LONDON
Printed in Aldersgate street at the signe
of the Starre.

Cum priuilegio.

PLATE V. COLOPHON OF HOLINSHED'S "CHRONICLES"

PLATE VI. Extracts from the municipal accounts of Aberdeen showing Lawrence Fletcher's name as comedian servitor to his Majesty and payment to the English players for their services and for their supper "the night they plaid to the toune."

Right Honorable.

The Hale you writte for I haue not But I haue
sent you a dowble Tent of more Rome then the
Hale was wishinge it may be vsefull vnto you.
if ther be any thinge els in my powre wch may
doe you serbise, That it may please you to comand
my dasyre is rather by performans then by
letter, to make you knowe your interest in me
wch I assure you is much more then I make shew
of, as by any good ocasione you shall haue
Tesdymony. And so for this tyme I leaue
remayninge.

Euer ready to doe you serdise

Willm Harvye

Saccoy. May. 3.
1603.

PLATE VII.   LETTER OF WILLIAM HARVEY TO SIR ROBERT CECIL

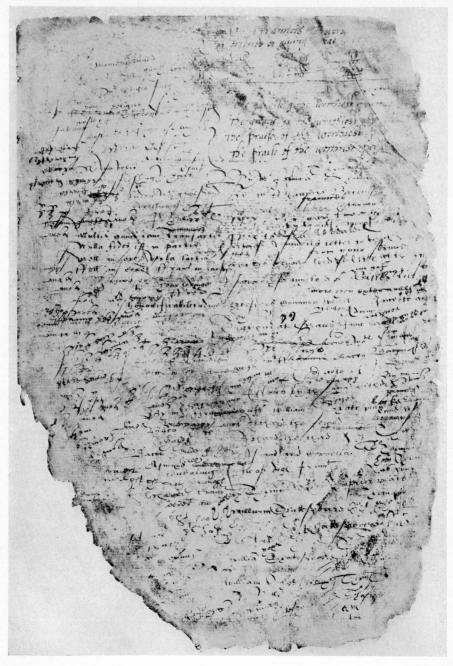

PLATE VIII.   COVERING PAGE OF THE NORTHUMBERLAND MS.

Mr. ffr Bacon of tribute
or giuing that wch is due

1 the praise of the worthiest vertue
2 the praise of the worthiest affeccon
3 the praise of the worthiest power
4 the praise of the worthiest person

A   C
B   D
2   1

A   Since we are mett lett me gouerne our leysure. B. C. D. com
euerie man do honer to that wch he esteemeth most and
praise. Þ o vaine metion and ignorance of tymes are not su
write then Dumms A obey

The praise of ffortitude

my praise shalbe dedicated to the noblest of the vertues. To
discerne betwene good and euill. Justice to stande indifferent
selfe-loue and societie temperance to deuide amygst betwene
reason theise be good innocent thinge. But the vertue of
vertue of resolucion or vertue of effect is ffortitude. for if
a man largely endued wth prudence the tempest of a
greate dannger and lett ffortitude absent then seise me
he of his wisedome. vnto se the power coteen to beholde
or to entende the remedye. or rather dothe not the first
disable him to take a true veiwe of the gitt. and the oth
the gitt so attache and seaze his senses that he cannott
for his deliueraunce revive the goodest groundes of rea
uarions of experience rules & precepts and Cautions
was wont at leysure to consider compare and reme
herested & confounded their printts are defaced.
a leame of perill gate no Aen mthius semit downe
inserte or else a lhef ye mind disordered subiectes
wisedome is the first thing that flies his spirit
tonarell in his braine are gone to succer yt
abandoned to his perills by the treas
dame would haue tould or

PLATE X. SHAKESPEARE'S SIGNATURES

(*Top*), On a legal deposition [1612]. (*Centre*), On flyleaf of Florio's Montaigne [1598]. (*Left centre*), On a house purchase [1612]. (*Right centre*), On a mortgage deed [1613]. (*Bottom*), On his will [1616].

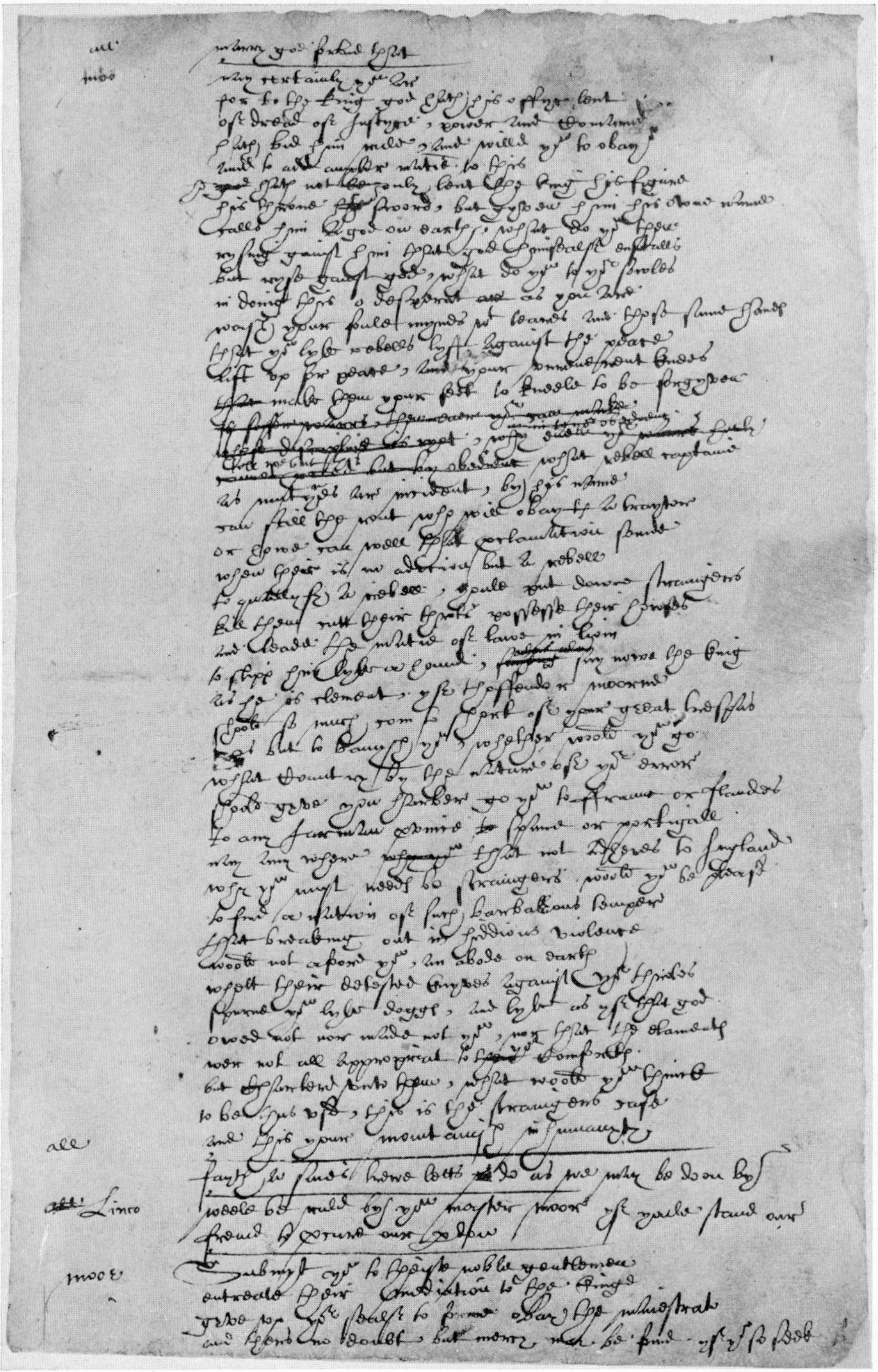

PLATE XI. SHAKESPEARE'S HAND IN THE PLAY OF "SIR THOMAS MORE"

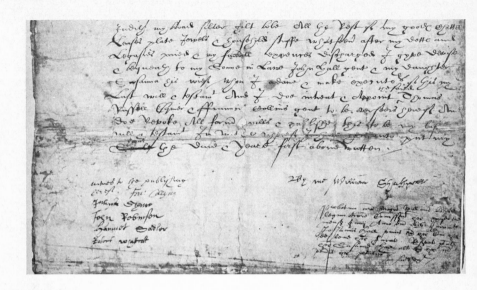

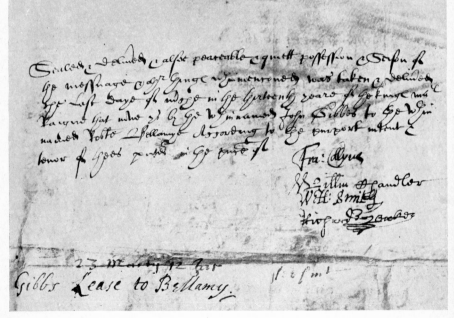

PLATE XII. *Top:* Concluding lines of Shakespeare's will.
Bottom: Lease made out and signed by Francis Collins.

APPENDIX

APPENDIX

BORROMEO'S SPIRITUAL TESTAMENT

The Spiritual Testament of Juan Phelipe Hernandez is given on the left hand column, that of John Shakespeare on the right up to the point in the third paragraph from whence, at the words "spiritually and in will" they become identical.

The Testament or Last Will of the Soul made in health for the Christian to secure himself from the temptations of the devil at the hour of death, drawn up by Saint Carlo Borromeo Cardinal of St. Praxedis and Archbishop of Milan.

The dangers to which human life is exposed being countless, and I Juan Phelipe Hernandez, knowing that I am a mortal man born only to die without knowledge at which time this debt will have to be discharged. In order that I may not be taken unprepared and that my flight may not be in winter or on the sabbath day as our Saviour says in the gospel, have taken thought with

In the name of the Father, Sonne and Holy Ghost, the most holy and blessed Virgin Mary, mother of God, the holy host of archangels, angels, patriarchs, prophets, evangelists, apostles, saints, martyrs and all the celestial court and company of heaven, Amen. I, Jhon Shakspear, an unworthy member of the holy Catholick religion, being at this my present writing in perfect health of body and sound mind, memory and understanding; but calling to mind the uncertainty of life and certainty of death, and that I may possibly be cut off in the blossome of my sins and called to render an account of all my transgressions externally and in-

303

the divine aid to prepare myself for that uncertain hour since God now gives me the time; and so with my whole heart being prostrate before the feet of Christ our Lord, as he hangs on the cross I declare unto the world my last will in the following form.

II

In the first place, as the foundation of all salvation, I, Juan Phelipe Hernandez, declare and confess in the presence of Almighty God, Father, Son and Holy Ghost, three persons in one God, the most holy Virgin and all the Court of Heaven, that I wish to live and die obedient to the Holy Roman Church, firmly believing all the fourteen articles of the Faith taught by the holy Apostles, all the interpretations and declarations made upon them by the Holy Catholic Church, guided by the Holy Ghost, has taught, defined and declared.

III

Item I protest in this same form that at the end of life I desire to receive the most holy Viaticum in order to unite me perfectly and peacefully with my Lord Jesus Christ by means of so divine

ternally, and that I may be unprepared for the dreadful trial either by sacrament, pennance, fasting or prayer, or any other purgation Whatever, do in the holy presence above specified of my own free and voluntary accord make and ordaine this my last spiritual will, testament, confession, protestation and confession of faith, hoping hereby to receive pardon for all my sinnes and offences, and thereby to be made partaker of life everlasting, through the only merits of Jesus Christ my Saviour and Redeemer who took upon himself the likeness of man, suffered death and was crucified upon the crosse for the redemption of sinners.

II

Item I Jhon Shakspear doe by this present protest, freely acknowledge and confess that in my past life I have been a most abominable and grievous sinner and therefore unworthy to be forgiven without a true and sincere repentance for the same. But trusting in the manifold mercies of my blessed Saviour and Redeemer, I am encouraged by relying on his sacred word, to hope for salvation and to be made para Sacrament; the which, if by some accident, I should be unable to receive, I now declare in view of that time that it is my purpose to receive it at least spiritually and in will

taker of his heavenly kingdom, as a member of the celestial company of angels saints and martyrs there to reside for ever and ever in the court of my God.

III

Item I Jhon Shakspear doe by this present protest and declare that as I am certain I must pass out of this transitory life into another that will last to eternity, I do hereby most humbly implore and intreat my good and guardian angel to instruct me in this, my solemn preparation, protestation and confession of faith at least spiritually and in will

Adoring and most humbly beseeching my Saviour that he will be pleased to assist me in so dangerous a voyage, to defend me from the snares and deceites of my infernall enemies and to conduct me to the secure haven of his eternall blisse.

IV

Item I Jhon Shakspear doe protest that I will also passe out of this life, armed with the last sacrament of extreme unction, the which if through any let or hindrance I should not then be able to have, I doe now also for that time demand and crave the same; beseeching his Divine Majesty that he will be pleased to anoynt my senses both internall and externall with the sacred oyle of his infinite mercy and to pardon me all my sins committed by seeing, speaking, justing,[1] smelling, hearing, touching or by any other way whatsoever.

[1]Jordan read "feeling" but the right word should be "gusting."

V

Item I Jhon Shakspear doe by this my present protest that I will not through any temptation whatsoever despaire of the divine goodness, for the multitude and greatnesse of my sinnes: for which although I confesse that I have deserved hell, yet will I stedfastly hope in God's infinite mercy, knowing that he hathe heretofore pardoned as many and as great sinners as myself, whereof I have good warrant sealed with his sacred mouth, in holy writ, whereby he pronounceth that he is not come to call the just but sinners.

VI

Item I Jhon Shakspear doe protest that I doe not know that I have ever done any good worke meritorious of life everlasting; and if I have done any I do acknowledge that I have done it with a great deale of negligence and imperfection, neither should I have been able to have done the least without the assistance of his divine grace. Wherefore let the devill remain confounded, for I doe in no wise presume to merit heaven by such good workes alone, but through the merits and blood of my lord and saviour, Jesus, shed upon the crosse for me most miserable sinner.

VII

Item I Jhon Shakspear do protest by this present writing that I will patiently endure and suffer all kind of informity, sickness, yea and the paine of death itself, wherein if it should happen, which God forbid, that through violence of paine and agony or by subtility of the devill I should fall into any impatience or temptation of blasphemy or murmuration against God, or the Catholik faith, or give any signe of bad example, I do henceforth and for that present repent me, and I am most heartily sorry for the same, and I do renounce all the evill whatsoever which I might have then done or said, beseeching his divine clemency that he will not forsake me in that grievous and painefull agony.

306

VIII

Item I Jhon Shakspear by virtue of this present testament I do pardon all the injuries and offences that any one hath ever done unto me, either in my reputation, life, goods or any other way whatsoever; beseeching sweet Jesus to pardon them for the same; and I doe desire that they will doe the like by me, whom I have offended or injured in any sort howsoever.

IX

Item I Jhon Shakspear do heer protest that I do render infinite thanks to his divine majesty for all the benefits that I have received as well secret as manifest and in particular, for the benefit of my Creation, Redemption, Sanctification, Conservation and Vocation to the holy knowledge of him and his true Catholike faith; but above all for his so great expectation of me to pennance, when he might most justly have taken me out of this life when I least thought of it, yea even then when I was plunged in the durty puddle of my sinnes. Blessed be therefore and praised for ever and ever, his infinite patience and charity.

X

Item I Jhon Shakspear do protest that I am willing, yea I doe infinitely desire and humbly crave, that of this my last will and testament, the glorious and ever Virgin Mary, mother of God, refuge and advocate of sinners, whom I honour specially above all other saints, may be the chiefe Executresse together with those other saints my patrons (Saint Winifrida) all whom I invoke and beseech to be present at the hour of my death that she and they may comfort me with their desired presence and crave sweet jesus that he will receive my soul into peace.

XI

Item In virtue of this present writing I Jhon Shakspear do likewise most willingly and with all humility constitute and ordaine my good Angel, for Defender and Protectone of my soul in the dreadfull day of Judgment, when the finall sentence of eternall life or death shall be discussed and given, beseeching him that as my soule was appointed to his custody and protection when I lived, even so he will vouchsafe to defend the same at that houre and conduct it to eternal bliss.

XII

Item I Jhon Shakspear do in like manner praye and beseech all my dear friends, parents and kinfolks, by the bowels of our Saviour Jesus Christ that since it is uncertain what lot will befall me, for feere notwithstanding least by reason of my sinnes, I be to pass and stay a long while in purgatory, they will vouchsafe to assist and succour me with their holy prayers and satisfactory workes, especially with the holy sacrifice of the masse, as being the most effectuall meanes to deliver soules from their torments and paines; from the which if I shall by God's gracious goodnesse and by their vertuous workes be delivered, I do promise that I will not be ungratefull for so great a benefitt.

XIII

Item I Jhon Shakspear doe by this my last will and testament bequeath my soul as soon as it shall be delivered and loosened from the prison of this my body to be entombed in the sweet and amorous havinge coffin of the side of Jesus Christ and that in this life-giveing sepulcher it may rest and live, perpetually inclosed in that eternall habitation of repose there to blesse for ever and ever that direfull iron of the launce which like a sharp cutting razor formed so sweet and pleasant a monument within the sacred breast of my lord and saviour.

XIV

Item Lastly I Jhon Shakspear doe protest that I will willingly accept of death in what manner soever it may befall me, conforming my will unto the will of God; accepting of the same in satisfaction for my sinnes and giving thanks unto his divine majesty for the like he hath bestowed upon me. And if it pleases him to prolong or shorten the same, blessed be he alsoe a thousand thousand times; into whose most holy hands I commend my soul and bodye, my life and death: and I beseech him above all things that he never permit any change to be made by me John Shakspear of this my aforesaid will and testament. Amen.

I Jhon Shakspear have made this present writing of protestation confession and charter in presence of the blessed virgin mary, my Angell guardian, and all the Celestiall Court as witnesses hereunto, the which my meaning is that it be of full value now presently and for ever, with the force and vertue of testament, codicill and donation inccourse of death; confirming it anew, being in perfect health of soul and body and signed with mine own hand; carrying also the same about me and for the better declaration hereof my will and intention is that it be finally buried with me after my death.

Pater noster, Ave Maria; Credo, jesu, son of David have mercy on me Amen.[2]

[2]Malone, *Shakespeare's Works* (Ed. 1790), Vol. II, pp. 162–66 and 330, 331. Collated with Herbert Thurston's transcript, published in *The Month*, November, 1911.

INDEX

INDEX

315

INDEX

316

INDEX

INDEX

INDEX

Whately, Sir Robert, 55 n.
Wheeler, Mr. 103
White, Roland, 276 n.
Whitfield, G. L., *Brief Life of Anne Lyne,* 225
Whitgift, Lord John, Bishop of Worcester, Archbishop of Canterbury, 53, 54 n., 56–58, 107–171 and n., 232–233
Whittington, Thomas, 40, 56 n., 60
Wilde, Oscar, 11, 162; *Portrait of Mr. W. H.,* 162
Wilkes, Thomas, 44, 47–49 n., 91
William I (The Conqueror), King of England, 243 n., 247
William II (Rufus), King of England, 246
William Shakespeare, by Sir E. K. Chambers, 211, 267
Willobie His Avisa, 158–159
Wilson, Dover, 125, 259, 282
Wilson, Thomas, *Arte of Rhetorike,* 23
Windesor, Lord, 47
Wingate, Edwarde, 49 n.
Winifred, Saint (Winifrida), 73–74, 307
Winstanley, 240
Winter's Tale, The, 71, 131
Wiseman, John, 226 n.
Witches in *Macbeth,* 194–197
Wither, George, 119

Wod, David, 207
Wood, Anthony, 24 n.
Woodcocke, Thomas, 261, 265
Woodfen, priest, 117 n.
Woodhouse, 226 n.
Woodhouse, Thomas, 19–20
Worcester, Bishops of, 15, 52, 54 n., 56–58, 170
Worcester, Earl of, 226 n.
Wordsworth, William, 134
World of Words, by Giovanni Florio, 6, 120 n.
Worsley, 216
Worthington family, 33 n.
Wray, Sir Christopher, 35
Wright, Mr., priest, 127
Wright, Hugh, 49 n.
Wright, John, 200 n.
Wright, William, 196 n.
Wriothesley, Henry, Earl of Southampton, *see* Southampton
Wriothesley, Mary, 178 and n.
Wyndham, George, 122, 198 n.
Wyse, John, 52

Yate, Mrs., 33
Yates, Miss Frances, 120
York, Archbishop of, 15
Young, Mr. Justice, 225 n.

323